Uti

A FIRE *to* WIN

ALSO BY JOHN LOMBARDO

Raiders Forever

A FIRE
to WIN

The Life and Times of Woody Hayes

JOHN LOMBARDO

THOMAS DUNNE BOOKS
ST. MARTIN'S PRESS
New York

THOMAS DUNNE BOOKS.
An imprint of St. Martin's Press.

www.stmartins.com

Book design by Jonathan Bennett

Library of Congress Cataloging-in-Publication Data

Lombardo, John.
    A fire to win : the life and times of Woody Hayes / John Lombardo.—1st ed.
        p. cm.
    Includes bibliographical references (page 265) and index (page 267).
    ISBN 0-312-32518-5
    EAN 978-0-312-32518-3
    1. Hayes, Woody, 1913–1987. 2. Football coaches—United States—Biography.
  3. Ohio State Buckeyes (Football team)—History. I. Title.

GV939.H35L66 2005
796.332'092—dc22
[B]
                                                                    2005048444

First Edition: October 2005

10   9   8   7   6   5   4   3   2   1

For Jane and Emma

CONTENTS

ACKNOWLEDGMENTS

Sincere thanks to my literary agent, Jim Donovan, who championed the idea of writing a book about Woody Hayes without hesitation.

Peter Wolverton at Thomas Dunne Books expertly shaped the finished product, adding balance, structure, and fairness where it was needed.

Rex Kern, Archie Griffin, Cornelius Greene, Dick Huff, and other former players helped me gain insight into their coach. Tom Baldacci was a vital source of assistance.

Ara Parsehgian, John Pont, and George Chaump provided invaluable access and information into the lives of major college football coaches. Others who provided key assistance were Kaye Kessler, Mary Hoyt, Wayne Duke, and Phil Lombardo. The friendly and helpful folks at the Ohio State University Archives, the Denison University archives, and the Tuscarawas County Public Library provided the foundation of my research. Barbara Scott at the Temperance Tavern Museum in Newcomerstown, Ohio, was of great assistance.

I'm also indebted to Greg and Karen Reichle, who cheerfully allowed me to disrupt their family life while graciously providing me a second home in Columbus.

Finally, unending appreciation to my wife, Megan, who never loses faith.

A FIRE *to* WIN

PREFACE

A generation has passed since Woody Hayes last stalked a sideline, but the mention of his name still conjures images of Saturday afternoons in autumn when Hayes and his Ohio State University football team would typically punish the opposition on their way to another win, sending victory throughout Ohio and further cementing the Buckeyes's reputation as a national football powerhouse. The wins weren't particularly stylish or technical. Instead they were mostly brutal, given Hayes's pounding strategy of sending wave after wave of top college football talent onto the field to beat the opponent into submission.

Those football Saturdays in Ohio were strictly reserved for the beloved Buckeyes. Any other activities during fall afternoons ran a distant second to the battles taking place inside the famed horseshoe stadium located next to the Olentangy River, that snakes through Ohio State's campus. Couples who scheduled weddings on a football Saturday afternoon in Columbus got a distracted guest list and perhaps a discounted dance hall offered to counter the lack of demand during the football season. Transistor radios were a prized commodity at events conflicting with the Buckeyes games, with small groups of people discreetly huddling around the transistor, one ear tuned to the event at hand, the other cocked toward the radio.

The obsession with Ohio State football existed well before Hayes came to Columbus in the early 1950s, but it was he who reigned supreme over the Buckeyes during college football's explosive growth from the 1950s through the late 1970s.

His dominant nature both on and off the football field captivated the world of college football and, although Hayes died in 1987, his commanding presence still resonates, not only throughout Ohio and Big Ten country, but through all of sports. He won 238 games and lost

72 as a college coach, including a remarkable 205-61-10 record at Ohio State University, putting him in the pantheon of college coaches with Paul "Bear" Bryant, Amos "Alonzo" Stagg, and Eddie Robinson. But it's not Hayes's impressive record that makes him so intriguing.

There is, of course, the singular memory of Hayes on a misty Florida winter night throwing a punch at an opposing team's player, that led so many to dismiss Hayes simply as a tyrant with a violent streak. He was far more complicated and complex than that. In fact, the more you learn about Woody Hayes, the more you discover the many dimensions that shaped the man who for twenty-eight seasons coached the Ohio State University Buckeyes football team to thirteen Big Ten championships, eight Rose Bowl appearances, and three national championships.

He was small-town Ohio, yet was befriended by world leaders, movie stars, and business icons. He was a man of compassion who would help anyone at a moment's notice, yet he spent little time with his own family and was fired from his job as coach of one of the most prestigious football schools in history because of the aforementioned infamous punch. He was politically conservative, yet he was one of the first big-time college coaches to actively recruit black players. He was a military historian who prepared his team for battle each Saturday afternoon by teaching them the lessons of wars past; yet he was incapable of learning the lessons of his own failed personal battles. He spoke in a high-pitched voice marked with a lisp, but was a legendary recruiter and a captivating public speaker. He was a coach who drilled his team to be in control of tough games in the face of unrelenting pressure; yet he could not control his own emotions when confronted by lesser threats, such as journalists and photographers who wanted nothing more than to take his picture and learn more about the man who led the storied Buckeyes to the pinnacle of college sports. He was a manipulative man who pushed his players to beyond the extreme. Nearly every player who ever played for Hayes suffered from the coach's almost intolerable demands and crueller punishment. Most hated their coach at one time or another during their playing careers, but their sacrifice was never forgotten; and their loyalty was returned whenever former players needed jobs, a business connection, or even medical care or financial assistance. Hayes's temper was legendary, but at times also contrived. He kept a desk drawer stocked with cheap watches to replace the ones he smashed on the practice field and the stitches in his baseball cap were sometimes strategically loosened to make it easier to shred the fabric to make a point in a fit of anger. Hayes preached self-lessness to his players and eloquently quoted Emerson at length, yet he had a raging ego and was world-class profane, not to mention being a notorious namedropper. He was a difficult man, loved by nearly every citizen of the state of Ohio and legions of football fans around the country, yet he would have been characterized as strange if not for one simple fact: Woody Hayes could win football games.

1

NEWCOMERSTOWN

Woody Hayes was entirely a small-town man. None of the national championships, the bowl games, fame, glory, and power that came from lording over college football would ever shake Hayes's firm belief that all that was right in the world came from rural America, where love of country, hard work, and loyalty made America great.

It was this philosophy that would send Hayes to speak at nearly every Elks club, Masonic lodge, and Moose hall that asked, giving him the chance to lecture his audience on the virtues of small-town life. In return Hayes would be honored with a key to the city, a chicken dinner, and a modest speaking fee. The fee invariably would never see the inside of his pocket. Instead, he often would donate the money back to the club, or sign the check over to the local high school football team that was invariably in need of new equipment. Even when the speaking fees increased well into five figures, he would quietly sign the money over to a hospital or a charity. Sometimes he simply tucked the check into his jacket, where it would be forgotten until the garment was sent to the dry cleaners.

"I speak at a lot of banquets in small towns, because small towns have so many great people," Hayes said during those boilerplate speeches. "All the presidents came from small towns. The largest town that a president came from was in that state up north," he said, referring to former president Gerald Ford, who hailed from Grand Rapids, Michigan. The standing joke would always bring a chuckle. So deep was his disdain for rival Michigan, that even during these friendly talks Hayes, who counted Ford as a friend, would refuse to mention the state of Michigan by name.

Hayes's own tenets were forged in rural Ohio, first in Clifton, a tiny mill town along the banks of the Miami River some seventy-five miles southwest of Columbus. It was there that he was born on Valentine's Day in 1913, the third and youngest child of Wayne Benton and Effie Jane Hupp Hayes. Woody was eight years younger than his sister Mary and two years younger than his brother Ike. Unlike his more independent older brother, young Woody was doted upon by both his sister and mother and stayed close to the women in the house.

"As the youngest, I don't think there was any doubt I was spoiled," Hayes said.

In 1915 Wayne Hayes moved his family to nearby Selma, where he took a job as school superintendent, another step in his career as an educator.

He was the visionary of the family, an intense man who, with his eleven brothers and sisters, was expected to work the family homestead in Noble County, Ohio. The family had deep Ohio roots. Woody's great grandfather David Hayes was a blacksmith and joined the Union army during the Civil War. He was killed during the Battle of Antietam in September 1862, leaving his father Isaac an orphan at eight years old.

Wayne was bright, ambitious, and resourceful, and the family farm wasn't enough to hold him. Most nights after chores and dinner, Wayne's mother would sit him down and school her son in reading and arithmetic, building the foundation for his future for a life off the farm.

He saw teaching as a way to better himself. During the early 1900s Ohio was still primarily a rural state, with small, unincorporated towns and hamlets dotting the countryside. High schools in these areas were either distant or absent altogether, so kids who completed the eighth grade could take the Boxwell Examination, that, if successfully completed, could serve as a substitute to a high school diploma. Wayne passed the test, posting a score high enough to qualify him to teach the eighth grade—beginning his long, slow march toward becoming a college graduate and a school superintendent. The Hayes family was serious about education.

Achieving high school equivalency by passing the Boxwell Examination was one thing, but attending college was for the wealthy and privileged, not for farm families from Noble County, Ohio. Though married and the father of three young children, Wayne was undeterred by family and financial hurdles that lay before his educational goals. He attended six different colleges at night and during the summers, before eventually earning a degree from Wittenberg College in 1919. Woody was six years old when he saw his father graduate from college. Wayne Hayes was thirty-eight. The memory would stay with Woody forever; his father's perseverance serving to motivate and inspire when things turned dark, as they often did, given Woody's high-octane, combustible personality.

The degree brought new opportunities and prosperity to the Hayes household, and in 1920 the family moved northeast to Newcomerstown, Ohio, population 4,500, where Wayne accepted a job as superintendent of schools. It was a sizable step up, compared to the tiny towns like Clifton and Selma where the family previously lived. Wayne earned twenty-eight dollars a month when he first began teaching in the early 1900s. By 1920 he had saved enough money to buy a modest white frame house at 488 East Canal Street, just east of downtown and near a stretch of water that used to be part of the historic Ohio Canal. After spending years working his way across Ohio, Hayes would never move his family again.

Woody was seven years old when his father settled his family in this quintessential 1920s small town, nestled in a valley along the Tuscarawas River. Hardworking folks lived in the village bisected by the Ohio Canal; outside the town limits farmland checkered the hilly countryside.

It was in essence a company town, with the Clows Pipe Works and the Heller Tool Company serving as the two main employers. The heavy industry, combined with the county's rural population, provided enough economic stimulus to make the town a bustling place. The country's interstate system was still a long way off from crossing through Ohio. Instead, Highway 21 funneled traffic through the heart of the downtown, helping pump commerce into the heart of Main Street. But travel was still difficult, and people who lived in Newcomerstown stayed put. There was a feed store, grocery, clothing store, hardware store, tannery, and even a cigar factory—all located within a few blocks of each other—where the locals spent their money, creating a self-sufficient place where one could buy whatever was needed.

Farmers would come into town on Saturday mornings to shop, eat, and perhaps, on summer afternoons, to linger to listen to a local band play uptown on Main Street. The locals would also hold town picnics at Mulvane Park. A summer social highlight was the tricounty fair held in the centrally located town, bringing together residents of Tuscarawas, Coshocton, and Guernsey counties, hoping to have that year's blue-ribbon–winning crops and cattle.

The local schoolchildren would swim in the river during the summer and ice skate on it during the winter, and if they collected enough bread wrappers from the local bakery, they could go to the movie house for free. Farmers and other rural folk would gather at the Grange Hall for meetings and dinners. Sunday mornings were for church, and afterwards families either went to a church dinner or to a neighbor's house for meals, dressed in their Sunday best. These get-togethers were formal affairs and provided a way of socializing after a long week of work, but they also helped establish a social pecking order within the town, a town so small that everyone helped each other, but also knew everyone else's business. Whenever a child contracted scarlet fever, the doctor would quarantine the family by placing a large red sign outside the house to serve as a loud warning of the then deadly disease, but also to signal to neighbors to leave food on the front porch of the unfortunate family.

There were dozens of towns in the Ohio Valley like Newcomerstown during the early 1900s, but the small village on the river had already made a name for itself, thanks to the baseball heroics of Denton "Cy" Young. Young grew up on a farm outside of town and moved back to his boyhood home after his Hall of Fame baseball career ended in 1911. He managed the local semipro team, sponsored by the Clows Pipp Works, in his retirement, and sometimes he would wear his old Cleveland Indians uniform to remind himself and the locals of his days of fame. The old lefthander would even break out his old Boston uniform on special occasions, like July 4th or Labor Day.

Young took a liking to Woody and hired the earnest youngster to do small jobs around the farm, paying him a nickel to groom the local baseball diamond. Cy's fame was not lost on the impressionable Woody. Young would regale him and other locals in farmyard smokehouses with stories of past stardom, of pitching duels against Walter Johnson, and of other glories that come from winning 511 big league games.

"That man could make me feel grown up when he said 'Woodrow,' and that's what he always called me," Hayes said. "Here's a man who would sit in front of Denver Reed's smokehouse and talk about pitching, and he pitched for twenty-two years. But he was a humble man. He never made himself look good. Never."

It was a time when sports began to enter the collective consciousness of America, with stars like Young, Johnson, Babe Ruth, and Lou Gehrig elevated to hero status. Listening firsthand to Young tell his stories instilled in Hayes an idealistic and virtuous notion of sports, one that would strongly influence the impressionable young man.

But it wasn't all ice-cream socials and Main Street bands. Newcomerstown could be a rough-and-tumble place, especially compared to the more prosperous neighboring town of New Philadelphia, the county seat located fifteen miles to the north. Life could get difficult in the seemingly idyllic village. Hard work didn't always pay off and faith wasn't always rewarded, especially when children got sick, or when jobs or farms were lost.

And while there may have been a vibrant Main Street, not everyone was welcome. There was a contingent of black residents brought to town to help build the company-owned houses and to work in the foundry that produced cast-iron sewer pipes that were used throughout most of Ohio. The blacks lived on the south end of town, segregated from the whites. Come Saturday night the police invariably would be called to the community house in "Clowstown" to break up knife fights and other violence that sometimes erupted after a backbreaking week of work in the plant.

When Wayne Hayes arrived in the summer of 1920, he was greeted with a combination of skepticism and hope that he could breathe new life into the town's school system.

From the clapboard house on East Canal Street, a half mile from the main square, the Hayes family settled into their new home—where it didn't take long for the new superintendent to establish himself as a man to be taken seriously.

He ran the school district with an iron fist, demanding that his teachers memorize textbooks while doing the same himself. He was a shrewd administrator, hiring promising young teachers just out of college, while weeding out those that weren't adapting to the evolving educational system that was moving the schools to a more modern curriculum. It wasn't long into Wayne's tenure that the teachers began calling their boss "Pappy," or "Pops," as a nod to his dominating management style.

"When Pappy hired me, I was still a senior at Ohio University, but he needed me to replace another teacher that was run out of town," said Robert "Gene" Riffle, who Wayne had hired to teach industrial arts. "I took the job, but I had to spend all summer building new desks for the students as part of my duties. So, not only did Wayne get a new teacher but he got new desks as well." Rules were to be strictly followed to maintain order and fairness. Right was right and fair was fair, with few exceptions allowed.

When neighbor Barbara Scott was to enter the first grade, her mother showed up on the Hayes's front porch with an appeal to allow her daughter to start school with her friends, even though her birthday fell just days past the December cutoff.

"My mother took me with her to his house to talk to him personally, and he firmly said no," Barbara Scott said. "He said that was the rule, and that was it. He was a very strict and very formal man."

Wayne was as strict and demanding at home as he was in the classroom. Self-educated and self-reliant, he expected as much from his children as he did from himself, and he took a formal approach toward his family, signing letters sent to his daughter Mary, away at school, "your father W. B. Hayes." He insisted that his children be a cut above the rest in their class, and he pushed them to achieve so much so that Woody once said, "I believe there is nothing tougher than being the school's superintendent's son."

But the demands were countered with a strong sense of fairness and respect. Truant officers would be dissuaded to visit the home of a family whose son or daughter was out of school. Wayne would pay the visit instead, sparing the family the embarrassment and shame from nosy neighbors.

There wasn't a lot of frivolity and waste in the Hayes household.

Work and sacrifice were expected to extend Wayne's small-town-school salary. The family paid cash for most everything. If there was an account balance at one of the local stores it was to be paid off promptly, with no debts to mark a man of standing in the community.

Education was honored as much as hard work, and religious teaching and much of the learning took place inside the house on Canal Street. Books filled shelves all over the house, and Wayne would often read aloud to his family, reciting poetry and Latin, trying to instill in his children the importance of academics and culture.

He was reaching the pinnacle of his career and commanding a nearly reverent status. Running the school system was considered a professorial life in rural Ohio, and he fit the part. He was a popular speaker throughout the county, espousing his views with a flair for the language, yet maintaining the respect of the community.

Wayne brought home the money, but it was his wife who expertly managed it. Effie was from a large rural Ohio farm family, and with nine brothers and sisters she learned at an early age the importance of marshaling a family's resources to make ends meet.

When her husband announced to the family that he would not attend his college graduation because of the ten-dollar cap-and-gown fee, Effie dipped into a secret stash she kept in a pitcher on the kitchen sideboard and insisted that the whole family attend.

She was a proud, practical, and hardworking woman, but she also provided a sense of balance in the household, a sorely needed quality, given the high level of intensity swirling about her husband.

While Wayne Hayes was well built and a good athlete, with fine features and a tough, no-nonsense approach, Effie was a large woman who was a steadying influence on her children. She would insist that her family spend Sunday afternoons at the dinner table that was set with linen, and that the kids be dressed in their Sunday best. Around the table, the family talked about sports, world affairs, and philosophies. They gossiped about the goings-on in town, and they talked politics, instilling in Woody his rock-steady Republican beliefs.

It didn't take long for the Hayes family to rise to the top of the local social circles, given Wayne's commitment to education, Effie's involvement in various social activities, and their children's burgeoning academic and athletic abilities.

Talent ran in the family. Mary was a singer who left Ohio after high school to pursue a singing career at the Ithaca Conservatory of Music and Dramatic Art. Sending her off to such a specialized school was no small feat. Wayne would spend summers teaching at Bliss College in Columbus, and would bring each of his children down to Columbus for a week to expose them to the city life, while earning extra money to help send those same children to college. It was a major achievement and a significant personal sacrifice to send Mary to music school, but the foundation was laid long ago; all of the Hayes children would go to college.

The investment paid off. Mary went on to star on Broadway during the late 1920s, playing the leading lady in *The War Song*. During the Depression she became the first female radio announcer in New York City and went on to write a series of radio programs. Despite the eight years difference in age, Woody was close to his sister and often went to her for advice, even later in his life, when his coaching career was already well established.

Before self-publishing a coaching manual, Woody shipped a copy to his singer sister in New York City, seeking her approval for what was nothing more than a bound set of offensive plays.

"I hope you will not dismiss the book as being too technical," Hayes wrote to his sister in 1969 just before he published his *Hot Line to Victory* manual. "I would appreciate your starting at the beginning, for you will understand much more than you expect—and I would like to have your reaction."

Woody was close to his sister, idolized his father, respected his mother, but he worshiped his older brother, Ike.

Ike was smarter, more athletic, and more popular than his younger brother, and Woody saw the gifts in his brother that he lacked in himself.

"He had a personal aura about him that was unbelievable, and I have to believe that if it weren't for his attitude and relationship to me I wouldn't have amounted to much. I was always second to him in everything I would try," Woody said.

Standing just five feet six inches tall, Ike was fearless, intense, and independent. Chafing under the constraints that can come with living in a small town with a father as a school superintendent, Ike rebelled at living up to his father's expectations, balking at going to college, despite graduating near the top of his high school class, while starring on the football team. Ike spent a few years knocking around northeastern Ohio after high school, working horses at his grandfather's farm and refusing to continue his education, despite his father's pleadings. The two brothers were so competitive that it took Woody's going off to college for Ike to accept a scholarship to Iowa State University, where he captained the football team and applied his love of horses to a career in veterinary medicine.

Woody may have publicly expressed that his brother was superior to him in every way, but one edge that he had over his brother was boxing.

Both shared a penchant for fisticuffs, and despite all the lessons of civility and the importance of education taught in the Hayes household, Woody and Ike were local town toughs, rough-and-tumble boys to steer clear of and to definitely have on your side in a fight. They were known as "Eastenders," since they lived on the east side of the railroad tracks. Those who lived on the other side of the tracks were known as "Westenders," and boys from the two sides battled furiously.

The combative nature, Woody insisted, came from his mother's side of the family.

"The Hupps were that kind of people," he said. "Her brother had been that way. They were prize fighters and oil well drillers, and they were really tough."

While Wayne, Effie, and Mary would spend Sunday mornings at the Presbyterian Church down on East Canal Street, the two brothers would clear out the parlor room furniture to make a boxing ring where they would slug it out until the rest of the family returned from services.

They eventually abandoned their parlor sparring and set up a boxing ring in a barn near the railroad tracks. These fights were more than schoolyard scrapes. They would take on all comers, fighting for the thrill of the punch and maybe a few bucks, entertaining the men at stag nights or at local, organized boxing matches.

"Out by Cy Young's farm up there in Peoli by the Elks club, where during Prohibition they used to have beer busts," Hayes later said, "they'd have prize fights and they'd have dancing girls too. Of course it was a stag affair. My brother and I were still in high school playing football, and we were both middleweight and we couldn't find anyone else to fight in our weight class, so we'd fight each other. I was a stand-up fighter and Ike was a weaving type of fighter, and we fought that way out there at Cy Young's farm and we put on quite a show. Over the hillside in Peoli was my dad, a school superintendent, giving a commencement address, and here were his two sons prize fighting at a beer bust. A member of the school board came up to my brother and said, 'Hey, does your dad know you're here?' Ike said, 'No. Does your wife know you're here?' "

One local poster dated 1931 lists Woody in a preliminary bout as a 160-pounder squaring off against a 155-pounder named Tommy Macmillan of New Philadelphia in a six-round match before the main event. No record exists of who won that bout, but Woody, a southpaw, was known to be an extremely aggressive boxer, foregoing style in favor of attacking his opponent with a flurry of left hooks looking for a quick knockout.

Local lore still circulating around town recalls a night when Wayne Hayes showed up at a speaking engagement only to find a mostly empty hall. Most of the crowd, it was said, preferred to watch the Hayes boys fight in a nearby boxing match held the same night as Professor Hayes's speech.

So deep was the respect for Wayne that it was probably the only time the professor was ever stood up in town.

The respect was rooted in his commitment to better each crop of students that matriculated at the high school. He was more than an administrator dictating policies from his office. He made it a point to know all of the students, and he took an active interest in seeing them at least graduate high school, while pushing the brighter students to attend college.

Though strict with the children in the classroom, Wayne sometimes would join in the baseball games after school, putting a wad of chewing tobacco in his mouth as he helped coach the boys.

Newcomerstown High School in the early 1930s was a handsome three story stone building located a mile or so from the Hayes's house on Canal Street. With a graduating class of fifty-one students, the Golden Trojans were typically outclassed on the football field, given that they were forced to round out their schedule against larger schools from bigger towns like New Philadelphia and Dover.

The football team was always shorthanded, with only fourteen or fifteen players on the roster playing teams with squads three or four times larger. The Golden Trojans' uniforms and equipment were tattered and their field was worse: cows routinely milled about, forcing the locals to chase the animals off the field an hour before the games so they could mark the gridiron with lime.

Woody played football, basketball, and baseball in high school; but, unlike his older brother, he wasn't a star. He stood six feet tall and weighed a muscular 160 pounds. He was slow, flat-footed, and tough, perfect credentials to play center on a lousy team that, in his senior year, won two games, with five losses and two ties. He captained the Trojans his senior season despite his mediocre talents, a nod to his natural leadership abilities.

Deliberate on the basketball court and lumbering on the baseball diamond, Woody was better suited for the football field, where he could channel his aggressive nature toward his opponents across the line.

"Woody wasn't much of a runner," said one of his former high school teammates. "But nobody ever ran over him."

His high school graduation picture depicts a self-assured young man dressed in a suit and tie, who not only played three sports but was class vice president, sang in the glee club, belonged to the Latin club, and was a member of the *Newcosean* yearbook staff, in charge of selling ads. His future, as predicted by his classmates in the 1931 *Newcosean,* saw no coaching jobs. Instead, recognizing his aggressiveness and fondness for the ring, it read that Woody would one day become a boxing champion.

His combative nature extended into the classroom. He had trouble getting along with some of his high school teachers, feeling that he knew more than they did; and that lack of respect resulted in an unremarkable academic performance.

"He always did his work," one of his former high school teachers once said. "If he hadn't done it, I probably would have remembered more about him."

Wayne Hayes may have hammered home the importance of learning, but it was a junior high school teacher named Clyde Bartholow who introduced Woody to what would become his love of history and of the practicality of English.

These lessons never left Woody, who as a coach often would reference the great historical battles he learned in grammar school to make a point to his sometimes-baffled players, as they listened to him lecture them on the battleground adversities faced by Leonidas or William the Conqueror.

"He was extremely interested in English grammar and the correct usage in expression in both speaking and writing," Bartholow said. "His papers had to meet his exacting standards, or he simply wouldn't hand them in."

It wasn't always Woody's idea to hold off turning in his work to his teachers because of a pursuit of perfection. Wayne often would insist on reading his son's written work before he handed it in, and there were many times that the homework was returned in shreds from the disapproving superintendent.

There was something else Woody was learning about himself, other than acknowledging his propensity for history and English. He hated to lose; and worse, he was a bad loser. He had a quick temper, was prone to screaming at referees, and was inconsolable after a loss. He'd miss a block or watch the other team score and he'd unleash a loud stream of profanities, screaming at his own and his team's failures. Even friendly backyard games could send him into a rage. Yet there was a natural quality about him that drew people in. Though he could erupt in anger with a stunning array of expletives, he was also a charmer when he needed to be, and he could certainly talk his way out of trouble. Woody, according to his yearbook, had the ability "to smooth over incidents such as breaking fences, and getting out of ditches."

Given the qualities noted by his senior classmates in 1931, Woody seemed destined for a life outside of football. No major football schools had much interest in a mediocre flat-footed linemen from a losing, small-town high school football team. That left smaller colleges for consideration, and with a push from a family friend named Richard Allison, Woody was headed to Granville, Ohio, to attend Denison University, a small liberal arts college that was hardly a football powerhouse. Granville is just thirty-five miles northeast of Columbus, but in football it is a world away from Ohio State University.

2

DENISON

In the early 1930s Denison University was a postcard of serenity. Tree-lined paths crisscrossed the small campus that sat on a hill above the quaint New England village of Granville, population 2,400, when Woody arrived in the fall of 1931.

The university was founded in 1831 by Baptists as a theological school, and until 1927 it was an all-male college. Enrollment stood at 848 students in 1931, and though the school's Baptist affiliation was falling away, it still focused on instilling a Christian education on its student body.

Traditionally, Denison was run by Baptist ministers, and its president in 1931 was a man named Avery Shaw, whose goal was to maintain the school's reputation as a Christian college. That meant mandatory weekly chapel attendance, vespers, and school organizations like the Student Christian Association.

The focus was mainly on academics. Organized sports existed simply to help round out the students' overall college experience, perhaps helping fulfill the "sound mind, sound body" philosophy.

Classes were small and attendance mandatory, with much of the school's social hierarchy centered on the Greek system. Students also belonged to clubs like the Maskers, and other literary organizations like the Franco-Calliopean Literary Society, that were prevalent at the school.

Most incoming male students were pledged to fraternities through sponsors or via "legacies" before they even stepped on campus in the fall. Richard Allison, the family friend, Denison alum and Sigma Chi, sponsored Woody, paving the way for him to join ten other pledges when he moved into the handsome stone dorm building of the Mu chapter of the fraternity.

The transition from a brash, small-town kid to a Sigma Chi freshman pledge wasn't all that easy for Hayes, whose aggressive personality
sometimes clashed with the upperclassmen. His roommates during his
freshman year were Bob Lowry from Chicago, and Robert Amos, a
legacy from nearby Cambridge, Ohio, whose father, brother, and uncles
had all attended Denison and were members of the local Sig chapter.

While the more worldly roommates sailed through the Sigma Chi
initiation, Woody chafed under the initiation process by his "brothers,"
who berated the pledges for various infractions.

"The discipline imposed was not to Woody's liking some of the
time, and his dislike only added to his woes in his relationships with
members bent on seeing him toe the mark," Amos said. He was cocky
around his male classmates, but awkward in the company of young
women, although he dated irregularly.

"He was not a ladies' man on campus," Amos recalled. "Soon after
our arrival, I introduced him to some girls who likewise were freshmen. Woody feigned surprise that they hadn't heard of him, saying,
'Surely you must have read about me in the newspapers.' The remark
was intended to be a joke, but the girls got the impression that he was
conceited."

It cost $125 per semester to attend Denison in 1931, not including
a $2.50 athletic fee and another $2.50 hospital fee. The school charged
another two to five dollars per student for classes (that included lab
fees) bringing the semester fees to almost $150.

It was a steep price for the Hayes family to pay. To defray the
tuition, Woody worked as a waiter at the Sig house and did mainte-
nance work around campus; and that work ethic carried over to the
football field.

He made up for his lack of agility on the gridiron with drive and
determination that made him a part-time player as a freshman, and he
cracked the starting lineup by the start of his sophomore season.

"There were better football players at Denison than I, but there
were only three of us in the class of 1935 that lettered for three straight
years," Woody later boasted.

Denison's coach during the 1931 through 1933 seasons was George
Rich, a former football star at the University of Michigan, who fielded

underachieving teams with average players too slow and small to play at larger schools, much less at giant universities like nearby Ohio State. Playing other small schools like Oberlin, Kenyon, and Wittenberg, the Denison Big Red won no more than two games in each of Woody's freshman, sophomore, and junior seasons. The 1932 squad was the worst, with the Big Red posting a sorry 0-4-2 record. The team was shut out that year three times, while scoring a total of eighteen points for the entire season.

The game, despite the team's misfortunes, was taking a greater hold on Hayes, thanks mostly to his relationship with an assistant coach under Rich named Tommy Rogers, who coached at Denison since 1926 and who was admired by the administration and beloved by the players.

Rogers made a strong impression on Woody early on, driving him to improve as a player while also treating him with respect. The two became close, and the influence deepened after Rogers replaced Rich as head coach after the 1933 season.

"Rogers was what every college student needs," Hayes later recalled. "Someone to admire, respect, and a man who could act as a father confessor."

Hayes was smart and tough on the field, but he wasn't all that durable, sitting out two games during his senior season with injuries. He was an aggressive player, challenging his teammates and opponents with equal energy. Outside of Granville, Denison football was obscure. Its teams were filled with small college talent. But the games took on a sense of importance for Woody that bordered on the extreme, seemingly out of context with his team's obscurity.

"He was musclebound and hence lacked appreciable speed, but his enthusiasm and leadership qualities made him a standout," Robert Amos said.

The team's fortunes made an immediate and dramatic improvement under Rogers with a 5-2-1 record. Woody's athletic success, combined with Rogers serving as his role model, began to stir aspirations in becoming a coach and, like his father, a teacher.

His academic load was heavy, with a double major in history and English and minors in Spanish and physical education, but Woody gradually adjusted to college life. He became an active student, joining the Student Christian Association, which supplanted the YMCA to coordinate the men's social and religious activities on campus. Hayes joined "D" Association lettermen's club, that, along with promoting school spirit, monitored freshman behavior on campus.

"That was accomplished, as usual, by the means of the paddle," according to the school yearbook, *Adytum*.

Hayes began a major transformation during his sophomore year, channeling his drive and energy into football and other sports. He played on the baseball team during his junior and senior years after Denison revived its baseball program, which had been disbanded for several seasons. He also taught boxing as part of his physical education curriculum. His academic achievement, however, was unremarkable.

"He was a good student in the classes he thought were important," his roommate Robert Amos said. "For those he didn't care for, he struggled a bit. But he had a photographic memory, and particularly amazing was his ability to remember names, dates, and other particulars about past events. He could stay up and cram all night to cover nearly the entire course work."

Woody got a new roommate in his junior year when he decided to room with Jim Otis, who transferred from the University of Michigan to Denison before the start of his sophomore year. Woody and Otis, the son of a physician from Celina, Ohio, had a lot in common. Both had fathers who expected a lot from their sons and both were high spirited. But the two couldn't have been more physically different. At five foot six and weighing 130 pounds, the closest Otis got to the football field was on sidelines as the school's yell leader. He was also a sharp dresser and, unlike his roommate, was popular with the girls on campus. Yet the two were nearly inseparable on campus, with Woody serving as Otis's protector.

"He was a boxer and I was his second in the ring," Otis said. "We would go out and beer up a little bit in the bars in Newark, and I'd get into fights and he'd settle them for me. He was protective, dependable, and a helluva fighter."

After his rough initiation, college became an idyllic time for Woody. The three-story Sigma Chi house that overlooked Deeds Field was one of the most attractive buildings on campus, with its two-story white columns framing the large front porch of the stone structure. Dubbed the "Old Stone Pile," the spacious fraternity house featured a large gathering area on the first floor and a wood-paneled library with a large fireplace, where the Sigma Chi members would gather to smoke, drink, and socialize. The Mu chapter was the center of Woody's social life, and competition between fraternities raged on the small campus, with each house vying for the best grades, the best athletes, and the best girlfriends.

Woody never smoked, drank only socially, and paid more attention to athletics than to the girls on campus.

"Socially, I had more to do with dating girls than Woody did, though I remember one time the house was having a dance and neither one of us had dates, so we spent the night in our room drinking orange blossoms, which was rye whiskey and orange juice," Otis said. "Woody really wasn't much of a drinker, but the most he drank in his life was with me."

His fraternity brothers nicknamed him "Kid Clutch," after his habit of shadowboxing, and mockingly called him "Alice," after a woman he unsuccessfully tried to court.

Woody grew more gregarious with each passing semester, regaling his fraternity brothers with stories and jokes, yet he still remained different from most of his classmates. For many students, college was a time to explore and shape different beliefs, but Woody was opinionated and stubborn, already seeing the world in mostly black-and-white tones.

"He was an independent soul and somewhat of a maverick, with definite likes and dislikes," Amos said. "And these traits didn't diminish as he grew older."

He was temperamental to such an extreme that it was fast becoming a defining characteristic, earning him the reputation of someone who could become violent if he lost his temper, according to Richard Mahard, a Denison professor during the 1940s.

"He was hard-boiled, a fighter, and a winner. Denison had intramural boxing and Woody was facing an opponent who landed a punch that surprised him. The punch made him angry, and Woody lost control of himself and began to beat the devil out of the guy. The inexperienced referee didn't get to him before Woody had pretty badly hurt the guy."

Woody had beefed up to 190 pounds by his senior year, and he was a mainstay on the line and a team leader. But his academic achievements were not nearly as impressive as his athletic efforts, ranking 131 out of 143 students in his graduating class. Still, the combination of his athletics and his double majors made him an attractive prospect as a teacher, and Woody had two job offers in the spring of 1935. One was to teach history at Dundee High School in rural Ohio, where he would coach the basketball team. The other was an English teaching job at Mingo Junction, where he also would work as an assistant football coach.

The basketball position paid more and was more prestigious, but his preference for football guided him to take the lower-ranked coaching position at Mingo Junction. It was a seemingly inconsequential choice at the time, but one that set the course for his coaching future.

Rogers had been steering Woody toward coaching, and with job in hand Rogers had helped arrange for him to attend a coaching clinic to extend his knowledge and skill level. On June 10, 1935, Woody received his diploma at Denison, said good-bye to his Sigma Chi brothers, and hitchhiked up to Toledo to participate in the clinic led by Richard Harlow, then the head football coach at Harvard, and by Francis Schmidt, who had just been appointed head football coach at Ohio State.

There, Woody would discover one of the most important qualities of a successful coach: the ability to make the right connections with other coaches that would pay off later.

3

THE APPRENTICESHIP

Mingo Junction, Ohio, sits next to the Ohio River, just across the West Virginia state line. In 1935, the town, named after the Mingo Indian tribe, was bursting at the seams with high-grade coal that lay beneath the hilly landscape, and while immigrant miners worked underground, the steel companies were quickly ramping up their factories the summer when Woody Hayes came to town.

Hayes had spent the past four years living in bucolic Granville, with his earnest Sigma Chi fraternity brothers. Now he was living in an industrial town anchored by steel factories. Mingo Junction was blue collar, smoke stacks, and coal dust. It was as unremarkable a place for Hayes to begin his coaching career as anywhere.

His first teaching assignment was to teach English to remedial seventh graders and to serve as assistant head football coach under John Murh for $1,260 a year. The teaching proved more rewarding than the football. Woody never jelled with Murh, and the team finished with a losing record.

But the year had its own rewards off the field, with Woody feeling like he had made a difference in his seventh grade classroom by helping motivate his slower-learning students.

"These youngsters were merely neglected learners," Hayes said. "I still feel that this may have been my best year of teaching. I liked those youngsters and they liked me."

Hayes was disaffected by the lackluster football program at Mingo High, despite the rewards that came from the seventh graders, and when the job of assistant coach opened up at New Philadelphia High School in the summer of 1936, he jumped at the chance to return to Tuscarawas County where he would be working just fifteen miles from his hometown.

High school sports, particularly football, captured most of New Philadelphia's attention during the mid-1930s. The NFL was still in its infancy, and though Canton, the birthplace of the NFL, was located just thirty miles from New Philadelphia, the pro game was still strictly a local draw. The Cleveland Rams played on Sundays up north, but with no television the games garnered little interest beyond their city limits. The fall sports pages at the *Daily Times* instead led with the fortunes of the New Philadelphia High School Quakers, with secondary coverage devoted to Ohio State football games. From preseason practice to the annual season-ending Thanksgiving Day game between the Quakers and the Crimson Warriors from nearby Dover, few details of the football team were left unreported by the paper, in order to satisfy the craving for football news from the locals who firmly embraced their team.

The players would be feted to a chicken dinner by a local family or restaurant the night before each game and before home games, the band mothers club would serve the team a pregame lunch of orange slices, baked potatoes, broiled steak, toast, celery, and tea. The local booster club arranged for special train service to transport devoted fans to away games.

Come game days, the local paper would compare the height and weight of each boy at each position from both teams, pointing out any discrepancies that would play in the Quakers's favor. Bonfires, parades, and snake dances—a student march from the school to the town square—were all part of the football pageantry, as the town turned out en masse to watch the games, many of which were held at night to maximize interest.

Each game was a community event, but none bigger than the season-ending game against Dover. The two adjacent towns had a deep rivalry that dated back to the early 1800s, when they fought over which municipality would serve as the Tuscarawas county seat. New Philadelphia won that battle, but the rivalry was fought on high school football fields for generations. The Thanksgiving Day game was treated as one of the top local news stories of the year by the editors at the *Daily Times*. Each starting lineup would be given top billing in the week leading up to the game, with various sidebars detailing injuries, schedules, and past performances. Even the marching bands' routines would be scrutinized by the local press. In 1939, the intrepid *Daily Times* disclosed that both the New Philadelphia and Dover bands—both of which had been practicing secretly for weeks to prepare for the big game—had unknowingly picked the same number, "The Darktown Stutters Ball," to be performed at halftime.

It should come as no surprise, given the number of newspaper column inches reserved for high school football, that Hayes's arrival in the summer of 1936 was big news. With just one season of coaching experience under his belt, but a salesman at heart, Woody was able to impress John Brickels, the highly regarded head coach, that he was the man for the job after the departure of assistant football coach Ike Truby.

Woody was only five years removed from his high school football days, but his name was still well known around the county. It would be a homecoming of sorts that would greatly impact him on both a personal and professional level.

Hayes made his official debut in late August 1936, when he opened football practice. The *Daily Times* called it "Toggery Monday," when Hayes welcomed the players to practice by handing out the equipment. He was one of four new coaches in Tuscarawas County that year, and he was handing out the uniforms only because Brickels was away in Chicago attending a coaching clinic. The local paper promised that the coach would "return from his classes with his head crammed full of new ideas in time to put the Quaker athletes through their paces."

Every successful coach has a mentor or a sponsor of sorts who supports and otherwise pulls younger coaches up through the ranks. Woody found his sponsor in John Brickels, who was already nearing legendary status when Hayes was hired as an assistant coach and history teacher in 1936. Brickels began coaching at New Philadelphia in 1930 after he graduated from Wittenberg College. He took over as head football coach after two years as an assistant coach, and during one dominant stretch his Quakers won thirty-six out of forty games.

Brickels would go on to a notable coaching career, leaving New Philadelphia to coach high school basketball in Huntington, West Virginia, and then moving on to coach basketball at West Virginia University. He returned to Ohio to help Paul Brown coach the Cleveland

Browns, and after that he would follow Hayes to Miami of Ohio, where he served as athletic director until his death in 1964.

"He taught me more about dealing with young people than anyone," Hayes said of his mentor.

Hayes still didn't consider coaching his true calling when Brickels hired him. Unable to apply to law school in the summer of 1936, Hayes instead enrolled at the graduate school of education at Ohio State University to better qualify him for an administrative job as a principal or superintendent.

He learned as much about football during his summers in Columbus as he did about public education. He roomed at the Sigma Chi house on the Ohio State campus, and his housemates during those summers were Brickels, Paul Brown, then the successful coach at Massilion High School, and Sid Gillman, an innovative young coach with progressive ideas about football that included offenses built around the forward pass.

The coaches would convene at the Sig house in the evening and discuss, argue, and steal each other's ideas, to be used when they went back to their respective coaching jobs in the fall. It was for Woody the equivalent of a football laboratory, as so much of his coaching philosophy can be traced to those skull sessions at the Sigma Chi house.

The 1936 season ushered in a new era both for Hayes and the New Philadelphia team. Playing in a newly refurbished stadium as part of the WPA program, the Red and Black rolled through its schedule with a 9-1 record and outscored their opponents 341–52, including a 73–0 win over nearby Urlichsville and gaining the county championship with a 14–13 win over Dover.

The next season proved as successful, with the Quakers posting another 9-1 season and Hayes taking on a bigger coaching role in his second season with Brickels, who allowed his assistant to develop his own more aggressive coaching style.

Their coaching styles couldn't have been more different. Brickels was a delegator, and he used a gentler touch in disciplining his players. He'd install the offense and then sit back in practice and observe quietly, calmly making adjustments. His patient demeanor and studious approach bred confidence in his players, and many times during the season the Quakers stormed back for comeback wins. Off the field, Brickels was warm and outgoing and always made time for speaking engagements.

Motivation through fear was Woody's biggest coaching tool, with the intricacies of the game still to be mastered. But his quick temper and demanding style were sometimes tough on the young high school players who were developing physically and emotionally.

Brickels saw Woody's talents early on. His young coach easily grasped the game's nuances, and he proved to be a quick read. He had developed a good rapport with his players for such a young coach, but if there was one quality that Brickels felt Hayes lacked, it was being able to control his emotions when a player made a mistake.

"He lacked patience," Brickels once said. "I tried to tell him that when he corrected a kid, he shouldn't make an enemy of the boy, but Woody had a hard time controlling himself and he drove the kids too hard."

Still, Woody's emerging coaching ability impressed Brickels enough to recommend his assistant as his replacement. Underneath the smoldering temper was the ability to instill confidence in his team. His sometimes harsh demands for perfection were countered by his knack of connecting with his players, fostering loyalty and a unified effort, and it was that connecting that was the driving force behind his development. Brickels saw that his assistant was fast separating himself from other young coaches, and he paved the way for Woody to take over as head coach.

Woody turned twenty-six years old the year he took over from Brickels. He was now a head football coach and his career was gaining definition. He had harbored the idea of going back to school to study law, but those thoughts were growing faint, because in the fall of 1938 he was completely focused on winning football games.

His first two seasons as head coach were impressive, with a combined record of 18-1-1. His 1939 squad was undefeated, with one tie, in one of the toughest schedules in the state. Woody's offense was simple: a straight-ahead run-blocking attack with limited passing. The resoundingly successful 1939 season caused many of the local boosters to quickly forget the beloved Brickels, particularly after the Quakers ended their season with a crushing 46–0 defeat over rival Dover on a rainy Thanksgiving Day in front of five thousand fans. It was the second undefeated season for the Quakers since 1934, and the devoted followers of the team had no quarrel with Woody's coaching ability.

"The great Ohio juggernaut will go down in history as one of the best—if not *the* best—football team ever produced by the Red and Black school," blared the *Daily Times*. "Their schedule included perhaps the most formidable array of foes to face a local team in many years, yet the club amassed 267 points and became the fourth-highest scoring schoolboy eleven in the state."

The 1939 season was bittersweet. Wayne Benton Hayes died of a stroke in his home on March 16, 1939, at age fifty-eight. Woody would mourn his father with six hundred other people who packed the First Presbyterian Church. The headline in the local paper read WHOLE TOWN MOURNS DEATH OF SUPT. HAYES, with a sidebar calling Wayne Hayes "A Man Among Men."

Woody was just twenty-seven when his father died. Though Woody's personality resembled his mother's confident nature, he was intellectually similar to his father, a student of history and a voracious reader. Woody's growing confidence in his coaching abilities was reflected in his development into a fine public speaker, a skill he inherited from his dad. Woody could inspire his teams with his recantations of famous battles, making the wars come alive to his young players, as though they too were about to take part in some Roman conquest for the ages.

Wayne Hayes's code of ethics was also deeply ingrained in his son. Woody was a tough, aggressive, and temperamental coach, but he was anchored in a foundation of honesty and fairness.

Just before he died, Wayne ordered his son to go down to the local Russell Bean department store to pay off a small balance that wasn't yet due.

"I paid the bill and a week later my father died," Hayes said. "That taught me a lesson. My father left this world without owing anyone a dime."

The undefeated 1939 season helped offset the sudden death of his father, and other aspects of Woody's personal life were mirroring his success on the field. He was now deeply involved with a local girl who could actually tolerate his addiction to football.

Anne Gross was an auburn-haired graduate of Ohio Wesleyan University, where she majored in sociology before returning to her hometown of New Philadelphia. They met when Woody was at Brickels's home. Anne, a longtime family friend, happened to stop by to drop off a basket of May flowers. Hayes took an immediate interest in Anne, so Brickels called Anne a little later and formally introduced her to Hayes over the phone. During their conversation, Woody boldly asked Anne for a date that same night, but the twenty-three-year-old declined. She already had a date for the evening.

Anne eventually would date Hayes, but it wasn't love at first sight. The two struck up a friendship; Anne enjoyed football, and, most importantly, understood sports. Her parents spent their honeymoon watching nine big-league baseball games in Cleveland and Detroit, and her college roommate was Mary Rickey, sister of pitching star Branch Rickey.

Anne was working in the Tuscarawas juvenile court when she met Hayes, and with her good looks and quick smile she had plenty of other suitors. Woody, however, did not. He spent all of his time holed up in his office, drawing up football plays. If Anne wanted to spend quality time with him, she had better learn the difference between a T formation and wing offense.

"Football was my game," Anne once said. "When I was in college I wouldn't miss a football or basketball game for love nor money. When Woody was an assistant at New Philadelphia, we'd go somewhere and scout. That was my date."

Woody's devotion to football left little room for romance, but there was a mutual attraction. Woody was handsome, and, while he was clumsy around women, he managed to relate to Anne in a way he had never been able to with other girls.

"On our first date, all Anne wanted to talk about was Bob Feller, the new pitcher for the Cleveland Indians," Woody recalled.

Anne, for her part, seemed to be able to see through Woody's headstrong and combustible personality, and she enjoyed being around the football team. He had a confident manner that held the promise of success, and Anne sensed in Woody good things to come.

They were a compatible couple, but Hayes would often find himself having to defend himself in the company of Anne. Her looks and personality often stood out in whatever room she occupied, and while Woody could be profane, he had little tolerance for anyone else using profanity around Anne.

"There were times when Woody, Anne, and my wife and I would be out for dinner and having a glass of beer or two when a guy would get into his cups and raise hell and start cussing," Otis said. "Woody could never stand that, and he'd cool the guy off with his boxing skills."

Woody was riding high in late 1939. His relationship with Anne was growing deeper, and he basked in the glory of leading the Quakers through an undefeated season. But trouble lay ahead. The powerhouse varsity was losing most of its players to graduation, depleting the roster and dampening the outlook for the upcoming 1940 season. Still, the locals had grown accustomed to winning, and the expectations ran high as practice began in September against the backdrop of World War II.

The Nazis had invaded France, Belgium, Luxembourg, and the Netherlands, and Winston Churchill was named British prime minister in May of 1940. A month later the Germans were bombing France into submission, and all over America eighteen-year-old boys were heading off to war, including many of the New Philadelphia graduates. Rationing was in full effect, while German U-boats sank merchant ships in the Atlantic. The same week Hayes was handing out football pads to his team, England was under siege as the German Blitzkrieg rained on London.

People in small towns like New Philadelphia raised the flag, bought war bonds, and burned less oil, in support of America's war-making machine that was cranking out bombs, ships, and tanks as fast as our factories could build them. None of this was lost on Hayes, the history major who was well-read about the great wars, and who firmly believed that football served as an extension of the battlefield.

He embraced the idealistic notions of heroism, bravery, and courage that could be found not just on the battlefield, but also on the gridiron. But to most others in New Philadelphia in 1940, high school football served as a simple distraction to the harsh realities of the war in Europe. Twenty-three varsity players had graduated, but Woody's first two successful seasons had blinded any Booster Club doubts, and hopes ran high for another impressive year for the Red and Black.

By midseason it was clear that the 1940 season would be as much a disaster as the 1939 team was a success. The team was undermanned and undersized and, given their dominance over the past decade, opposing teams took no mercy on the inept Quakers team that just a season earlier was hailed as one of Ohio's all-time greats.

The Red and Black went 1-9 in the 1940 season, the failure of the lost season magnified by past successes. Hayes grew more frustrated with each loss and worked his players harder, placing more pressure and showing more impatience on far-less-talented players who couldn't satisfy his demands. No matter how hard he pushed his players, they couldn't respond. They simply weren't talented enough. Practice became torturous for those young boys. Hayes would vent his anger with profane outbursts and sometimes hit players in frustration over fumbles, missed assignments, and the overall ineptitude. The season ended with a whimper. The Quakers lost to their Dover rivals 19–0, putting an end to their misery on the field.

Off the field, Woody's problems were just beginning. Rumors had been slowly but steadily spreading about his harsh behavior toward his players, and it took just a few days after the season ended before school superintendent H. S. Carroll acted on the raft of complaints surrounding Woody's behavior. On November 26, a banner headline across the *Daily Times* screamed QUAKER GRID COACH MAY LOSE POSITION.

The article informed the readers that Carroll had notified Hayes that he would not recommend he be retained for the 1941 season, based on reports of his abusive behavior in practice. Carroll claimed that Woody had been warned about the use of profanity for the past three years, and now he was forced to take action against the head coach.

The announcement caught many by surprise, and it infuriated

Hayes, who in the past three years had carefully cultivated support from various school board members. The members called Woody in support, and they suggested that he appear before the school board to challenge Carroll's recommendation. The day after Carroll's announcement, the school board granted Hayes a full hearing to allow him to defend himself, buying him some time. The football players also rallied around their coach, announcing plans for a protest strike by skipping class.

Hayes publicly convinced his players to call off their protest, a move that only helped his cause. He then issued a blistering statement to the *Daily Times* in an effort to save his job and reputation.

"Since Mr. Carroll has made no effort to definitely establish authenticity on the rumors on which he has based his complaint, and since he has completely ignored any testimony I should wish to give, I have appealed to the board of education for a hearing on these charges," he said in the statement.

"Several times during the season, I have invited Mr. Carroll, or a capable representative, to attend our practices so that he would know that I was complying with his wishes. At no time did he accept this invitation.

"I regard this attack upon the members of the team as unfair and unfounded, and it is my contention that I have had the full support and cooperation of my squad at all times. Needless to say, I am deeply sorry that such a situation has arisen; but since Mr. Carroll's accusations are of such personal nature, I feel, in fairness to my squad and myself, the only satisfactory means of vindication lies in the method which has been chosen. I am grateful to the members of the board for the open-mindedness they have displayed in granting me this hearing."

There was no response in the paper by Carroll, and the paper's coverage worked in Woody's favor. There was public outcry over his pending dismissal as football coach, with members of the New Philadelphia Booster Club packed into the city council chambers in support of a resolution that was passed on November 30 to reinstate Hayes. During a special school board meeting on December 2, Carroll publicly reversed his decision to fire Hayes in front of fifty local merchants, four hundred booster club members, and dozens of parents.

"I told Mr. Hayes that I would not recommend him for reappointment, but since that time you folks have been very much disturbed, even more so than I was," Carroll said in the meeting. "After a long conference [I am] convinced that perhaps we should go another mile with Woody. We are ready to go that mile with him."

The sudden reversal came with some assurances that Hayes "will refrain from the use of profanity in the presence of his boys, and that he will do all he can to discourage the use of foul and profane language by the boys, and that he will attend to his duties as coach at the time provided for the purpose and leave administrative functions where they belong, in the hands of the principal."

Carroll then assured the crowd that his actions had nothing to do with the team's lousy season.

"We all agree that [Hayes] has a perfect right to discipline his boys for impudence," he said. "We will back our coach, regardless of the team's wins or losses. We are not concerned with the win-and-loss record of the team, but we are concerned with how athletics are conducted and played."

Hayes and Carroll then shook hands and the embattled coach rose and defiantly addressed the crowd.

"In the last week I said a lot of things which I am glad I do not have to repeat here tonight," Hayes said. "Several times during the year I have disciplined my boys and at times severely, but when they came back, we agreed to let bygones be bygones, and I believe they were better boys for the discipline. I expect to cooperate one hundred percent. I could have left town and saved a lot of confusion, but I believe I had a case and I still do. I feel sure that we can go on as if these things had not happened."

Hayes then promised a better team in 1941 and thanked his supporters, who gave him a standing ovation.

Despite the public agreement to "let bygones be bygones," the incident took its toll. Woody was hurt and angry over the charges and the perceived damage to his reputation, and he questioned whether he wanted to continue coaching the Quakers. His options were limited. Law school was already out of the question, he hadn't yet completed his master's degree in educational administration, and his relationship with Anne was still undefined after years of sporadic dating.

But the war was still raging in Europe, and serving in the military presented an honorable way to leave New Philadelphia on his own terms. Hayes thought about it for a while and then decided to enlist in the navy. There was a war to fight, he figured, and almost everyone of his generation was going to war, and he may as well as do his part. So, in March of 1941, he finished coaching the Quakers' spring practice, and installed the T-formation that he learned from one of the coaching clinics he regularly attended. But Hayes would never see the new offense in game action. That summer he said good-bye to Anne and headed for the navy. He would never coach at the high school level again.

4

DENISON AGAIN

The road back to Denison began at the massive naval base in Newport News, Virginia, where Hayes was assigned to a physical fitness program headed by former world heavyweight champion Gene Tunney.

Sports during the war struck an odd chord in America. Athletes and young coaches joined the war effort, yet there was a hesitation on the part of the government in sending high-profile athletes to the front lines. The last thing the war department wanted was to give the enemy a morale boost for killing one of our nation's heroes, as well as keeping the nation's morale from plummeting over the loss in action of one of America's stars. Yet these same heroes were valuable on another level, given their ability to draw attention to the war effort and to help raise millions of dollars in war bonds. So there was a compromise of sorts. Programs like the physical education training program were headed by men like Tunney. The ex-champ had joined the marines in 1918, served in the navy from 1940 to 1945 and was charged with leading the training program, which allowed many athletes and coaches to fulfill their military obligations while staying out of harm's way.

But during the war, and particularly after the bombing of Pearl Harbor, there was a small group of sports stars who saw real combat. Ted Williams survived two crash landings as a fighter pilot, and there were others who wanted real action, instead of safer stateside duty. Detroit Tigers slugger Hank Greenberg enlisted in 1941, even though he could have gotten a medical exemption for flat feet. He missed almost five seasons while he served. Warren Spahn was a member of the infantry and earned a Purple Heart. Yogi Berra saw action during the D-Day invasion at Normandy. Nile Kinnick, the University of Iowa football star and 1939 Heisman Trophy winner, crashed his fighter and was lost at sea.

Thanks to Tommy Rogers, Hayes's friend and former coach at Denison, who was well-connected to some navy brass, Woody entered the navy as an assistant boatswain's mate and shortly thereafter was commissioned as a junior-grade officer. The Tunney Program was teeming with like-minded men, and it was there he met Rix Yard, a bright young graduate of the University of Pennsylvania, where he was a star tackle on the 1940 football team. The two struck up a friendship as they taught physical fitness to platoons of new recruits. Yard was impressed by Woody's football knowledge and Hayes recognized and appreciated Yard's football background.

"He was very involved in football," Yard said. "I was coaching a six-man football team and was there for eight or nine months, and we got to be good friends and we talked football a lot. Then we both got shipped out."

Yard was sent to Boston to train as a submarine officer. Woody would go on to another navy fitness program, this one run by commander Tom Hamilton, who was a former football star at the naval academy and another friend of Tommy Rogers.

Again it was soft duty drawn by athletes and coaches, including Hayes and a tough young southerner named Paul "Bear" Bryant, who was coaching a football team on the base.

Woody still held lofty ideas about serving the country and fighting the war, and he wanted more from the navy. Life on the base was stifling. Woody rarely drank, didn't play cards, and wasn't content to while away his duty leading platoons of sailors through mindless exercise. He was itching for some real action at sea, and got it by befriending the yeoman assigned to the commander charged with approving sea duty orders on the base. The trick, he was told, was to make sure his orders were at the bottom of the stack, because the number of orders to be approved was so large that the commander only looked at the first few at the top of the pile and then hastily signed the remaining papers.

The strategy worked. In late spring 1942, Hayes finally got his orders to ship out. But before he would embark, he called up Anne and proposed. The two had dated on and off for six years before Woody finally asked for her hand in marriage. The wedding took place on June 19, 1942. A week later he would be shipped off to sea.

"We never kept steady company," Anne said. "In fact, we were never engaged. He had some leave time due. I accepted his proposal over the phone, he came home, and we were married."

The marriage hinged upon Anne's ability to stand up to her husband, to be strong enough to put him firmly in his place when his outbursts exceeded reasonable levels. Anne's pleasant temperament ran counter to Woody's explosive nature and gave balance to the marriage.

"We've never had an argument, but we fight a lot," Anne said. "We never have time for a really good fight, though. When you're off base emotionally, you don't think right." Her logic, though, was clearly lost on her husband.

When they'd argue things could get comically ugly. Once, during a fight, Anne locked herself in the bathroom and took a long bath to escape his wrath. After a while, he calmed down, broke into the bathroom, sat on the toilet, and served his wife a peace offering of champagne.

"How can you stay angry with a man who serves you champagne in the bathtub?" Anne once told a local women's club. "It was funny. It was delicious. The problem was that I don't like champagne and neither does he, but we drank it."

Anne also took a keen interest in Woody's players, serving as counselor, den mother, and confidant. She would throw open her house for the team, cooking dinners, lending moral support, and offering occasional housing. Her homey touch helped the players through personal problems and helped them get over the pressures of playing for her husband. In return, the players developed a firm sense of loyalty to Woody and Anne, helping counter his demands on the football field.

"It gives us a chance to get to know them well," Anne once said of her famously warmhearted approach to the players. "And if a boy has a problem, sometimes we can help before it becomes a big one. That's where my role as coach's wife ends though. I let Woody do the coaching."

There was also a practical nature in their relationship. Woody had little interest or skill in running a household. Anne was the boss at home, paying the bills and giving her husband her undying support, which allowed him to focus solely on coaching. Through all the battles

Woody would fight, she was his biggest ally, and she would later become a popular public figure in her own right throughout Ohio.

"Anne was a lovely lady with a great personality and she helped Woody considerably," Otis said. "They were different, but they really had little animosity between them."

Anne's shopworn line, delivered at countless speeches, summed up her life with her husband.

"Divorce Woody? Never," she would deadpan. "But there were times I wanted to murder him."

Ten days after his wedding he reported for duty and spent the next three years earning rank on two ships, Patrol Chaser *1251* in the Palau Islands invasion in the Pacific, and the USS *Rinehart*, a destroyer escort ship that carried three hundred seamen.

It was aboard the *Rinehart* that Hayes would define his naval career. In April 1945, he was assigned as executive officer of the *Rinehart*, as it plied the convoy lanes in the Atlantic theater. The job was among the most challenging on the ship. Basically, the duties of the executive officer were to serve at the pleasure of the ship's commander. It could be a difficult assignment to satisfy a commanding officer's often arbitrary demands, but Hayes made an immediate impression on Lt. Cmdr. Aubrey Engle, who knew nothing of his subordinate's background.

"I was expecting a guy named Wayne Hayes and I got Woody," Engle said. "It's not easy being an executive officer. You have to do everything, and Woody was the best I had on six ships that I commanded. He knew his way around the ship he'd never been on before."

Hayes's duties as executive officer also included being the navigator of the *Rinehart*. The destroyer was 306 feet long, with a thirty-six-foot beam and a displacement of 1,400 tons. Its 12,000-horsepower turbine engines generated a cruising speed of twenty-three knots, and it was armed with six sets of triple torpedo tubes. The *Rinehart*'s main duty was to escort the troop ships from New York Harbor to Europe, and with the war in Europe ending in April 1945, the *Rinehart* turned to the Pacific to help guard Wake Island.

Each morning Hayes would rise an hour before dawn and help set the ship's course. Then he would hear reports on the running of the ship from each of the ship's division leaders, and then take any disciplinary action deemed necessary. Serious matters were reported to Engle.

"Woody would come up often to my quarters, but he was a good leader," Engle said. "The men liked him and he had their respect. He was cautiously social with the crew, and though I didn't know of his shore habits, he was an intense, driven guy."

Hayes's straightlaced nature ran counter to most of the sailors, but he developed a good rapport with the ship's crew, breaking up the monotony of the cruises by taking out a medicine ball and throwing it around the deck with the enlisted men. He never talked football with Engle.

"He wasn't a football coach, he was a naval officer, and that was all he cared about," Engle said.

The war was over in September 1945, just as Lieutenant Commander Hayes reached the pinnacle of his military career, replacing Engle as commanding officer of the *Rinehart*. Hayes would serve in that post until the ship was decommissioned in 1946. The promotion was fully earned. Engle gave glowing evaluations, but he did no favors to help Hayes climb the ranks.

"Woody was strictly by the book, but he also had a human side to him," Engle said. "It seemed that it was just his nature to be a commander."

Woody would see little of Anne during his years in the navy, and while he was away she gave birth to Steven Benton Hayes in October 1945. Woody wouldn't lay eyes on his son until the baby was nearly nine months old. Still, military life suited Woody well, despite the prolonged absences from his family. He thrived on the discipline and order of the military, where there was no questioning your superiors and the chain of command was to be respected at all times.

With the war raging and with so many young men off fighting during the mid-1940s, many colleges around the country suspended their sports programs, especially football. Denison University was no different. With head coach Tommy Rogers headed for the navy and the number of able bodies needed to field a team dwindling, Denison athletic director

Walter J. Livingston decided to shut down the football program in 1943. But in 1945 Livingston felt it was time to bring back varsity football. Available talent was no longer a problem. Thousands of ex-servicemen were flocking to colleges and universities for a college education funded by the GI Bill.

Thanks to Uncle Sam, Livingston wouldn't have a problem fielding a team for the 1946 season; but first, he would have to find a new coach. Rogers, who had taken over the Denison program in Hayes's senior season in 1934, would not be returning to the Granville campus, and the departure left a big hole in the program. Not only would Livingston have to revive the football program after four years of inactivity, but he would also have to do it with a new coach.

He began to consider a number of replacements, but Rogers had already decided whom he would recommend as his successor. But timing was a problem. The USS *Rinehart* was anchored in Long Beach, California, while Lieutenant Commander Hayes readied his ship to steam to Panama on the way to Boston where the *Rinehart* would be decommissioned and put into dry dock. It took a month for Rogers's letter to catch up to Hayes with the news that the Denison job was open, and asking if the former lineman would be interested in taking his old coach's job. Hayes immediately sent word to Rogers that he wanted the job, and the news was passed on to Livingston, who knew Woody from his playing days and was familiar with his high school coaching record. The job would not be filled until the summer of 1946, when Hayes could get back to Granville for an interview.

After quickly winning approval from the school's faculty committee and from the university president, Hayes was offered a two-year contract to coach football and to teach physical education.

A decade had passed since Hayes left Denison. Now, the former student who had graduated near the bottom of his class returned to his alma mater as a member of the faculty, and he was charged with reviving the moribund football team. It was a fresh start for Hayes, who had left his last coaching job under a cloud of controversy, and he was determined to take advantage of his newfound opportunity.

The first task was to hire an assistant coach. Denison's limited football budget allowed for just one full-time assistant, so choosing the right man for the job was essential. Both coaches would work side-by-side in close quarters, for hours at a time, during the football season. Whoever Hayes hired would have to have a good understanding of the new head coach, and both men would have to enjoy each other's company. The success of the team would depend on their combined abilities and the cooperation between the two coaches. Hiring the right assistant would be crucial in Hayes's development. He had never been a college coach, and he would soon discover that trying to motivate college athletes was an entirely different task than coaching a bunch of compliant high school kids.

There wasn't much time for Woody to ponder over a long list of candidates for a job that wasn't all that appealing. Denison was a small school, and on top of that Woody had little time to recruit players, so talent was a big question mark.

But Hayes had some advantages. Before he enlisted he was a regular on the coaching clinic circuit among the colleges, enabling him to build up a network of contacts. The Tunney program also provided another source of candidates, given that it was full of coaches and athletes. With the war over, there would be an ample number of potential candidates. One name stood out: Rix Yard, Woody's friend from his early navy days. Since leaving the navy as a lieutenant, Yard was coaching high school back in Pennsylvania. He was inexperienced, but he fit the profile: he was young, smart, and most importantly, he could get along with the mercurial Hayes. Unfulfilled as a high school coach, Yard readily agreed to work as line coach under Hayes, and he hastily moved to Granville to help jump-start the Denison football program.

The recruiting focus was mainly local. In nearby Newark, Ohio, which fielded strong high school football teams, Woody convinced Bob Shannon and Billy Fleitz to attend Denison, after surprising them at their summer jobs at a local 4-H camp where he worked them out on the spot to better evaluate their talent.

"He came out before lunch and made us run a series of forty-yard dashes," Shannon said. "I had to be honest with him, I wasn't that great a player, but Billy was. But I was a good student, and he kept hounding me. I was headed to the service, but he said I should come to Granville."

Shannon and Fleitz couldn't afford the Denison tuition. The school offered no athletic scholarships, but Hayes had tapped into a network of local businessmen, including his old coach Rogers, who now owned a local radio station, and a local hardware man and good friend named Mike Gregory, who would quietly pay the players' bills, helping attract talent.

"There were people in Newark interested in seeing Billy and I go to school," Shannon said. "Remember, the NCAA wasn't like it was today. I got a grant and a job for my meals, and everything else was paid for. My dad was a mailman and I was just a little old farm boy, and the day I enrolled, I went to the last table to get my bill and it was already stamped 'paid.' "

Denison's 1946 roster was an odd mixture of eager young freshmen hoping to make a good impression on their new coach and a group of older players fresh out of the service. The veterans were men who had enough discipline and regimentation to last a lifetime. The last thing they wanted from their unproven new coach was a military-like approach to football. They were fed up with having to obey orders barked at them by superior officers and they were tired of being outranked. Plus, most of these veterans smoked and drank their way through the war, and they weren't about to break their habits for some coach they'd never heard of.

On Monday, September 3, 1946, Hayes appeared in front of the players to conduct his first team meeting. Half of the team wouldn't arrive until the end of the week, but Woody wanted an early start to the training. He firmly laid out his plans for the season, making it abundantly clear that he would not tolerate anyone failing to meet his demands. The grizzled veterans rolled their eyes at the hard-line approach. Already, the season was off to an inauspicious start.

"We had all these veterans returning, but a lot of guys didn't train," said Dick Huff, a former navy man who was a freshman in 1946. "These guys didn't want to take orders from anyone, including Woody."

Another problem was brewing in the preseason practices. Hayes and Yard had decided to install a T-formation offense to replace the wing formation offense that was prevalent at the time. The transition wasn't easy for the players. Unfamiliarity bred confusion, which in turn led to a ragged offense—sending Woody into a rage and frustrat-ing the players, who struggled to learn the new system.

Some of the older players began to openly challenge their new coach. Some even threatened to fight him if he didn't back off. Dur-ing one practice, a tough-as-nails fullback named Bernie Wentis, a for-mer captain in the Marine Corps, grew tired of the screaming and came after his coach on the practice field. Woody, the former boxer who never backed down from a challenge, wisely chose not to fight his fullback.

"It wasn't good," said Bill Wehr, a center and one of the ex-servicemen who enrolled at Denison. "Woody was going around act-ing like a commander, and at the same time we were all half-polluted before games and practices."

Woody struggled to maintain control of his team. The night be-fore each game he would house the team in the school's infirmary to keep them from getting drunk. He had a different strategy for Wehr and Billy Hart, two of the most uncontrollable players on the team. The two free-spirited players couldn't be trusted to keep curfew in the infirmary, so Woody would sometimes bring them to his house on South Mulberry Street the night before games. There, they'd eat din-ner under the watchful eye of their coach. Come bedtime, Anne would send them to their rooms with a full stomach and a handshake that se-cretly included a few cigarettes.

"He didn't quite trust some of us, and we had to stay," Wehr said. "And Anne was a big factor to the whole thing. She was the only girl in the world who could stand Woody. She'd load up the refrigerator for us and we'd sleep there so we could make curfew."

Hayes's keen interest in the personal lives of his players had yet to make him more likable. His driving nature and aggressive coaching style had an unnerving effect on the team, and there would have been a mutiny, if not for Yard's calm and understanding demeanor.

The young assistant was the perfect counterbalance to Woody's harsh nature on the field. The players would turn to Yard when Hayes's frustrations became intolerable, and Yard's steady nature would usually diffuse the anger.

"It took awhile to get everyone on together, because we had such a mixture of former military people and high school players," Yard said. "There was only one way to do things and that was Woody's way. On the field he was the boss and there was no questioning him, so the kids would come and talk to me."

Yard's influence was obvious very early in the 1946 season and to Woody's credit, he was not threatened by his assistant coach. The two became more like co-coaches than the typical top-down relationship that usually develops between head and assistant coaches. Woody leaned heavily on his assistant coach and, as a result, Yard quickly gained the respect of the players.

"Rix was more introspective," Huff said. "He could sense a problem with us and he'd come over and talk to you quietly. He was like our team psychologist in a way. He helped us adjust to Woody, and I don't know how that first season would have gone without Rix."

Even with Yard acting as team counselor, the Big Red of Denison were underachievers. The team opened the season against Otterbein and lost 18–13 on a last-minute touchdown that spoiled Hayes's coaching debut. The team would go on to lose the next four games before beating Capital University 14–13. But that week the team was shut out by Ohio Wesleyan, losing 39–0. The season ended the following week with a 31–0 win over Wittenberg. But it was a hollow victory, and the players were elated to finally put an end to a miserable 2-6 season in which they were outscored by a total of 139–90.

The players knew they could compete. The end of the war flooded colleges and universities with hordes of ex-servicemen, sending college coaches around the country into a recruiting frenzy to meet the pent-up demand for players. Hayes, a natural recruiter, was able to bring in some talent.

Most of the losses came when the team faltered badly in the fourth quarter, when the players' fatigue allowed opposing teams to pile up yardage. Hayes's harsh practices also took their toll as he would try to whip the team into shape. As a result, many of the team's starters were injured during the season. It was rare for the Big Red to have its full complement of starters in the game. During the team's loss to Washington and Jefferson, Denison had five out of its eleven starters out of the lineup due to injury.

Just as the returning veterans hadn't played football in years, Woody hadn't coached since 1941, and now he was installing a new offense with an unfamiliar group of players.

"Woody was erratic that year," Huff said. "We had good material to work with, but frankly, he took a while to get used to."

It took the Denison faculty some time to adjust as well. Sports was not a major priority on campus. Hayes knew that taking the job, but he still pushed for more of a commitment, financial and otherwise from the faculty and he wasn't shy about letting the administration know that he wanted their support. But his behavior during games did little to impress the administration. With the football team playing poorly, Hayes's profane tirades directed at his players echoed around Deeds Field.

"Woody had a voice like a bullhorn. You could hear him swear all the way to Columbus," Shannon said. "And our president was a Baptist minister who went to all the home games."

Resentment among the faculty grew and many were turned off to this hard-nosed, inexperienced coach who was boldly demanding that football be placed higher on the administration's agenda.

"Football wasn't important to the administration, and the dean and the tenured faculty didn't care much for Woody," Huff said. "They thought he was disruptive and he was invading their turf."

Although the 1946 season ended with a shutout win over Wittenberg, the players were tired of Hayes and he was fed up with the futility of coaching the team. Yard wondered if he had made a mistake leaving Pennsylvania to help coach a mutinous squad of unmotivated players. Even Woody was discouraged. His return to coaching was a disaster, and he knew he would lose his team completely if he didn't figure out a way to diffuse the dissension.

There was little chance of the players escaping Hayes following the 1946 season. The campus was so small that they could hardly walk to class without seeing their coach. Many of the players were enrolled in Hayes's physical education class and as a result were forced to endure their coach even during the off-season.

But Hayes was a different man away from the football field. He treated his players kindly, took an interest in their lives, and got to know them. It was a strange transformation for many of the players. In the classroom Hayes was patient and jocular, quite opposite from the same person who could be so abusive on the practice field.

As the players recovered from their troubling first season, Hayes spent hours reviewing the disastrous performance, trying to pinpoint exactly what went wrong and how he could repair the damage.

He knew his team was poorly conditioned, which clearly was a factor. But the team also lacked the will to win, a foreign and inexcusable concept, but one, nonetheless, that he realized was plaguing his team.

He couldn't scream any harder at his players. The more he had yelled during that first season the less the team responded. Yet he knew that he could not allow a lack of discipline to infect the squad, just to appease the players. Easing up would make the players happier, but it would also cause the team to lose a measure of respect, and that would be worse than anything to Hayes.

The answer wasn't found in any off-season coaching clinic or any coaching manual. Woody instead turned to five players and created a quasi-counsel to act as a buffer between himself and the team. He would meet regularly with the group and get them to believe in his system, and he hoped that they would then influence the rest of the team, no matter how demanding or senseless it may have seemed.

Hayes also knew he had to back down a bit. He would still demand as much, if not more, but he'd do it in a way that was more palatable. He would still push his players to their limits and beyond on the practice field, but he would try to be a little more calm in his approach.

"Woody got up in front of us in chapel and said how bad it was for all of us, and that it was his fault. He then talked with us and told us what he decided to do. That first year was a bad season and Woody was tough, but he took the time to find out about all of us and he could get inside you," said Wehr, who went on to star as a Little All-American at Denison. With the truce in place by spring practice of 1947, Hayes and Yard sensed that the team was coming around to their new system.

"Woody did mellow a bit," Huff said. "He had humbled himself, and a sense of respect developed both ways. He worked with the team instead of ordering us around like he was our commander. We finally got to know him and learned when to ignore him and when to listen to him."

Still, the players entered spring practice in March full of skepticism. They needed to be convinced that Hayes was changing his ways to fully believe that things would be different. Hayes knew that more than the players, and he galvanized the team by allowing the team's starting halfback. Eddie Rupp to also play on the golf team. Rupp was a war veteran and wanted no part of the discipline. All he wanted to do was to go to class and play golf. But he was a talented runner and had deep ties to the football program. His father captained the football team and then coached the team in the late 1920s. Hayes, who desperately needed Rupp in the backfield, played upon Rupp's family history and convinced Eddie to join the team by allowing him to split time between golf and football. It was an almost unthinkable arrangement, given Hayes's ironclad demand that his players fully commit themselves to football.

Another defining moment for the players came during a spring scrimmage. Rupp, the conflicted halfback, ripped off a long run and was loping back to the huddle when Hayes halted the scrimmage, motioned his halfback over, patted him on the back, and rewarded Rupp by excusing him from practice in front of his incredulous players. The gesture would have never happened a year earlier, but Hayes badly needed to build some trust between himself and his players.

Hayes's theatrics with Rupp seemed to kick the remaining spring practice sessions into a higher gear. The team was executing the offense with precision and confidence. The players, especially the returning serviceman, had finally knocked the rust from their military days and finally were in football shape—especially after responding to Hayes's demands for increased conditioning.

There was also an up side to having former servicemen on the squad. Those ex-GIs had now been given another year to adjust to life outside the military. Some of the players were now into their midtwenties and they exuded a sense of maturity and confidence, qualities that Woody would learn to rely on throughout the season. The 1947 Denison team counted nine of the eleven starters who had military experience, including quarterback Glen "Whitey" Culp, a former navy commanding officer, who wouldn't back down from Woody, especially since he'd held the same naval rank as did his coach. Bill Wehr was an ex-navy pilot who, as center, directed the line play with a calm and confident manner. The team's fullback was Wentis, the former battle-hardened marine. At left tackle was Walt Cheslock, a former navy captain who had played for Woody at New Philadelphia High. Huff, the former navy man, was the left guard, and playing right halfback opposite Rupp was a former army man named Jerry Gainer, who was also a top student. The team was loaded with talent, in great shape, and mature enough to keep its cool on the field.

Woody was also more seasoned, and he had firmly adopted what would become his famous work ethic—the thing that drove him harder than anyone else. During the season, he'd start his day before eight A.M. and work well into the night, and he expected everyone else to do the same. Many nights Hayes would show up unexpectedly at Yard's house and demand that his assistant coach join him in his excitement for drawing up new plays.

"He'd walk into my home in the evening to get me to work, and he'd find me reading a magazine and he'd climb all over me," Yard said. "He say, 'Goddamnit Rix, what are you doing wasting time reading. We've got work to do.' That was how intense he was. There was only one way to do things and that was his way."

The successful spring practice whipped up expectations inside the team for the 1947 season, but outsiders had no clue about the changes made in the off-season. Opposing teams circled the name "Denison" on their schedules as an easy win; but when they got on the field it was soon made clear that the Big Red had undergone a major overhaul during the winter.

The Big Red opened the season at Deeds Field in a fortuitous fashion, by thumping a weak Rio Grande College team 48–0. The game was so lopsided that Hayes held off on opening the playbook, and instead stuck with a few basic off-tackle plays. He knew that his team was being scouted by coaches from Washington and Jefferson University, the perennial conference power, and he didn't want to tip his hand to Big Red's upcoming opponent.

Hayes had prepared all year for the upcoming Washington and Jefferson team, led by Dan "Deacon" Towler, who later became a running back for the Los Angeles Rams and later on, a minister. Towler could have played football at any major college, but attended Washington and Jefferson in order to study for the ministry. He clearly outclassed the players in those small Ohio universities, and in the previous season's big game with Denison, he piled up big yardage while leading his team to a 12–7 win.

During the summer, Woody regularly sent his players weekly letters outlining off-season conditioning drills, and other correspondence to help prepare them for the upcoming season. Hayes would end each letter by penning, "I wonder what 'The Deacon' is doing today," to motivate his players to do their summer running.

Hayes knew after the Rio Grande game that, if the Big Red could beat Washington and Jefferson it would set the tone for the rest of the season and erase any doubts the players had in his demanding methods.

Denison played the first quarter as if they never prepared for revenge. Penalties, missed assignments, and a general lack of execution marred the first quarter and they fell behind 7–0 in the game, being played on a searing-hot late summer Saturday. The team's improvement over the previous season became apparent during the second quarter, though. The players kept their poise and settled down to tie the game 7–7 at halftime.

Hayes also showed his increased savvy. He brought his team out to the field for the second half, but found that Washington and Jefferson was engaging in a bit of gamesmenship by staying in the cool of their locker room for at least ten minutes, while the Denison players waited outside in the heat. With no shade in sight, Hayes had his eleven starters sit on the bench while circling the others around the bench to help keep his starters out of the sun. He then convinced the officials to levy a fifteen-yard penalty against Washington and Jefferson when they finally returned to the field.

Bolstered by the improved field position on the ensuing kickoff, Dension scored. Then they added a second touchdown with a play action pass over Towler to go up by two touchdowns. Towler avenged his mistake on defense by scoring a touchdown on the next possession. But Denison managed to hold on to win 19–14, in what was one of the school's biggest upsets in years.

It was a watershed game for Hayes. He had done a masterful job of motivating and preparing his players; and while his methods were at times unbearable, they had paid off. His once-mutinous team now firmly backed their coach no matter how much punishment he meted out to the players during practice.

"What Woody did that year was figure out the talent and where to put people in different places to succeed," Huff said. "Then we worked constantly on execution and technique. He made sure that all of us knew what everyone else was doing on every play, and we were a smart team with a bunch of Phi Beta Kappas."

The Washington and Jefferson victory gave the team a shot of badly needed confidence, but the next week was supposed to be just as tough a test against Beloit College. Beloit, which, the previous season, had scheduled Denison for their Homecoming Day to assure a win, was an infrequent and out-of-state opponent. The low-budget Denison team had enough trouble convincing Dean Livingston to pay for new pads, much less for travel to Beloit, Wisconsin, located just over the Illinois state line.

To prepare for the game, Woody called on his older brother Ike to scout Beloit. Ike had been an All-American guard at Iowa State, and was now a veterinarian living in Iowa, so Woody banked on his brother's football expertise to give Denison an edge. Ike's scouting report was grim. The Beloit team was much bigger, and Ike felt that Denison would be overmatched.

When Woody and the rest of his team got off the bus in Beloit, Ike was there to greet them with words of warning, but Denison pounded Beloit 50–7, completing a three-game stretch in which the Big Red outscored their opponents 115–21. If there had been any doubts about Woody's ability to put a team together, they were erased by the first three games of the 1947 season.

Woody took his team to Chicago after the game, where they would stay at the Bismark Hotel. Even though Denison had a minuscule football budget, he insisted that his team travel first class. Coats and ties, top hotels, the best restaurants. That's how winners traveled, he figured, no matter how costly.

Spending a Saturday night in Chicago was a big deal for the Denison players. A big night out in Granville for the players meant drinking in the bars in nearby Newark, Ohio, which, compared to Granville, was a big town. Hayes was aware of the temptations posed by the bright lights of Chicago, but he wanted to give his players a break from the monotonous campus life. A dinner, a movie, a few drinks in big city nightclubs would do wonders for team morale, so he convinced the administration to approve the trip, though it meant more criticism from the faculty, who believed that football was becoming a bigger priority than academics. But Hayes had some distinct leverage, because Denison president Dr. K. I. Brown's son was a member of the football team. Of course, that didn't stop Hayes from criticizing Brown's approach to sports on campus: "He didn't know football from a pumpkin," Hayes once said about Brown.

Hayes made sure his boys would take advantage of their trip to Chicago, and knowing that a few of the players couldn't afford a night on the town, he discreetly reached into his own pocket.

There was little or no NCAA oversight in the mid-1940s, but Woody wasn't trying to cheat the system with his cash donations. He wanted to spare his players, who had no money, the embarrassment of not being able to afford a night out in Chicago.

On the field, Hayes owned the players and treated them harshly if they didn't satisfy his demands. Off the field, he was a friend and a father to many, and if some couldn't afford a night on the town in Chicago, he saw no reason why he couldn't help.

"Woody always ran a clean program; but when we got to Chicago he knew there were five or six guys who didn't have money," Wehr said.

Hayes was also becoming much more personally involved in his players' lives, whether they wanted him to or not. He'd consistently monitor their grades, their girlfriends, and their drinking habits. He'd go to the fraternity houses to talk to certain players, and he'd get to know their problems, their parents, and their interests outside of football. Notoriously, he had that nearly photographic memory and an amazing ability to recall details of a player's personal life, and he'd often ask about a player's mother or father by name. He knew each player's grade-point average and he'd even go to the student union and shoot pool with the students, many of whom were his players looking for a little distraction away from school and football.

He did everything to keep them in school. He helped players pay tuition out of his own pocket if they couldn't afford it, and when one member of the team told Woody that he would have to drop out of school, he invited the player to live at his house for the semester free of charge.

The generosity was afforded to any of his players, good or bad. The player who lived with Woody was one of the least talented on the team, but he was, as Hayes would say, "a 110 percenter," and that was all that was required.

"Woody helped any way he could, and it wasn't because this guy could help Woody, it was simply that sometimes guys needed help, and Woody felt they deserved it," Huff said.

Hayes's involvement not only drew him closer to his team, but the members sometimes came to feel, unhappily at times, that they were part of his family, like it or not. If a player's grades were suffering, he'd find himself staying with Hayes on South Mulberry Street, where Woody and Anne would serve as his mandatory tutors.

Many of the nonmilitary players at Denison received grant-in-aid packages to help pay for school, and if a player's grade-point average slipped below a 2.0, they would lose their financial aid. Bill Fleitz, one of Woody's favorites, lost his grant after struggling academically. Hayes moved him into his house and spent hours tutoring his star player to keep him eligible. Fleitz, who was drinking too much and coming dangerously close to flunking out of school, spent most of his freshman year living on South Mulberry Street.

"One day I came back from class and Woody was in my room on campus packing my bags. I asked him if he was sending me home and he said 'no, just get in the car,'" Fleitz said. "We pulled in front of his house and he told me I had to stay there. I had to check in at eight P.M. on weekdays and eleven P.M. on weekends."

If nothing else, the thought of having to live off campus with the Hayes family was enough to drive even the laziest student to the library.

"He knew what kind of home life you had, and he'd do anything for you if you produced; and we had produced for him," Wehr said. "That was just that way he was."

The players were now beginning to return some favors. They

knew all too well that Woody wasn't easy to live with either on the field or at home. Woody and Anne lived on the first floor of the three-story house just a few blocks from campus. It was up to Anne to run the family and she was by herself for much of the time, especially during the season, so the players would run errands for her and help in any way they could. During the winter, they would stop by the house to shovel coal into the furnace, knowing that the chore would likely fall to Anne anyway.

"We really did become kind of a family to Anne and Woody," Huff said. "They both thought of the Denison players as the ones who gave them their start."

It was becoming obvious to the team following their win over Beloit that their fast start wasn't a fluke. But maintaining the momentum was a chore. Denison placed a high priority on academics and the players were cut no slack no matter how taxing it was playing for Hayes. The older military veterans were also serious about getting their education and getting out of college as fast as they could to get on with their lives. Most of them had already spent four years in the service and didn't want to waste any more time in school than necessary. Football was simply sports, and it held little future, and Hayes had to battle to keep motivating players to try to reach his impossibly high expectations.

Hayes also had responsibilities other than simply coaching the football them, though he managed to incorporate his own coaching duties into the classroom. As a faculty member of the physical education department, he had to teach—which also took him away from focusing solely on the team. But he found a way to minimize the distraction by teaching "Theory and Practice of Coaching Football" in the fall of 1947 and loading the course with football players. Even the lab portion of the class was oriented toward his team. Non–football playing students in his class were required to attend football practice, chart the plays, and shag balls for the team. Employing students to shag balls meant that the players who otherwise would be assigned those duties could run more plays or improve their technique. In essence, he turned those nonplayer students into de facto team managers under the auspices of academics, giving some members of the faculty even more reason to become concerned about too much emphasis on football.

The Big Red was brimming with confidence, and after the Beloit game, the team rattled off two consecutive shutouts, by beating Wooster University 28–0 and Oberlin College 33–0. The team's sustained, dominant play wasn't surprising to Hayes. He knew that the key difference to the strong first half of the 1947 season was the team's excellent conditioning. Knowing that fatigue played a big part in the previous losing season, he ran his players to near exhaustion and ordered that there be full contact during much of the practice week. There was never any water on the practice field, and his players practiced in full pads, even though the starters played both offense and defense.

The players still complained and went to Yard to intercede, but they knew that Hayes was pushing himself just as hard. Hayes would hole himself up for hours inside the office he shared with Yard in the basement of Cleveland Hall, drawing up game plans and charting new plays for that week's opponent. The filming of games was still relatively new to the college ranks, but Hayes was already devoted to the new coaching tool, and he spent hours breaking down the game moves, detailing every player's performance, and charting every identifiable tendency on the part of players. Just as the players were developing as a team, so too was Woody as a coach.

Film sessions were more like classes for the players, with "professor" Hayes at the lectern, pointing out the good plays on film and adopting an instructive tone when the film caught the mistakes of a player. The game plan prepared for each opponent was meticulous, with new plays inserted in the offense—an offense invariably named after the opponent it was designed to attack.

"Woody would sit up there at the front of the room and tell you all about the certain players on other teams, and we named the plays after the players he was talking about. For the Muskingum game, the star was a guy named Moses, so that week the plays became the Moses Series," Huff said. "He made it personal."

Come Saturday, the hours of intense preparation and attention to detail erased much doubt among his players on the field. Most of the situations they'd run into during their games had already been drilled into their heads during the week.

"He was always working, always going over personnel, so that during our games there was never a hint of indecisiveness when it came to making decision on the sidelines," Huff said.

The team was battling overconfidence with just three games to play in the 1947 season. They had to come from behind only once, at that was during the second week of the season, when Washington and Jefferson scored an early touchdown. Denison countered quickly with a score of their own to tie the game.

They had shut out three opponents and allowed only twenty-one points in five games. Each game seemed to get easier until Denison played Muskingum College, a team that barely beat the pathetic Denison team a year earlier.

But overconfidence faded quickly after Muskingum scored two touchdowns and shut down Denison's powerful offense during the first half. It was as if the Big Red reverted back to form from the previous inept season, and when the team entered the locker room at halftime they expected Hayes to launch into a tirade. But when Hayes closed the locker room door, he was strangely quiet as he went over adjustments, quietly explaining how his team could overcome the deficit. The players were stunned. They had steeled themselves for one of Hayes's outbursts, and instead he acted as if they were the team that was holding a comfortable lead.

They responded to the quiet show of confidence by running up twenty straight points and shutting out Muskingum in the second half.

The 20–14 come-from-behind win was a galvanizing victory and Hayes's handling of the team at halftime a master stroke of psychology, instilling in the team even more faith in their coach.

"We knew then that we had come a long way," Huff said. "From what we had been through, we knew we had a team."

There was no stopping Denison after the Muskingum game. They handily defeated Capital 56–7 and ended the season with a 12–6 win over Wittenburg. In one season, Hayes had taken 2-6 team, filled with mutinous players, and turned them into a juggernaut that posted the first undefeated season at Denison in fifty-eight years.

Not only were the players convinced of Hayes's coaching ability, but so was the administration. The school gave him an extension on his two-year contract, even though some members of the faculty had battled with Hayes over the increased attention spent on football. They also rewarded him with a new set of luggage, presented at the football banquet held after the season, while each player received a framed team picture commemorating the unbeaten season.

"If you would have given me the luggage last year, I would have been worried," Hayes said when presented with the new suitcases, sending the room into fits of laughter.

To prepare them for the upcoming season, Hayes continued to send a regular stream of letters to his players during the summer of 1948, but it was wasted postage. In 1948 the team would lose Culp, their starting quarterback, and the starting fullback, Wentis, graduated.

But their replacements were as capable as the departed seniors in running the offense. Hayes again relied on his excellent line blocking to run the ball, but the halfback option pass had become a regular staple of the offense, and most of the passing was done by the halfbacks out of the T formation. It was a much more inventive offense than Hayes would become known for, but it was easy to open up the passing game and give his team's total dominance over their opponents. The Big Red opened the 1948 season with a 38–7 blowout of Otterbein and steamrolled through the rest of the season. Winning was now expected, with the players extremely confident but not cocky. Their age and experience combined for a matter-of-fact approach to each game as they plowed through the season unchallenged, and there was little celebrating the winning streak.

"It was just business as usual for us," Huff said. "The attitude was that we were just doing our jobs and that was the way it was supposed to be. But it was amazing to me what you could do when you have total confidence."

Hayes had little to complain about. The team went undefeated for the second consecutive season, and the unshackled offense was devastating, as the Big Red outscored their opponents 347–45. With one less game on the 1948 schedule, Denison scored 119 more points and allowed nine points less than during their 1947 season.

The season wasn't as satisfying to the players as the previous year. They hadn't overcome nearly as much adversity during the season, so their achievements seemed less rewarding to the team. Many of the players who started with Woody still had another year left before graduation, and they assumed that the winning streak would continue as long as Hayes kept the same system in place.

Denison's stunning success, even by small college standards, did not go ignored within Ohio's coaching fraternity. Hayes was just another aggressive and ambitious coach looking to climb the ranks when he took the job at Denison. While his success was remarkable, it was at a small college where he didn't have to face the pressure of a bigtime program, where politics was as much a necessary skill as actual coaching ability. What set him apart from other successful small school coaches was that his burning ambition was matched only by his ability to sell himself. Woody already had gained a great reputation for being able to recruit and keep key players in school. Bringing Flietz, a bigtime college prospect, to Denison was a major coup. His ability to keep players academically eligible was a skill all its own. Not many coaches were willing to personally tutor players who were struggling in the classroom. Even fewer were willing to house them, as Woody did, with the aim of protecting both his and his players' futures.

Most importantly, he had begun to make deep connections for a relatively unknown coach, thanks to some off-season coaching clinics, which gave him exposure outside the state.

Every summer Woody would go to these clinics that were a staple of the college football coaching profession. It was where he could rub shoulders with other big-name coaches, who not only could pocket some extra money for leading the clinics, but could also check out up-and-coming coaching talent. These clinics were as much about networking as they were about football strategy. A young coach could make a name for himself at these relaxed events, and Woody was part of the circuit. Coaches he knew in the early days were now moving up the ranks, including Paul Brown, who was already an Ohio coaching legend, with stints at Ohio State before moving into the NFL. Then there was his old coach Johnny Brickels, who in 1949 had joined Brown to help run the Cleveland Browns franchise. But Woody also knew to align himself with other, lesser-known but equally influential power brokers that could protect him. Men who were key members of alumni boards, and local businessmen whose generosity gave them access and influence, and other administrators who could broker other connections. One of those administrators was David Reese, commissioner of the Mid-American Conference, which counted Ohio schools such as Xavier, Cincinnati, Dayton, Ohio University, and Miami University of Ohio as members. The schools in the Mid-American conference were larger than Denison and most were state-supported, with budgets large enough to field competitive sports teams. For an up-and-coming coach like Hayes, coaching at schools in the MAC was the next logical step, given the better players, bigger budgets, and better exposure.

In the early winter of 1949, Hayes was again engrossed in the planning for his fourth season at Denison. The thirty-six-year-old coach by now was firmly entrenched in the school's athletic department, and for a man of ambition like Woody, entrenchment could be a dangerous thing. You didn't want to spend too much time coaching at a small college, no matter how much success you achieve. There was a danger of getting pigeonholed, or even institutionalized into the football program at Denison, and with two consecutive undefeated seasons and a growing reputation, the time was right to consider new opportunities. Though he wouldn't admit it publicly, Woody would use the administration's gift of luggage sooner than they had realized. There was a job open at Miami University of Ohio, and he had already received a call from its president, Dr. Ernest Hahn, asking if he'd like to come down to Oxford to talk it over.

5

PROVING GROUND

Oxford, Ohio, lies 160 miles southwest of Granville, a distance that gave Hayes plenty of time on his trip down to Miami University to think about how he could convince the school's administration that he was worthy of succeeding highly regarded Sid Gillman and popular George Blackburn, the two previous Redskins coaches. On the face of it, it wouldn't be easy. Gillman coached the Redskins in 1947, leading his undefeated team to the Sun Bowl, where they beat Texas Tech 13–12. He had also compiled an impressive 31-6-1 record as head coach at Miami from 1944 through 1947. After the 1947 season, Gillman left Miami to join Earl "Red" Blaik at West Point as line coach for Army. It was a plum job for Gillman even though he was leaving for an assistant's position. Army was a national football power in the late 1940s under the legendary Blaik, who was a 1918 graduate of Miami University. Gillman, like other bright coaches including Vince Lombardi, saw their West Point tenure as a launching pad to better college coaching jobs or to the professional ranks. Miami assistant coach George Blackburn was hired to replace Gillman, and he too was a success, leading the Redskins to an 8-1 season in 1948. But Blackburn would go to West Point after the 1948 season, replacing Gillman, who took the job as head coach at the University of Cincinnati. The domino effect of Blackburn's sudden departure created the opening that quickly sparked Hayes's interest.

Miami University, with its handsome colonial buildings and manicured lawns, more than matched Denison in its beauty, but that's where the comparisons ended. As a public institution, Miami University was supported by state funds, and unlike the Denison faculty that was indifferent toward athletics, Miami's administration had no misgivings about the changing role of sports at colleges and universities during the postwar boom. Miami president Hahn, an economist and an authority on public finance, realized that the way to fund the school's growth was to engage a more active and involved alumni; and what better way to attract alumni contributions than having a successful football team? So, while Hahn increased the school's library budget and oversaw the development of Miami's graduate school, he also believed in emphasizing athletics while maintaining the school's academic mission. It was a far different mentality than what Woody had experienced at Denison, and one that would encourage his drive to build a winning program.

On paper there were dozens of other coaches more qualified than Hayes for the Miami job, but Woody came to the interview with something the others couldn't match: clout. His connection with Reese, who was commissioner of the Mid-American Conference, certainly bore influence upon those who would get the job. Reese's friendship with Hayes began at Denison where Reese was an influential member of the alumni club. Reese had also been a key booster during Woody's early days in Granville, when he looked overmatched during the disastrous 1946 season. Reese liked what he saw in Hayes at Denison, and he gladly sent Hahn a glowing recommendation about Hayes's coaching ability, adamant that he was right for the Miami job.

Hahn sensed the value in his new coach having a connection to the conference commissioner. The friendship wouldn't hurt when it came to making bowl-selection decisions, or any other key football decisions that fell into the hands of the commissioner's office.

The link between Hayes and Paul Brown also held weight with Hahn. Their relationship dated back to when both roomed at the Sigma Chi house during graduate school at Ohio State. Brown, also a Miami graduate, had deep ties to the school and was well on his way to legendary coaching status.

The two heavyweight recommendations trumped any other candidates, and Hayes was offered the job on February 23, 1949. His contract was for two years, beginning on March first, with an annual salary of $7,500, including a one-month vacation. He was also offered the rank of Associate Professor of Physical Education.

Hayes took the job, but leveraged one condition from Hahn, who wanted the remaining football staff retained. The staff could remain, Hayes agreed, but he insisted that he be able to hire his own assistant coach. Hahn allowed the request, and Hayes immediately offered the job to his trusty Denison assistant, Yard. But Yard wanted more out of his career than following Woody around Ohio, working night and day for little money and little recognition.

It was a job better suited for a young, single coach. Yard was married, and his wife wanted some semblance of a normal life, so he returned to the University of Pennsylvania to earn his doctorate. Woody understood. He knew Yard's value to his football team, but he knew that it would be a disaster if there were any second-guessing by his assistant in coming to Oxford. They parted amicably.

"Woody sent my wife Godiva chocolates on her birthday for years after I left," Yard said.

Hayes then quickly turned to his old friend and mentor John Brickels, who was working with Brown as an assistant with the Cleveland Browns professional football franchise. Brickels was interested, but he took the job only after Hahn had written a promise to hire Brickels as the head basketball coach.

"Pursuant to our understanding, you are also given the privilege of selecting an assistant football coach," Hahn wrote in his offer letter to Hayes. "Accordingly, I telephoned Brickels of Cleveland, offering him the position of assistant football coach, and eventually appointment to head basketball coach, as soon as the staff adjustment could be made at Miami University."

Wrangling the hiring of Brickels out of Hahn would be a big advantage. There were about five thousand students at Miami in 1949, five times the size of Denison, and that meant there would be higher expectations. Oxford, for all its greenery and natural beauty, would be Woody's proving ground. He had no interest in ever returning to the comfortable world of private school football. Failure would stall—or even derail—his burning ambition. He badly needed someone he could trust in his new job, an ally who had no loyalty to any previous member of the Miami athletic department.

Hayes accepted the Miami job immediately after receiving Hahn's letter, and he had one week to move to Oxford in order to start on March first. He quickly informed Livingston of his new job and then met with his old football team. The Denison players had established themselves as one of the best teams in school history, and leaving them wasn't going to be easy.

"He came into the room and said some kind things and then just thanked us," Shannon said. "I kind of figured it would happen. We had two undefeated seasons and he was becoming a hot ticket, especially since, before he got to Granville, the team never did anything. One of the things he told us was that there were two jobs he would leave for: one was for Miami, the other for Ohio State."

But his sudden departure dealt a blow to the team. The players were bitter, particularly the ones that started with him as freshmen in 1946 and were now seniors. They had hoped to continue the string of back-to-back undefeated seasons, and they had become disciples of Hayes's gospel of commitment, loyalty, and maximum effort. Hayes had become extremely close to his team, despite his harsh and demanding coaching style. Now their coach was abandoning them for a bigger and better job, and while there was no fault in moving up, it was all so sudden.

"I was surprised and frankly ticked at him for leaving," Huff said. "In my case, my father had passed away during school, and though Woody wasn't all that much older than me, he had become a sort of father figure to me and to others. I felt he was deserting us."

The Denison administration wasn't nearly as upset to see him go. In their eyes, football was getting too much attention, and with Woody and his blustery personality now in Oxford, the administration could put sports back into what they felt was its proper place.

"They didn't want any more teams like the ones Woody had," said Shannon, who would go on to coach track at Denison for forty years.

When Woody arrived in Oxford a few weeks before the team began its spring practice in March, he found that he had inherited a depleted roster. The Redskins were 8-1 in 1948 under Blackburn, and at least six starters had transferred after the season to follow Gillman to the

University of Cincinnati. Woody would have to spend his first season rebuilding the team with backups, who had to learn a new system. It was a grim way for a first-year coach to start at a school where the stakes were considerably higher than at Denison, and it stoked the fires of the fierce rivalry between Hayes and Gillman.

The two men did not like one another. The bad blood began during Woody's first season at Denison over the recruitment of Bill Fleitz, the superstar from Newark High who had forty offers from colleges around the country. Fleitz was bound for Miami of Ohio to play for Gillman, until Woody stepped in during the summer of 1946 just after he accepted the Denison job. Though Fleitz was committed to Gillman, Hayes, ever the salesman, continued to woo the local star, until he convinced Fleitz to change his mind and go to Denison. Gillman, bitter over losing his prized recruit, never forgave Woody.

"I guess I started it," Fleitz said. "I had my room and everything at Miami, but I was Woody's first recruit at Denison, and I changed my mind."

Gillman, who had served as a line coach at Denison during the late 1930s, was in many ways the opposite of Hayes. Woody was an undistinguished lineman in high school; Gillman was a high school football star who went on to become a star end and captain at Ohio State. Sid's coaching style emphasized speed and intricate passing plays. Woody trusted the run and preferred power over speed. Strength versus speed, the run versus the pass. The only similarities between the two on the practice field was the demand for perfection. Both would stress precise execution from their players, but even that differed. Woody would harangue players over the wrong block at the point of attack, or he'd explode in frustration over fumbles or missed assignments. Gillman would quietly rebuke players for a line split that was off a few inches, or an extra half step taken by the quarterback during a three-step drop.

"Sid's approach was that he'd tell you once and tell you a second time, and if he had to tell you a third time he'd forget your name and ignore you," said Mel Olix, Gillman's starting quarterback at Miami, who also played for Woody during his senior year. "Sid was speed, speed, and more speed. Woody was power, power, and more power. Woody would banter and rave, but he only did it to get your attention.

If Sid stopped talking to you, then you were better off joining the soccer team."

Gillman was Jewish, Hayes a Presbyterian. About the only thing both had in common off the field was that they were both English majors. Woody emulated the way Coach Neyland did things at the University of Tennessee with repetition and strength. But Gillman did his own thing.

Woody's football field was a battleground, Sid's was a laboratory. Woody would put the game in his fullback's hands to pound out first downs, while Gillman would hand the quarterback the keys to the offense, creating multiple formations and options for the wide-open attack to confuse defenses more accustomed to a basic running game.

But some of their biggest battles were fought off the field. With Gillman now at Cincinnati and Woody at Miami, the schools were just twenty-five miles apart, and that meant that they both recruited many of the same players. Their styles were predictibly opposite. Hayes was the high-minded salesman preaching education. Gillman's style was more slick, and whenever Woody lost a recruiting battle, he believed it was because Sid had skirted the rules.

Hayes opened his first spring practice facing two problems. The biggest challenge was his depleted roster and the players' strong loyalty to Gillman, whose presence and influence still lingered on the team, though he had been gone for a full season. The other problem was that Hayes came to campus with little respect. The players were unimpressed with his success at Denison. To them, Denison was a small-time football school that was just a step up from the high school ranks. Only a season removed from the Sun Bowl, the Miami players felt Hayes had little pedigree.

"Woody who?" was the response from most of the players when learning that they had their second new head coach in as many seasons.

Hayes did not go out of his way to make a good first impression. He was direct, firm, and some of his first encounters with his new players left them cold. In one instance, he went up to a group of football players who were hanging around the handball court and said, "you young men will have to gain some weight," leaving the players scratching their heads at the awkward introduction. "Didn't the team just finish the previous season at nine and one?" the players wondered aloud as they watched their new coach abruptly walk away.

It took just a few days of drilling for the players to despise their new coach. He figured that punishing practices would make the players forget about their old coach. Every practice was in full pads with full speed contact. Like most coaches of the era, he allowed no water, no breaks, and little patience for any mistakes on the practice field. Instead of lessening the sting of Gillman's departure, it only made the players miss their old coach even more.

There was a silver lining for Hayes, despite the departure of some key players. World War II was over, but plenty of veterans still flocked into colleges across the country. Enrollment at Miami had swelled to four thousand one hundred students, of which two thousand were ex-servicemen, creating a vast talent pool for the Miami football coaches to use to build a roster.

With little oversight from the NCAA, Gillman ran the program by suggesting that if anyone was interested in playing football they should strongly consider attending summer school. Along with classes came six full weeks of football practice in pads. Of the one hundred players that began the summer session, only forty remained, as the coaches weeded out the veterans with grueling three-hour practices. Bob Kappes was a seventeen-year-old freshman center during the summer of 1947. When he lined up with the team at the start of the session, he found thirteen others at the same position. Six weeks later, he and one other center were the only ones left.

In 1948, more than three hundred players tried out for the Miami freshman football team. Blackburn divided the players into four teams and held scrimmages to pick the best fifty players to make the cut. One of those players who made the freshman team was twenty-year-old John Pont, a scrappy halfback from Canton, Ohio, who walked onto the team after Gillman refused to offer him a scholarship. Another player on the team was a sophomore tackle from northeast Ohio named Glenn Schembechler, who as a member of the baseball team was spared Hayes's wrath during spring practice. But when fall practice opened, Schembechler and Pont were skeptical whether their new coach could earn the respect of his team and their doubts only intensified.

"When Woody got to Oxford he had to win over the players, un-like when a new coach comes into a losing program and is seen as some sort of messiah," Pont said. "The players loved Sid and followed him to Cincinnati, and they also loved George. Now here comes Woody from a small school, and it just took time. He had to really work to win."

Hayes spent most preseason practice in 1949 installing the offense that ran counter to Gillman's wide-open approach. Hayes instead ran a basic power offense, with much of the skill and responsibility given to the halfback, who had to play flanker as well as the traditional halfback position. Hayes would call plays that were snapped either to the quarterback or to the halfback, with the motion used as a way to confuse defenses. But Hayes did incorporate passing into the offense. Where Gillman would average around twenty-five pass plays per game, Hayes's team that first season passed an average of twelve to fifteen times per game.

"We ran a bit of everything," Pont said. "I ran direct plays from the center, and we also threw the ball. It was not as conservative as you'd think."

But the players believed that they were taking a step back.

"Several of the fellas didn't think Woody's system was updated," Olix said. "Sid wanted smaller, faster players, and he spent more time on technique. With Woody, well it took us about two nights to learn his play book and blocking schemes."

Miami was hardly a football factory. Most of the players worked for room and board, and these were real jobs. The administration allowed little preferential treatment for Woody's players, who would work as dishwashers or busboys in various dormitories or fraternity houses. Most had to work each meal, except on game days, and got one weekend off a month. Nearly all the players were part of the heavily Greek system, and during pledge week Hayes would pay a visit to the various fraternity houses, making sure that his players were in bed by eleven P.M.

"We were mixed in with the rest of the students, and we weren't just jocks," Pont said. "We were recognized for who we were; and when the games and practices were over, we went to class. There was just a great intermingling with the players and the rest of the students, and, really, it was a idyllic time."

Hayes's debut opened with the Redskins traveling to Wichita State and winning 23–6 in a game highlighted by Pont, in his first play on the varsity team, returning the opening kickoff for a touchdown.

But Miami lost the next three games against tougher competition against Virginia, Pittsburgh, and Xavier. Losing was something that neither Hayes nor his new players were used to. Woody was coming off consecutive unbeaten seasons at Denison, and the Redskins had lost just one game per season in each of the previous three years.

The frustrations over the offense, which that season was dictated by Woody but headed by Brickels, were now at the boiling point. During the Pittsburgh game, the Redskins were trailing by three touchdowns in the second half when Olix got fed up with the predictable game plan and switched to Gillman's offense.

"We were twenty points down and started using some of Sid's maneuvers and Brickels allowed us to do it, which was unheard of," Olix said. "But Woody was so excited about us scoring that he didn't recognize what we were doing. He was just happy we were scoring."

The week following the Pittsburgh loss, the players clamored for a return to Gillman's system, but Woody refused. Olix, the senior quarterback who was set to attend medical school, had no qualms suggesting a change back to Gillman's way.

"Why he wouldn't use it I don't know, but I really don't think he understood it," Olix said. "Woody just couldn't put his finger on it."

But neither could other coaches. After he graduated, Olix was invited to play in the Blue-Gray game, where seniors showed their skills to professional scouts. Each day of the week-long practice schedule, Rip Engle and Ray Elliott, both college coaches, would make Olix meet with them for an hour after practice and ordered Olix to go over Gillman's offense so they could copy it.

"That was the only reason I was invited," Olix said. "That's all they wanted from me."

As the 1949 season progressed, Woody worked harder than ever. Eighteen- and nineteen-hour workdays were common while he rebuilt the team. Each morning he would huddle with the coaches to review the day's practice schedule. The plan was to keep practices to two hours, but many times during that first season the team toiled into the darkness, until Hayes was satisfied with their efforts.

The players, confident in their talents, weren't easily intimidated by Woody. They learned to avoid his wrath by simply knowing their assignments, which weren't all that difficult to begin with. Sometimes, the players could barely contain their laughter at his blowups.

There were times during practice when Olix would be running the offense under the direction of Brickels while Hayes was working with the defense. Woody would call out the passing coverages, forgetting that his quarterback could hear every coverage and accordingly make adjustments. Olix would tee off on the defense, easily moving the offense down the field. After each completion Hayes would grow more frustrated, and he punished the defensive players by making them run a lap around the field every time a pass was completed. The more Olix threw, the madder Woody got—and the more the defense ran. By the time the drill was over, Woody's screaming was echoing all over the practice field, while the exhausted defensive players glared at their quarterback.

"I would look at Brickels and he'd just tell me to keep doing what I was doing," Olix said. "I think one day I had twenty-five consecutive completions. Woody never knew."

After practice, Woody would go back to his tiny six-by-eleven-foot office in Withrow Court and spend hours watching film, calling recruits, and planning for the next day—while also dispatching one of the players to his apartment above Tuffy's Sandwich Shop, on the corner of High Street and Tallawanda, to tell Anne that he would again be late for dinner.

Anne, like always, would defer to her husband. She long ago had accepted his absence and would raise their son Steve as both his mother and his father. It couldn't be any other way if she wanted to stay married. Instead of fighting Woody for his time, Anne attached herself fully to his rising career. She knew how to put Woody in his place, but outside of the house she was fiercely protective of her husband. She either stood up to any criticism of her husband, or diffused it with her bountiful wit and charm.

She would also play a big role in counseling the wives of the assistant coaches, women who no doubt heard from their husbands about their mercurial boss. It wasn't easy working for him. He had no qualms about being away from his family and expected his coaches to feel the same way, so it could be a lonely life in Oxford for those women, especially the ones with young children. During the football season the wives would barely see their husbands, so Anne would befriend the spouses. She'd organize coffees, lunches, teas, and other social outlets to break up the monotony and difficulty that many of the wives would face.

Anne had already been through Woody's difficult first year at Denison, and now he again struggled to win over his players. She knew that fostering a sense of unity among the team would prove valuable. She'd spend time with the players' parents after the games, as they milled outside the locker rooms waiting for their sons, establishing a rapport.

It was a natural effort, but it also helped smooth over the bitterness and anger that at times during the season all the players felt toward their coach.

"She really was an asset to Woody that first year," Olix said. "She wasn't pushy like Woody could be. She made an big effort to get to know us and our families."

Woody needed all the goodwill Anne could muster among his players. The Redskins struggled to end the season with a 5-4 record and lost the all-important season-ending game to Gillman's Cincinnati team. It was a crushing 27–6 loss. In the late 1940s and 1950s the rivalry between both schools was intense. In 1949 the game took on an extra measure of intensity because of the dislike between the two coaches. The feud began with Hayes stealing a recruit during his Denison days and deepened when Woody got to Miami. He believed that Gillman deliberately raided the Miami program, when so many players followed the ex-coach to Cincinnati. Subsequent recruiting wars only added to the bad feelings. The loss only added to the bad blood.

"It was the worst season we ever had in our class at Miami," Olix said. "It was just difficult. We thought Woody's football was way behind, but really, anyone who followed Sid would have been behind."

The season's end didn't ease the workload. Through the winter, Woody camped in his office, lights off and film projector whirring, resolving to chase the ghost that haunted the season.

There would be no peacekeeping meeting with his Miami players, no promises of understanding, and no vows to ease up on his demands. One of the first changes he made during the off-season was to assemble his own staff—one that allowed him to put his own stamp on the program.

Brickels was now head basketball coach, and he was also appointed the school's athletic director in 1950, a move that further boosted Woody's standing within the athletic department.

With a freer hand to hire who he wanted, Hayes offered a recent Miami graduate named Ara Parseghian to coach Miami's freshman team. Parseghian barely knew Hayes, but he had made a good impression in his first encounter with Woody in early 1949, while back at Miami to work on his master's thesis. He also hired a bright graduate from the 1949 team named Bill Arnsparger to coach the line. The hires proved Woody's uncanny eye for discovering coaching talent. Both Arnsparger and Parseghian would go on to notable coaching careers.

Parseghian was an unlikely coach. He had been a star player at Miami, and he followed Brown to the Cleveland Browns, where as a rookie in 1949 he got hurt. Parseghian was trying to hang on with the Browns when Woody called him in December of 1949. Brown had already made it clear to Ara that his days were numbered as a pro, so he decided to return to Miami and set a new course for himself as an assistant to Woody and as the coach of the men's golf team. The only problem was that Ara had no coaching experience whatsoever. But he was bright and intuitive and he flourished as part of Woody's five-man staff. Each morning the assistants would meet with their head coach, and then Ara would be off on a separate field with the freshman players, free to develop his own style. He was instructed to install Woody's power offense, but since the freshmen were apart from the varsity, he could do it his own way without being influenced. The setup allowed for a great deal of freedom, and as a result he developed more quickly than he would have, had he needed to follow orders as a varsity assistant.

The freshman team won all of its five games in 1950, and when

Hayes called on the freshman to run the scout team, the younger players often gave the varsity all it could handle. Though Woody would
seethe at the scout team's success, he recognized how well they were
coached. Parseghian, however, sometimes was baffled by what he saw
on the practice field.

"Woody was the most emotional guy I'd ever seen, and he got madder than hell at his players," Parseghian said. "He'd get so emotionally
involved and explode. He'd punch kids and yell at them, but off the field
he was like a father to them. He was really like two different people."

Woody welcomed back the varsity players in 1950 with a new purpose. For one thing, most of the players who were loyal to Gillman and
Blackburn were gone, and with a full season and another spring practice
under their belts, the players were far more comfortable with Woody,
who that winter turned thirty-seven years old. Hayes loved handball
and he'd play against his players and assistant coaches, the lumbering
former lineman working the angles of the court. Hayes was still an im-
mensely strong man and as tough as his players. Running into him on
the confined spaces of the handball court was like running into a telephone pole. You couldn't budge him on the handball courts, just as you
couldn't make him do anything that he didn't want to do himself. So it
was a stubborn and determined Hayes that drove his players before their
1950 season opener against Bowling Green. The practices were crisper
and better organized and limited mainly to two hours, with many of
the returning starters in sync with Hayes's strategy—a strategy that was
now stressing a more balanced attack.

The Indians would pound the ball, but Hayes opened things up by
using Pont and Carmen Cozza as both receivers and runners. The pass
was just as much a threat as the traps that Hayes loved to ram down the
opposing defenses.

The first game showed just how explosive Hayes's offense could
be, with a stunning 54–6 win over Bowling Green. The Indians scored
nearly at will, racking up yardage both on the ground and in the air.
After losing 7–0 to a strong Xavier team, the Indians blew through the
rest of their regular season schedule with a staggering display of scoring thirty-four points against Western Michigan, thirty-nine against
Wichita, and a sixty-nine-point barrage against Western Reserve.

Hayes's approach to the team was shifting. He now trusted his offense and took advantage of their talents, using Cozza as quarterback and Jim "Boxcar" Bailey at halfback to spread the field. He would still thunder along the sidelines during games, not dressed in what would become his familiar baseball cap, but wearing a felt Stetson hat or a fedora that matched his suit and tie, in a nod to the stylish Paul Brown. He grew more relaxed with his team. He would invite players into his home, small groups at first, and eventually to the point where he had team dinners that would force Anne downstairs to Tuffy's for more hamburgers.

Any sense that Woody was relaxing came to a crashing end during the final week of the 1950 regular season as he prepared the Indians for their annual grudge match against Cincinnati. The bad blood between the two coaches was still flowing freely, with Hayes still feeling the sting from the previous season's loss.

The Indians this time around were well prepared for Gillman's speedy squad. Not only did the backfield in Pont and Cozza anchor the offense, but Cozza, a tremendous all-around athlete, was one of the best defensive backs in the Mid-American Conference. His ability to defend against Gillman's varied passing offense would be crucial to the Indians' chances of winning the game and bringing the Indians a probable bowl invitation.

The weather forecasters were calling for cloudy and cold conditions on Saturday, November 25, with possible snow flurries. With weather seemingly a nonfactor, Hayes knew he'd have to somehow slow down Cincinnati's revved-up offense. With the Indians averaging well over twenty-five points per game, he figured that they would get their points, so the concern was more about stopping the Bearcats. But that Saturday morning the game plan went out the window. A surprise blizzard was raging across central Ohio, and though Cincinnati was south of the center of the storm, freezing rain was quickly turning to ice and snow. High schools and colleges across the state were scrambling to reschedule their games, but a few schools opted to play in the miserable conditions. Up north in Columbus, Ohio State and Michigan would play in the blinding snowstorm. So too would Miami and Cincinnati. Hayes wanted no part of a postponement. The Indians were better suited to the winter conditions than the more speed-oriented Cincinnati team, and by the time the game started, a sheet of ice and snow covered the field. In the locker room Hayes gave his team a simple instruction.

"Take small steps," he commanded.

With Gillman's passing game grounded by the wintery conditions, Cincinnati had a difficult time moving the ball, and the Indians dominated with a convincing 28–0 win.

Gillman, caught up in the bitter taste of defeat, accused Hayes of instructing his players to sharpen their cleats while on the sidelines, a charge that only deepened the hostilities between the two coaches.

"That was ridiculous," Arnsparger said. "All we did was have the lineman shorten their stances to get better control of their feet. We just took advantage of the ice."

The win was even more satisfying to Hayes after the Indians were invited to play in the Salad Bowl in Phoenix against the Arizona State University Sun Devils. It would be Hayes's first bowl game, and one that would bring redemption and respect.

The bowl season was growing in national stature by 1950, with major bowls like the Sun, Rose, and Orange bowls already around for decades. But postseason games, like the Salad Bowl in Phoenix, the Raisin Bowl in Fresno, the Harbor Bowl in San Diego, and the Oil Bowl in Houston, were around only for a few years, mainly in the late 1940s to early 1950s, and just before the age of television took the games to new heights. Though the Salad Bowl was considered a major bowl game, it was a far cry from the Rose Bowl, which in the 1950s was living up to its reputation as the granddaddy of them all.

None of that mattered to Hayes. Whether the game was played in a huge stadium or at a high school field, going to a bowl game was an accomplishment for Hayes, who was just two years removed from his days at Denison and one year away from his subpar season at Miami. No matter what the status of the Salad Bowl, Hayes was glad to be invited. Miami may have been a midsized school, playing in a relatively small-time conference, but traveling to Phoenix meant that Hayes would get exposure outside the state, and a win over a school like Arizona State would do even more to raise Woody's thus far only local profile. No one outside of the Mid-American Conference knew who he was, and beating a West Coast school like Arizona State would at least put his name in newspapers outside of southern Ohio.

The game was supposed to be a reward for the players after a long season, but the only goal was to leave Phoenix with a win. The game wouldn't be played until New Year's Day, but Hayes practiced his team hard during the month after the regular season. They would practice in the Quonset hut behind Withrow Court, with two big potbellied stoves blazing to try to simulate the Arizona heat. Then Woody would move the team into the more spacious Withrow Court gymnasium, where they'd work on the finer points of the game plan.

Going to Phoenix was no vacation; it was *work,* an opportunity to win yet another game. And that's precisely what the Indians did, beating the Sun Devils 34–21 in front of twenty-three thousand people at Montgomery Stadium.

The game was never really close, as "Boxcar" Bailey ran for two touchdowns, including a fifty-yard score in the fourth quarter that put the game out of reach.

"All Woody did was hand the ball to Bailey and he did the rest," Arnsparger said.

The Salad Bowl win would be the pinnacle of Hayes's career in Oxford. He didn't know it then, but Hayes had earned his spot in what would become a remarkable roster of coaches who earned their stripes at Miami, dubbed "the cradle of coaches."

It wasn't overblown public relations fodder. The school's remarkable list of coaches at Oxford dates back to 1918, when Earl Blaik graduated and went on to national fame by coaching at Army. Also included are: Walter Alston, who went on to manage the Brooklyn Dodgers; Weeb Ewbank, who was head coach of the Super Bowl champion New York Jets and Baltimore Colts; and Paul Brown, who was both a college and professional coaching legend. And, of course, there was Gillman. Years later there would be more alumni to follow, including Parseghian, Pont, Arnsparger, and Schembechler.

But in the early winter of 1951 it was Hayes's time to make his mark and earn the right to be mentioned next to his old foe Gillman. Their dislike and distrust of each other would continue for years beyond the few seasons they spent competing on the football fields in Oxford and Cincinnati. But time and mutual accomplishment would help repair the breach between the two men. Years later, each in the twilight of his career, both men found themselves early one morning in the coffee shop of a Chicago hotel. Hayes and Gillman exchanged a few cursory greetings and then Hayes, awkwardly but resolute, asked Gillman if he wanted to spend some time explaining the concepts of his passing offense. It was Hayes's stubborn way of extending an olive branch. A surprised Gillman agreed. Eight hours later, the two took a dinner break.

"You know," Hayes told friends after spending the whole day listening to Gillman. "I still don't know what the hell he was talking about."

6

A NEW BEGINNING

The November 25, 1950, blizzard that hammered Ohio would have a profound impact on another football rivalry. Up in Columbus, Michigan and Ohio State met in Ohio Stadium as the storm was raging. By the time the Ohio State athletic director Dick Larkins and his Michigan counterpart Fritz Crisler decided to play on through the weather, six inches of snow had fallen with no sign of letting up. There was really no chance to call a postponement. The last thing Michigan wanted was a return trip to Columbus, and with almost eighty thousand tickets presold, the gate was already assured. Though the city was paralyzed by the storm, the reported attendance was more than fifty thousand, a remarkable number, considering that at game time the temperature was hovering around ten degrees, with the wind howling at thirty miles an hour. Visibility was almost impossible for the players, much less for the brave fans, who sat anywhere they pleased inside the massive horseshoe-shaped stadium. The Buckeyes, under coach Wes Fesler, were 5-1 in Big Ten play entering the Michigan game, and they were six-point favorites. The Big Ten conference title and a trip to the Rose Bowl was hinging on a win over the rival Michigan team, a team that came to Columbus with a 3-1-1 record. The game figured to be a mismatch. Ohio State was averaging nearly thirty-five points a game, compared to Michigan's anemic seventeen, so it was no wonder that Crisler and the rest of the Michigan football contingent didn't protest playing the game in conditions that figured to generate very little offense. And that's exactly what happened. Both teams struggled mightily to move the ball even a few yards per possession, with both teams content to punt, even on first and second downs, to protect field position. Ohio State punted the ball twenty-one times, while Michigan punted twenty-four times—and won 9-3 in one of the strangest games ever to be played in college football. Michigan never gained a single first down, but still managed to win—not with a series of field goals as the score would suggest, but with a safety and a touchdown from a blocked punt that Michigan recovered in Ohio State's end zone. Ohio State scored on what still may be one of the most remarkable field goals in history after Vic Janowicz successfully booted a thirty-eight-yard attempt into the teeth of the howling wind on a snow-covered field.

"I could see the goal posts but not the stands behind," Janowicz said later. "Conditions weren't so bad in the first half. If it had been in the second half it would've been impossible."

From the newly built press box, Kaye Kessler, a young writer for the *Columbus Citizen,* who managed to make it through the snow to the stadium, had to scrape the inside of the frosted press box windows with a silver dollar in order to see outside. Down on the field, volunteers were quickly rounded up and given brooms to sweep sidelines markers and goal lines throughout the game.

"The storm didn't really come on until noon, and by then Crisler and Larkins had already decided to play the thing, and it was the damndest game I ever saw," Kessler said. "It was played in gale-force winds and you couldn't see a thing."

Games played in extreme conditions often are decided not by spectacular plays but by mistakes that become magnified as a team's ability to execute gets bogged down—in this case, by the snow. And one of the biggest mistakes was made by Fesler with less than a minute to play in the first half, with the Buckeyes leading 3–2. It was third down with six yards to go for a first down, with the ball in Ohio State territory, but Fesler ordered Janowicz to punt the ball. Janowicz had already had one punt blocked for a safety earlier in the game, and with forty-seven seconds on the clock and two downs remaining, the Buckeyes could have run out most of the clock. But Fesler figured a punt to be a safer play, until it was blocked by Michigan center Tony Momson, who recovered it for the game's only touchdown, giving Michigan a 9–3 lead as the teams headed to the locker room to thaw out during halftime. Adding to the surreal nature of the play was that Momson's younger brother Bob started at tackle for Ohio State that day and recovered a fumble that led to Janowicz's field goal.

"It was only third down, and Wes punts, and sure enough it gets blocked," Kessler said. "It was incredible. He could have easily just run out the clock."

Neither team could score in the second half, and the game mercifully ended with Ohio State gaining a total of forty-one offensive yards and three first downs to Michigan's twenty-seven yards, with no first downs. Even with Janowicz (who at the end of the season would win the Heisman Trophy) the Buckeyes passing offense consisted of three completions out of eighteen attempts for a total of twenty-five yards, while Michigan failed to complete a pass in their nine attempts.

"It was like a nightmare," Janowicz said after the game. "My hands were numb. I had no feeling in them, and I don't know how I hung onto the ball. It was terrible. You knew what you wanted to do, but you couldn't do it.

Given the inability of either team to generate offense in the frightful weather conditions, Fesler's coaching blunder at the end of the first half was all the more critical and generated howls of criticism, not only from the fans, but more importantly from the administration that demanded that, no matter what the regular season record, Ohio State at all costs must beat Michigan. Making things even worse for Fesler was that the upset win sent Michigan to the Rose Bowl instead of the Buckeyes.

"Imagine having a great team like Fesler had and then not being able to use it because of the conditions," Michigan coach Bennie Oosterbaan told the press after the game. "Naturally I'm happy to have won, but the conditions were such that it wasn't a fair test of football."

The "Snow Bowl" loss added to the already mounting pressure on Fesler, who in the late 1920s had become the Buckeyes' first triple-letterman, winning a total of nine letters in football, basketball, and baseball. He was one of Ohio State's all-time great athletes: a three-time all-American halfback, an all-Big Ten guard in basketball, and a baseball player who could play any position. He was also a well-known man about town, with his matinee idol looks and his affable approach, making him a popular figure in the local papers. Kessler would play golf with Fesler in the summer and cover the team in the fall. And people still remembered Fesler for his heroics as an undergraduate star, adding to his popularity. As a coach, Fesler was knowledgeable, but had one fault.

"He was too nice," Kessler said. "He was just a helluva nice guy."

Since taking over as football coach in 1947, the Buckeyes had a 21-13-2 record, but Fesler had never beaten Michigan, losing three times and tying once. His blunder during the "Snow Bowl" loss to Michigan proved too much for him to handle. The papers from Cleveland to Cincinnati unrelentingly criticized his strategy, and fans were calling his house night and day to harangue the former hero who they felt single-handedly cost their Buckeyes a trip to Pasadena. On campus, students and even some faculty members kept up the barrage of outrage aimed at Fesler. After two weeks of constant criticism, Fesler was unraveling. He couldn't sleep with the public outcry ringing in his head. Instead of dismissing the game, Fesler kept focusing on what had happened, re-playing the game over and over until, nearing a nervous breakdown, he resigned on December 9, 1949, citing the damage the pressure was caus-ing to his health and his family. He remains the only Ohio State coach who stopped coaching the Buckeyes without being fired.

"That Snow Bowl game just killed him," Kessler said. "That was his demise."

Down in Oxford, the thirty-seven-year-old Hayes was busy prepar-ing his team for the Salad Bowl when he heard that Fesler was out in Columbus and that the search was on to find a replacement. Few at Miami had the slightest inkling that Hayes would be considered, much less interviewed to replace Fesler. It was a job that would attract top candidates from across the country, given the prestige of Ohio State football, the reputation of the Big Ten, and the vaunted rivalry be-tween Ohio State and Michigan.

From the 1920s to 1934, the Buckeyes had fallen on hard times, failing to win a Big Ten championship. But the Buckeyes would take a huge step in regaining prestige. For the first time in school history, Ohio State went national in looking for a new coach, and the school's recruiters settled on Frances Schmidt, who had led Texas Christian University to two Southwest Conference titles in five seasons. Schmidt had no previous connection to Ohio State. He had played college football at Nebraska, and now he was so highly regarded by Ohio State officials that they gave him a three-year contract, the first multiyear deal in the school's history. He almost immediately returned Ohio State to glory.

The 1935 game against Notre Dame in Ohio Stadium was a classic, though the Buckeyes gave up eighteen fourth-quarter points to lose 18–13. But the Buckeyes went on to share the Big Ten title with Minnesota, and fans still flocked to the games despite the Depression. From the mid-1930s through 1940, the Buckeyes were cranking out all-Americans, as Ohio State dominated the Big Ten. By 1940, Schmidt left under pressure and Brown, the Ohio hero, was hired, beginning his ascension into coaching legend.

By 1942, the Buckeyes were national champions. In 1943 Brown enlisted in the navy, but still kept the Ohio State job in absentia, while he assigned temporary head-coaching duties to an assistant named Carroll Widdoes. The war years didn't stop the Buckeyes. They went undefeated in 1944 and played in front of large crowds and national radio audiences. In 1945 Brown snubbed the Buckeyes by accepting the head coaching job for the Cleveland entry in the All-American Conference, paving the way for Fesler, a nine-time letter-winner during his playing days at Ohio State in the early 1930s, to return to Columbus as head football coach in 1947. Three years later, the job would be open again.

There was no shortage of applicants for the six-member screening committee formed to consider a replacement when Fesler resigned. The committee was headed by Larkins and formally included two university professors in Hermann Miller and Frank Strong, a university vice president named Bland Stradley, a well-connected and generous alum named Frederick Mackey, and a student named Walter Donham. Also informally joining the committee were tens of thousands of self-appointed experts who believed that it was their birthright to weigh in publicly on each potential candidate and to mount hiring campaigns for their personal favorites.

By January the screening committee had compiled a confidential list of thirty-eight candidates that included some of the biggest coaching names targeted by Larkins. There was Charles "Bud" Wilkinson of the University of Oklahoma, Army coach Colonel Earl "Red" Blaik,

Paul Bryant, then an up-and-coming coach at the University of Kentucky, and even William Orwig from the enemy camp known as the University of Michigan. Number three on the list was Paul Brown. Number ten was Sidney Gillman from the University of Cincinnati. And number twenty-nine on the list was W. Woodrow Hayes, a late addition who again used his connections to push his way into consideration. The link that would bring Woody to Columbus was a postcard from Dr. Dan Eikenberry, who had been a graduate adviser to Hayes during his summer graduate work in the late 1940s, when Hayes was coaching at Denison. In 1948 Hayes presented his master thesis in educational administration in front of Eikenberry. Shrewdly, Eikenberry had invited Larkins to sit in on the presentation to give Hayes exposure to a big-name athletic director that perhaps someday could help Hayes. That day came late in January, when Hayes got a postcard from Eikenberry. He was in Mexico, and he had heard about Fesler's resignation and thought that his old student might be interested.

"If you are interested in his position, please let me know and I will contact Dick Larkins on your behalf," Eikenberry wrote to Hayes.

Hayes didn't think twice. He immediately informed Eikenberry that he was very interested. In early January, just after the Indians' win over Arizona State in the Salad Bowl, Hayes met with Larkins at a coaches convention in Dallas and was assured that he would at least get the chance to interview for the job.

Woody's friends, however, were less than thrilled when they learned of his interest. They felt Woody was too inexperienced to handle the pressure that was inherent in coaching the Buckeyes, and he begged him to stay in Oxford where he was just beginning to prosper. Woody, filled with blind ambition, dismissed the concerns.

"When the job was open, I spent an hour and a half trying to dissuade him, telling him about the wolves. But he wouldn't listen. It was a challenge," said Woody's old friend Mike Gregory.

In mid-January 1951 the screening committee first narrowed down the list to eight candidates, and then scheduled interviews from January 19 through February 10. Ohio State assistant coach Harry Strobel would be the first to interview, followed by University of Missouri head coach Don Faurot, Drake University football coach Warren Gaer, Massilion

High School coach Charles Mather, and former Ohio State coach and current Cleveland Browns coach Paul Brown. Springfield, Ohio, coach James McDonald followed Brown and then came W. Woodrow Hayes. Gillman would be the last to be interviewed.

The minute Brown's interest was made public, he became the anointed one to succeed Fesler. Groups of Brown supporters openly campaigned to get their man the job by the time the former Buckeyes coach made his return visit. The vast majority of fans wanted a big name to take over their team, someone experienced and accomplished enough to hold up under the pressure. Brown was the perfect choice. He had already proved that he could handle the job. From 1941 to 1945 he had coached Ohio State to an 18-8-1 record before leaving to join the navy. After the service he founded, then coached, the Cleveland Browns to a string of championships. A newspaper poll ran heavily in favor of Brown, while the Ohio State Football Coaching Association was publicly endorsing Brown for the job. When Brown came to Columbus to interview for the job, he was greeted by a band and hundreds of cheering students. All over campus, signs were posted urging the athletic board to BRING BACK BROWN.

"There was this human cry for Brown," Kessler said. "He was championed for the job, but he wouldn't get it no matter how popular he was."

The problem wasn't Brown's coaching record, it was his arrogance. He may have been the overwhelming public favorite, but key members of the administration, including Larkins, held deep resentments against Brown, who as owner of the Cleveland franchise that he named after himself, had signed a number of Ohio State players before their eligibility expired. Larkins and a few other members of the faculty club never forgave Brown for the shady dealings with Ohio State players, and a few minutes after the four-hour interview they scratched his name off the typed list.

Instead the committee focused on Don Faurot, who at the University of Missouri was the architect of the split-T formation offense that in 1941 helped Missouri lead the nation in rushing. The T formation was introduced by Stanford University coach Clark Shaughnessy; but Faurot, a former basketball star at Missouri, patterned the split T, or the "sliding T," after the two-on-one fast break in basketball, where the defender was forced to make a decision to stop the ball. The formation was the precursor of the option-style offense so prevalent in college football. Faurot's offense called for the linemen to use wider splits to open up the line of scrimmage. The quarterback, instead of turning his back away from the line for hand-offs, would slide along the line of scrimmage instead, either keeping the ball or pitching it to the trailing halfback, thus creating the option.

Under the split T, Faurot's Missouri Tigers went 8-1 in 1941, losing only to Ohio State 12–7 in their opening game of the season. Over the next decade, Faurot regularly scheduled his Tigers to play Ohio State in Columbus, and, as a result, Larkins and others in the athletic department were very familiar with his impressive coaching talent. Bud Wilkinson, who as coach of the University of Oklahoma used Faurot's offense to build a powerhouse program, said in 1950 that the split T formation was "the most original and significant contribution to offensive football in the past ten years."

None of Faurot's accomplishments were lost on the selection committee. A decade earlier, Ohio State nearly lured Faurot from Missouri to coach the Buckeyes, but instead decided to hire Brown. Now, Larkins wanted a big name and offered him the job. Faurot initially agreed to the offer, but changed his mind when he returned to Missouri, where he was met with a suddenly more generous athletic board.

Larkins and the rest of the administration were stunned. Nobody turned down a chance to coach at Ohio State, at least not after accepting the job. With Brown and Faurot out of the picture, there weren't any more big names to consider. There was the highly regarded Gillman, but he had never run a major program like Ohio State's.

Faurot's rejection put Larkins in a bind. It had been two months since Fesler's resignation; and with Faurot out of the picture there were no marquee names to hire to deflect growing public criticism over the length of time it was taking to find a coach. The committee certainly couldn't start the search over, not with spring practice just a month away. Larkins went back to the list of candidates that they had already interviewed. Of the six remaining candidates, Woody Hayes stood out. Hayes had interviewed in Columbus in early February, and in front of the board he'd delivered one of his best recruiting pitches of all time. But instead of convincing the parents of some high school star to send their son to Oxford, Hayes sold himself. He delivered a no-nonsense pitch, pointing out his accomplishments and explaining the coaching philosophies he utilized, based on discipline and power. What Ohio State needed, he said, was to abandon Fesler's single-wing offense, which was becoming antiquated, and install the T formation. Then he launched into his expectations of success and bluntly told the board that under Fesler the team had lacked training and the will to win. Under his command, Woody said, those days soon would be over.

The meeting played right to Woody's strengths. His natural gift of persuasion made him sound more like a coach who had led teams to countless Rose Bowls, than like a relatively inexperienced coach at a mid-sized school, with just one trip to something called the Salad Bowl.

"Before I went to see them, I didn't think I had a chance, but after talking to them for three hours I knew I had the job," Hayes said later of his interview.

With nobody else left to consider seriously, the board—confident enough to give Woody the shot of a lifetime—recommended Hayes and turned the matter over to the board of trustees for official approval. But just as everything about the hiring process proved difficult, so too would getting the trustees to approve the decision.

The committee's recommendation sparked outrage. So strong was the public support for Brown that the local papers called for Larkins to be fired for leading the committee's decision to bypass Brown in favor of Hayes, while other pro-Brown supporters sent telegrams and called Hayes's house back in Oxford to try to harass him out of the job. Despite the recommendation, there was still some hope left for the pro-Brown forces.

The committee had voted unanimously to appoint Hayes as head coach for one year "at a salary of $12,500, with the possibility of advancement of $500 per year in succeeding years until the maximum of $15,000 had been reached," according to records from the committee's meeting, held at nine A.M. on February 12 in Stradley's office. The board then recessed until Stradley returned around noon with the news that the trustees would hold off on a vote.

"Because three members of the board have found it impossible to be present, and feeling that a matter of this importance should have the consideration of a larger representation of the board, a special meeting has been called for Sunday, February eighteenth, at four P.M."

The four P.M. meeting was delayed for nearly three hours to allow Sen. John Bricker, one of Hayes's allies on the board, to fly in from Albuquerque, New Mexico. Bricker was stuck in St. Louis due to bad weather, and the meeting was postponed until he could arrive. Bricker got to campus at 6:42 P.M. and at 6:45 the meeting began, with no guarantee that the board would approve Hayes. So tenuous was the board meeting that Larkins and the rest of the committee huddled in a nearby office to be able to act swiftly in case the board rejected their recommendation.

At 8:11 P.M. the board ended their deliberations and called in Larkins to end his suspense. With one board member absent, the vote was unanimous to hire Hayes. Ohio State president Dr. Howard Bevis then made the official announcement.

"Hayes has a one-year agreement, like all our contracts," Bevis said. "But it's a general understanding that it is to be a continuous agreement."

Hayes's $12,500 starting salary was what the university paid Fesler when he was hired in 1947. Apparently there was no consideration by the university of inflation between the years 1947 and 1951 when the board offered Hayes the job, though the $500 annual raise would in five years bring Hayes's salary to $15,000, which was what Fesler was making when he resigned. It was at the time the highest salary ever paid to an Ohio State coach, and by hiring Hayes the head coach's salary structure could be pushed back by four years.

Hayes was well aware of the pressure Larkins was under, but he didn't leverage a better deal for himself. It was the prestige of the job, not the money that mattered. Not only did he fail to ask to be paid what Fesler was earning when he resigned, Woody didn't even demand to be paid what Fesler was paid in his first season four years earlier. When asked by Larkins what he thought he should be paid, Hayes answered that he figured $10,000 would be sufficient.

Bevis also added one detail of Woody's agreement: "He has a free hand in selecting his assistants," Bevis said.

The message was supposed to be clear. Hayes would be free to run the football program as he saw fit. But it wasn't entirely true. Hayes could certainly hire his own assistants; but once Miami officials were informed that Hayes was hired, they reacted swiftly to protect their interests. Just before going public with the announcement, Larkins and Hahn reached a tacit agreement that prevented Hayes from raiding the current Miami of Ohio football staff.

Because of the turmoil that hit the Miami program when Gillman took some of the Miami players with him to Cincinnati, Hahn warned Larkins that, while he'd allow Woody to leave Oxford, he did not want to see other Miami assistants following Hayes up to Columbus. If Larkins didn't agree, Hahn feared that any bad blood between the two schools could spill over to the state legislature and threaten state funding.

"No doubt you recall that only two years ago we lost Gillman and a situation developed, with the resentment running high on our campus" Hahn wrote in a February 8 memo to Larkins. "If you were to take Woody from us at the present time it would be very unfortunate to have him take other members of our staff, because both Ohio State and Miami have alumni in the legislature, and, as you know, appropriations are important to both institutions, as situations might easily develop over which few of us would have any control. I am sure that members of your committee, as well as the members of the staff at Miami, would regret such a development. In the event, therefore, of your selection of Woody, I would recommend that some understanding be reached in advance that would safeguard Miami against any repetition of our experience with the University of Cincinnati. I do not wish to stand in the way, but we might as well be realistic about the whole thing and recognize that both institutions have influential alumni."

Larkins agreed and Hayes was introduced by Bevis as the nineteenth head football coach in Buckeyes history. Woody Hayes had turned thirty-eight years old during the frenzied week of his hiring. He would be the second-youngest coach to take the job. Only Paul Brown, who was thirty-five when he began his tenure in Columbus in 1941, was younger.

The announcement ended seventy-one days of the long and con-troversial search that saw Ohio State officials essentially hire their sec-ond choice. But no one was happier in the hiring than the relieved Larkins, who had been feeling pressure from both the public and from the administration over the protracted process in replacing Fesler. By the time Woody took over, Fesler had recovered from the strain of the past season and was hired as head football coach at the University of Minnesota.

With Fesler now a forgotten man, the Buckeyes faithful was ready to embrace their new coach—if they only knew who he was.

"Columbus's little world-within-a-world today was ready to again recognize the world situation, the onrushing baseball season, and the outrageous price of pepper. Ohio State had named its new football coach," Kessler wrote in introducing Hayes to his *Columbus Citizen* readers, while taking a swipe at the city's obsession with Ohio State football. "Wayne Woodrow Hayes, a broad-shouldered guy with an in-tense desire to win football games, was booked as the Buckeyes head grid boss."

7

WELCOME TO THE MACHINE

There were no banners to greet the Buckeyes' new coach in late February 1951. Any plans for welcoming parades reserved for Paul Brown's triumphant return were summarily shelved, along with the "Bring Back Brown" banners, after the announcement of Hayes's hiring. The general sense of disappointment allowed Woody to slip quietly into Columbus just a month before the opening of spring practice that was set for March 27. Not long after arriving in town, Hayes took Anne and six-year-old Steve to Ohio Stadium and the three stood inside the imposing structure that seemingly reached to the sky. The sheer emptiness of the huge stadium made the field seem to stretch for miles, from goal post to goal post.

"Isn't that the same size as the one at Miami?" Steve asked his father.

"Yes," Hayes said. "The field is the same, and the game is the same wherever it is played."

But Woody knew football at Ohio State was not at all like it was at Miami, where the program was operating in a tier well below the Big Ten football stratosphere. Hayes had a nice team at Miami in 1950. But even if he lost there was still far less pressure in Oxford, where only a polite weekly newspaper was assigned to cover the Indians, compared to Columbus, where two daily papers were fighting for every scrap of football news.

"In Oxford, there were no reporters around and once a week, the coaches would maybe go to Cincinnati or Dayton to talk to reporters, and that was it," Pont said. "It was quiet in Oxford and it was a pretty good atmosphere in which to coach."

It was the exact opposite in Columbus. As Fesler's replacement, Hayes was walking into a job considered to be the "graveyard of coaches." Counting Fesler, the Buckeyes in 1950 had run through six coaches in the past twelve seasons, a track record that almost certainly meant little job security for Woody. There was no doubt that the job was one of the most prestigious in college football, but along with the prestige came almost impossible expectations from the Columbus faithful, who worshiped the Buckeyes. Each Buckeyes game was a rite of communion for the eighty thousand fans that packed themselves inside the imposing horseshoe-shaped stadium along the banks of the Olentangy River. But losing was a sin for which there was no forgiveness. Ohio State University was a public institution receiving millions of dollars in annual funding, and that was enough for the taxpaying citizens of Ohio to believe they had every right to have their say in the school's interests, particularly in matters related to the Buckeyes football team.

After scouting the area, Anne and Woody bought a house in Upper Arlington, a quiet, upscale suburb due west of Ohio Stadium. The unassuming two-story white frame house with green shutters on 1711 Cardiff Road was about two miles from the football facility on the edge of the massive Ohio State campus. It was a wise choice. Woody wouldn't have to waste time commuting to work, allowing him to spend even more time at his office, located north of the stadium and in relative isolation from the rest of the campus.

Each spring, the burning question in Columbus was who was going to be quarterbacking the team. But in the spring chill of 1951, nobody really cared about who was going to lead the Buckeyes. The bigger question was, "Who in the hell is Woody Hayes?" It was a good question. Hayes had gotten the job more by a stunning convergence of luck, connections, and persuasiveness, than by his reputation and experience. As a result, people in the state of Ohio were mostly unaware of Hayes, and they were still stinging from the administration's decision not to hire Brown. Skepticism and doubt shrouded their confidence in Hayes's ability to lead the Buckeyes to conference championships and Rose Bowls, not to mention victories over Michigan.

Woody spent the few weeks before spring practice making the rounds in town, building public support, speaking to local business and alumni groups, and promising to deliver a "tough team" that wouldn't "back down from any challenges." His boilerplate speech was devoid of any guarantees of victories. Instead, he would rally the Buckeyes faithful with promises of toil and effort.

"We may not win them all, but we'll show you the fightingest team you've ever seen," he would say, whipping up support. "I promise you we'll never be outconditioned."

He failed to mention his history of difficult first seasons in each of his previous jobs.

With just a month before spring practice, he put together his coaching staff, blending some remaining assistants, like Esco Sarkkinen and Ernie Godfrey with new young blood including Doyt Perry and Bill Arnsparger, Woody's young assistant at Miami.

Arnsparger was the only member of the Miami staff allowed to go to Columbus as part of the "understanding" between Hahn and Larkins. Others hired by Hayes included Harry Strobel, Bill Hess, and Gene Fekete. In the fall Bo Schembechler would come to Columbus as a graduate assistant. Parseghian was named to replace Hayes as head coach at Miami.

By now Woody was an expert at the organizational aspects of running a college football program. He was thorough, expert at preparing his coaches, and adept at installing an effective system of controls, patterned after his days on the USS *Rinehart,* where as executive officer he would deliver departmental reports first thing in the morning. During the morning coaches meeting, Woody would go down the line, grilling each position coach about their respective players' grades, class loads, study habits, or anything else that could threaten their eligibility. Hayes and the coaches would then go over the day's practice plans and adjust accordingly, depending on the day of the week.

The assistant coaches also had to teach physical education classes in addition to the coaching responsibilities, so after the coaches meeting they'd head off to teach, and reconvene in the afternoon to begin practice. After a two-hour practice that began at three P.M., the coaches would meet and watch film, breaking down that week's opponents and creating game plans. There would be a break for the coaches to go check on their players, some paying visits to dorm rooms or apartments to make sure the players were studying. After making their rounds, the coaches would meet again, and sometimes they wouldn't leave the football facility until midnight. Overseeing every minute of it was Woody.

During the season, their families became almost an afterthought to the coaches. They worked constantly, and the weekends were consumed by the games. Even on Sundays, the coaches would return to their offices after the game to begin breaking down film. Woody didn't give the brutal hours a second thought. Though his son Steve was now almost ten, Woody was rarely home. During the season Woody would sometimes bunk in his office, even though he lived about two miles from the football facility. This left the job of raising their son mostly to Anne.

"We worked hard, but you knew that Woody was working just as hard, and you knew he wouldn't ask you to do anything he hadn't done himself," Arnsparger said. "But you really had to make sure the players were studying. There were no academic advisors back then. We were the ones who monitored in detail the players' studies."

The nine-man staff was far more coaching assistance than Hayes had ever had at his disposal, but in those early years he also demanded to be involved in every aspect of the team, even though veteran coaches like Godfrey and Strobel could easily run the team without his interference. Each coach quickly developed a thick skin to protect against Woody's mercurial nature.

"His outbursts never lasted long, and you knew it wasn't personal," Arnsparger said. "And he was doing it because you probably deserved it."

Woody's first task at hand was to back up the bold promises he made to the athletic board. He would scrap the single-wing formation and install the T formation to give the Buckeyes a more up-to-date offense. It was a good theory. New coach, new offense. A fresh start. Except that Fesler's antiquated single-wing offense was built around the prodigious talents of all-American Vic Janowicz, who led the Big Ten in scoring and total offense in 1950 and was a star safety on defense. He rushed for 938 yards and scored sixteen touchdowns that year. Despite losing to Michigan in the Snow Bowl, Janowicz was voted the Big Ten's most valuable player and won the Heisman Trophy, going away as a twenty-year-old junior, garnering more than double the number of votes over runner-up Kyle Rote of Southern Methodist University.

Fesler called him one of the best athletes in Ohio State sports history.

"Vic excelled in every phase of the game," Fesler said. "He not only was a great runner, passer, and blocker, but he did all of our kicking, including punting, field goals, quick kicks, kickoffs, and extra points."

But Hayes wanted his own offense installed, even if it meant moving Janowicz to halfback.

On March 27 Woody got his first look at the 1951 team that, on paper, was loaded with some of the best high school talent at nearly every position. The players' view of Woody was far less impressive. None were recruited by Hayes, and most had never heard of their new coach until he was named as Fesler's successor. These were players who were used to winning. They went to the Rose Bowl in 1949 and they felt they should have gone in 1950 as well.

Spring practice was a vitally important time for most major college football programs. In the six weeks between late March and early May, the coaches would put together the depth chart for the fall and settle on starting lineups. As a result, it was a time of brutal competition among the players, as they battled to impress their coaches. Woody not only had to evaluate players with whom he was not familiar, but he also had to install his offense. The combination made for a miserable spring practice, as the players struggled to adjust while learning his new system.

A year earlier the Buckeyes were led by the easygoing Fesler, but that approach was soon forgotten. Under Woody the players discovered that toughness was rooted in pain. Already exhausted, the practices now ended with laps around the field in the Ohio heat. With no water on the field, players would routinely collapse from heat exhaustion.

Like other coaches of that era, Woody saw no harm in his methods. The Buckeyes' morale, already low with the loss of Fesler, plummeted under the new hard-line approach.

The team was ranked seventh when the season opened against Southern Methodist; nevertheless, the Buckeyes barely won 7–0, as a miscast Janowicz struggled to duplicate his Heisman Trophy form.

The Southern Methodist game was a harbinger of things to come for the rest of the season. The Ohio State offensive was stuck mostly in neutral, and the team struggled to win just once in their first four games.

The players were miserable, especially Janowicz, who grew frustrated in accepting his lesser role. Along with the brutal running and conditioning, Woody held endless team meetings that drove the players crazy. By nature he was a worrier, and holding meetings was his proactive way to exert at least some control over his anxieties.

"I believe in overlearning," Hayes said. "That way you are sure."

But some of the players resented the overpreparation. "We set a record for meetings. We had meetings about meetings, and when we weren't in a meeting we were out running some more. When we finished running, we had a meeting about that too," said tackle Dick Logan.

Woody was undeterred by the growing disenchantment among the players.

"He just knew what he wanted to do, and he never lacked confidence," Arnsparger said. "He had definite ideas, and he wasn't going to change for anybody. He was like that from the first time I met him. It didn't matter that it was his first year at Columbus. He just knew what he wanted to accomplish."

The team struck back on November 17, at home against Illinois. Before the game the Buckeyes players locked Hayes out of the stadium locker room and held their own pregame talk in defiance of their coach. The players-only meeting worked, with the Buckeyes holding the heavily favored Illini to a scoreless tie.

The Buckeyes finished the season with a 4-3-2 record, including a 7–0 season-ending loss to Michigan. Public sentiment railed against Hayes, who still had to fight against the fans' preference for Brown. During the last home game a plane flew over Ohio Stadium pulling a WOODY MUST GO banner. It had been a season where Hayes had turned one of college football's most talented players, Janowicz, into a mere mortal, while alienating the rest of the team.

The Buckeyes scored just 109 points in 1951, forty-seven of which came in one game, in a blowout win against Iowa. The 109-point total was less than half of what it was in the 1950 season, when the Buckeyes scored 286 points. Janowicz's performance was miserable. The year after he won the Heisman, he gained 376 yards rushing and completed just seven of twenty-five passes for seventy-four yards and two touchdowns, compared to his Heisman season, when he accounted for 939 yards of offense. It was a disappointing end to his remarkable college career. Only five-eight and 180 pounds, Janowicz has been called the greatest athlete to play at Ohio State. But he may also be the most hard-luck player to come out of Columbus.

Following his disappointing senior season, Janowicz spent two years in the army and then signed a $25,000 bonus contract to play baseball for the Pittsburgh Pirates—even though he hadn't played baseball since high school. Forced to play in the big leagues due to the bonus-baby rule—a rule that required big bonus players to play in the big leagues for two years—Janowicz faltered and played little in 1953 and 1954. He returned to football in 1955 by signing with the Washington Redskins, and despite not playing the game for two years, Janowicz finished second in the NFL in total scoring.

But Janowicz couldn't outrun heartbreak. After a preseason game in Los Angeles in 1956, he suffered a severe head injury in an automobile accident and was forced to retire. Redskins owner George Marshall added to the disaster by refusing to pay Janowicz's salary after the accident; but the Redskins players chipped in to help pay his medical bills.

Then, demonstrating his loyalty and his dichotomy as a coach, Hayes stepped in. He had failed to take full advantage of Janowicz's prodigious talents during the 1951 season; but Woody showed his appreciation and loyalty in 1954 when a disheveled Janowicz showed up at the Breakwater Hotel in Chicago where the Buckeyes were staying before playing Northwestern in nearby Evanston. After the game, Hayes put Janowicz on the plane back to Columbus and arranged for rehabilitation care for his former player. Janowicz eventually overcame the brain damage suffered from the accident and moved back to Columbus where he worked as an auditor for the state of Ohio. He died in 1996 from prostate cancer.

★　★　★

There were no bowl games and no Heisman Trophies awarded to Hayes's underachieving 1951 squad. Instead, the Buckeyes earned a disappointing fifth-place Big Ten finish. It was an inauspicious yet familiar inaugural season for Woody, given his experiences at Denison and Miami of Ohio, only this time there was a nearly limitless amount of resources at his disposal. He needed to stock his program with players that fit his game of strength and power, a game that was well-suited to the Big Ten, where pounding ball control and stout defense mattered more than innovate offensive strategy.

In 1952 Ohio State was awash in money, influence, and power. The school's football budget was immense compared to Miami of Ohio, and Ohio State's sphere of influence reached not just across the state, but all over the Midwest, and even to both coasts, through powerful and well-connected alumni. A well-organized network of football supporters who lent their power and their checkbooks in support of their beloved Buckeyes football team was already in place when Woody arrived in Columbus. Members of the network, called "Frontliners," identified and steered recruits to Columbus. These men typically were local prominent businessmen who, staying mostly on the right side of the NCAA's recruiting rules, would bring in blue-chip prospects by arranging summer jobs, buying dinners, and otherwise keeping tabs on the players until an assistant coach or Woody himself could step in and extract a commitment from the player. It was a sophisticated operation, with Frontliners assigned to specific areas in Ohio and around the country, that made it almost impossible for a player to slip under the Buckeyes' radar. Ohio State may not have signed every top player, but they almost never missed the opportunity to try to woo them to Columbus. The Frontliners would also lend formidable financial support to the football program. In return for their efforts and donations, the Frontliners, later to be called "Committeemen," got to rub shoulders with the coaches, attend team functions, sit in the best seats at games, and otherwise feel as if they were part of the team.

Hayes was at the top of the recruiting organization, with most of the details handled through Ernie Godfrey, who in addition to his assistant coaching job was also the Buckeyes' recruiting coordinator. Information from the Frontliners on top talent would flow through

Godfrey, who in turn would oversee the efforts to bring the player into the Buckeyes fold.

Each assistant coach was assigned different areas of the country and would keep track of the top players in their area. When it was determined that the prospect was worthy of serious consideration, the assistant coaches would make contact and work to get a commitment to Ohio State. The process usually ended with the player making his official visit to Columbus, where he'd spend the weekend with a dozen or so other recruits attending a campus party, eating at Columbus's finest restaurants, and going to a football game. Then, just before leaving campus, the high schoolers would be granted a few minutes with Hayes. The speech was nearly always the same. Hayes would explain how lucky the prospect was to be considered worthy of playing for Ohio State, and then he'd make only one promise.

"If you're good enough, you'll play," Hayes would tell each one.

It was an honest pitch. There were no guarantees of any playing time, and in most cases, there was no promise of a specific position. Nearly every high school player who came to Ohio State was a high school superstar, and he soon discovered that all-state running backs made for great defensive backs and high school fullbacks made great linebackers. Hayes generally had his pick of the young prospects, but he would also hit the road to woo the player who was either waffling or so full of potential that it required a more personal touch.

Hayes was a master of the home visit: He wouldn't waste much time recruiting the kid. He had already seen enough film to know he could play at Ohio State, so he zeroed in on the parents. It was a thing of beauty. Hayes wouldn't talk about the glories of Ohio State football, of past Heisman Trophies, national championships, or Rose Bowls; instead, the avuncular Hayes would preach to the parents about the value of an Ohio State education and the connections that would come with a degree. He'd promise the parents that, by God, he'd do everything in his power to get the kid the diploma that would set him up for life.

The delivery was full of charm and folksiness, vital parts of what made Hayes a natural salesman. There was none of the harshness that so many players and parents had heard about. He was the exact opposite of what the parents had come to expect. And, unlike with so many other coaches, there were no discreet offers of cash, or cars, or jobs, or any special treatment. Ghetto, or country club suburb, it didn't matter. Hayes felt at home in either surrounding. He was the ultimate closer, and once he stepped foot into the parents' kitchen it wouldn't be long before another blue-chipper would be headed to Columbus.

When necessary, Hayes would also turn to some of the state's most influential leaders to win over the hottest prospects, in essence delivering a lethal one-two recruiting punch to bring in the best talent. To truly impress a prospect, and more importantly the recruit's parents, Hayes would call on John Galbreath, the fabulously wealthy Ohio industrialist who also owned the Pittsburgh Pirates and presided over the regal Darby Dan farm outside of Columbus, where he bred top thoroughbreds. It was also a working farm, with some three thousand acres of corn and soybean fields, along with acres of blue grass pastures for the horses to roam. Galbreath also brought some exotic animals to his land—zebra, buffalo, deer, elk, and antelope roamed freely in large, fenced pastures.

It was an impressive place to bring a prized recruit, or to entertain influential alumni. Galbreath, an Ohio University graduate, was nonetheless devoted to the football fortunes of Ohio State. He would not only lend his financial support to the Buckeyes, but he would also bring the bluest of the blue chips out to his farm, impress upon the player the importance of the connections that would be made by playing for the Buckeyes. He'd also arrange summer jobs for some of the team's top players at one of his numerous construction jobs around town, and he'd use his influence to help former Buckeyes in need.

It was no coincidence that Janowicz was given a big bonus to play baseball for Galbreath's Pirates after the Heisman Trophy winner left Columbus. And it was Galbreath who helped Hayes reel in Columbus Central High's Howard Cassady, who was one of Ohio's best all-around athletes. Hayes nearly passed on recruiting Cassady, when the 155-pound running back failed to impress him in a sloppy high school football game. But his great speed attracted other schools, and Hayes finally decided to offer him a scholarship. It wasn't as if Woody had much to worry about. Cassady was the first in his family to even graduate from high school, so the thought of leaving town to go to college was very much a foreign concept to Cassady. Though he had earlier scholarship offers from a number of other schools, Cassady had little intention of leaving Columbus.

He made an immediate impression. Nicknamed "Hopalong" for his shiftiness on the football field, Cassady weighed no more than 170 pounds in his freshman year, 1952, and even Hayes, who despised playing underclassmen, couldn't keep him off the field when the Buckeyes opened the 1953 season with another new offensive scheme.

After spending a few weeks during the spring in Norman, Oklahoma, to learn the split T offense from Bud Wilkinson, Hayes installed a new split T formation, in hope of reviving the anemic offense that scored only 109 points in the previous season. The split T was originally designed by Faurot at Missouri, Larkins's first choice to replace Fesler in 1951. Ohio State didn't have Faurot as its head coach, but at least it had his offense.

Even with Cassady at halfback, the Buckeyes offense sometimes sputtered early that season. Part of the problem was the new split T, but Woody had also made a major personnel change. He decided to switch senior Tony Curcillo, the two-year starter at quarterback, to linebacker to make way for unproven sophomore John Borton, who Woody felt would be a better fit for the split T.

With Janowicz gone, much of the team's offensive success now rested on Cassady's slight shoulders, and immediately he proved he could carry the load. During the Buckeyes' first game against the Indiana Hoosiers, Cassady scored three touchdowns and the Buckeyes won 33–13. It was a dazzling performance that merely hinted at what was to come.

After the impressive win over Indiana, the Buckeyes lost at home to Purdue, thanks to three second-half turnovers. But a week later Ohio State upset number-one-ranked Wisconsin at home in a hallmark win for Hayes. The performance was a nearly perfect demonstration of Hayes's coaching strategy. The offense clicked, scoring long, sustained drives that kept the ball out of Wisconsin's all-American running back Alan Ameche's hands. The defense showed a newfound toughness. Ameche couldn't score against the aggressive defense, patterns that held the Badgers offense five times on downs inside Ohio State's 20-yard line. The Buckeyes won 23–14.

It was a big win for Hayes, easily the most important since coming to Columbus. But his team was inconsistent. The week following the huge win over the Badgers, the Buckeyes scored 35 points in a blowout of Washington. But then Ohio State was shutout at Iowa 8–0, an embarrassing defeat, considering that the Buckeyes were twenty-one-point favorites going into the game. The team recovered to beat Northwestern 24–21, but then the seesaw season continued, with a 24–21 loss against Pittsburgh, followed by a 27–7 win against Illinois that set up the season-ending game against Michigan.

The inconsistent Buckeyes were underdogs against Michigan, which going into the game had dominated their rivals by winning thirty-six of the previous forty-eight games. But the Buckeyes were razor sharp, with Borton throwing for three touchdowns and the defense forcing eight turnovers, as the Buckeyes dominated in a 27–7 victory. It was Hayes's first win over that despised team "from up north," and it quieted for the moment any talk of his dismissal, as the team was headed to a 6-3 season's ending, for a third-place finish in the Big Ten.

The win over Michigan eased some of the pressure on Hayes, but the season was marred by the death of Woody's mother. Widowed since 1939, Effie, seventy-four, died in her home on East Canal Street in Newcomerstown, after weeks of a lingering illness. Mary Hayes, Woody's sister, had moved back to Ohio from New York City to take care of her ailing mother. But Woody had spent little time in Newcomerstown since leaving to begin his college coaching career at Denison. With Effie gone, there was even less reason to visit.

Given the relative success of the 1952 season, hopes were running high for the following year. Hayes was counting on Cassady and Borton to lead a formidable offense. The season began with two easy wins against Indiana and California, stoking the expectations for a Big Ten championship and a trip to the Rose Bowl. But the wins disguised what was a weaker Buckeyes defense. Against Illinois, Ohio State gave up 41 points to Illinois in blowout 41–20 loss at home. Worse, the Buckeyes lost their prolific passer in Borton to injury.

With inexperienced sophomore Dave Leggett replacing Borton,

the offensive sputtered against a much weaker Penn team in a 12–6 win. Leggett gained confidence in the next two games and led Ohio State to wins over Wisconsin and Northwestern, setting up the 5-1 Buckeyes to play the defending national champion Michigan State Spartans, who also were 5-1 when they came into Ohio Stadium. It was a game that would define the Buckeyes season. An upset would answer any doubts that last season's win against powerhouse Wisconsin and Michigan were flukes. But the Buckeyes defense again faltered, and Hayes got conservative when he ordered four consecutive running plays—plays that stalled the offense when the Bucks trailed just 14–13 in the fourth quarter. Two late touchdowns by the Spartans put the game out of reach, and it ended in a disappointing 28–13 loss. Now 5-2, the Buckeyes beat Purdue, easing some of the sting of the Michigan State loss, and setting up their visit to Ann Arbor with the hopes of salvaging their season with a road win against a weak Michigan team.

Expectations were soaring in Columbus that Ohio State would win at Michigan—something the Bucks hadn't done since the 1937 season. There was no Big Ten title on the line, but all the week leading up to the game the pressure mounted for Hayes. Leggett's steady improvement at quarterback made the Buckeyes overwhelming favorites, but the team played arguably their worst game under Hayes. Six offensive turnovers, including five interceptions, and a lack of any running game, sunk the Buckeyes, in a humiliating 20–0 loss. Any goodwill that came from last year's win over Michigan was long gone, and support for Hayes was faltering.

The vast majority of Buckeyes fans didn't want Hayes hired in the first place. Now, with three seasons behind him, Hayes had a 16-9-2 record. At most other schools, Hayes would have been rewarded for the respectable record. But in Columbus Hayes was still a pariah. The public still pined for Paul Brown, and only a Big Ten title and a trip to the Rose Bowl would quiet the call for Hayes's ouster—a call that seemed to grow louder each day after the season ended. Following the 1953 season Woody no longer answered the phone at home. Invariably, the calls that flooded the house after the season were from complete strangers who felt it was their right to phone at all hours of the day and night to bid good riddance. Anne, Woody's first and truest line of defense, would answer the phone and firmly tell the callers that under no circumstances was the Hayes family considering leaving town anytime soon.

Hayes, in typical fashion, was motivated by the criticism. He simply buried himself in work, while Larkins fended off the mounting cry for his ouster. Anne ran the house and understood.

The nearly desperate push was fueled by an unmatched level of intensity. The only answer was to work longer hours, watch more film, have more meetings, and recruit better players. Consumed by football and desperate to save his job, Hayes turned inward. His gregarious and charming nature that so often mesmerized banquet audiences was lost in a new intensity. There was little time for even his small but loyal knot of friends. Football transcended everything. There simply was no other option but to succeed.

8

THE DRIVE

A few weeks before the start of the 1954 season, Hop Cassady paid a visit to teammate Dick Brubaker to talk to the stellar Buckeyes end and senior co-captain about the upcoming season. Brubaker, who two years earlier showed up at Woody's office unannounced asking for the chance to play football, had become one of Ohio State's most unlikliest leaders. In doing so, he had earned the respect of everyone on the team, from superstar Cassady down to the last man on the squad.

Before transferring to Ohio State, Brubaker had played end at Ohio Wesleyan, and wanted to prove to himself that he could play Big Ten football, so he boldly knocked on Hayes's office door and asked for the chance. Hayes greeted him with the usual charm, the trait that was so effective in wooing players to come to Columbus.

"I walked into his office and said, 'Mr. Hayes, I'd like to try out,' but he had no idea who I was," Brubaker recalled. "But Woody was kind and empathetic and took me right in to to see the coaches."

After exchanging pleasantries, Hayes passed him off, instructing end coach Esco Sarkkinen to check out the potential new player. Sark sensed something in the slim end from Shaker Heights, who wasn't a blue chip player steered to Columbus by one of the Frontliners. Though Brubaker played on his state championship high school football team, he wasn't a star player and wasn't anywhere close to being considered by Ohio State. Coincidentally, Brubaker had already met Hayes when, as a senior in high school he and his friend Robin Brown, Paul Brown's son, took a trip to Oxford to check out Miami University. The introduction was made during Hayes's regular handball game with his assistant coaches, and left no lasting impression.

Hayes assigned players different-colored practice jerseys to sort out the myriad of talent. Red was for the starters, blue for second string,

followed by orange, yellow, and finally white, a color used to designate
the obscure walk-ons and scrubs who were nothing more than cannon
fodder for the starters. Brubaker drew a white shirt the first day of
practice and stood around doing nothing. The next day, not knowing
enough to check the list, he again donned a white jersey. But Hayes
had upgraded him that day to yellow to allow the coaches to give him
a look. Unaware that his chance was at hand, Brubaker was with the
scrubs. Afterward, an incredulous Sark implored him to check the list,
leaving a crushed Brubaker feeling that he had blown what little chance
he had to move up the depth chart. The next day, he again drew yellow
and though he anxiously checked the list every day, he never again wore
white as he quickly became one of Woody's favorites.

Smart, tough, reliable, and disciplined, Brubaker was Hayes's type of
player, one who could learn fast and easily handle his coach's direct
methods. In just two seasons he would go from wearing a white jersey—
the ultimate symbol of football obscurity—to being named team cocaptain. He and co-captain John Borton fit perfectly into Hayes's
definition of a team captain. Hayes felt flashy players and superstars made
lousy leaders. Instead, Hayes wanted his captains to be mature, and most
of all unflinchingly loyal, just as he had been during his own playing days.

"The best lead by example," Hayes said. "Our captains have all been
the rather quiet type—not the 'holler guy' nor the 'personality boy.' Just
good, sound men. We ask these captains to carry water on both their
shoulders, for not only are they responsible to the squad's welfare, but
they are also responsible to the head coach."

Brubaker and Cassady, two of the team's key players, gathered in
Brubaker's house and talked of the team's chances. Though they never
spoke directly about it, the budding all-American Cassady and the reliable Brubaker knew that Hayes's coaching destiny was in their hands
as they handicapped the upcoming season. The Buckeyes had an unremarkable 6-3 record in 1953, and the sportswriters, seeing little improvement, picked Ohio State to finish fifth in the Big Ten. But as
Cassady and Brubaker talked, they both sensed that the team had more
talent than the experts knew.

"We just sat there and talked about how we really could have a
great team," Brubaker said. "I knew we had players that were damn

good, and we had Hop. He was just a junior, but he always seemed to be able to shift gears to fit the situation. He could always somehow ratchet it up, and he was a winner."

Some of the younger players had better spring practices than any outsiders expected, and the team was as tough as any Hayes had ever coached.

But one of the big problems for Woody was his quarterback. Senior cocaptain John Borton was never the same after a devastating leg injury that he suffered against Illinois in 1953. Borton, who was a talented passer, was beaten out by Dave Legget, but the position was the season's big question mark, and Hayes worried whether Leggett could meet his demands. He hated inexperienced quarterbacks, and though Leggett had started six games in 1953, Hayes preferred to have Borton start. But after spring practice it became clear the Leggett would run the offense.

At fullback was one of the most talented of Buckeyes, a guy named Hubert Bobo, who was just a sophomore, but he had the combination of speed and size that Woody loved. Bobo had a linebacker's mentality and loved to clear the way for Cassady, while also posing a triple running threat for the Buckeyes. Bobo ran hard off the field as well as on it. He hailed from tiny Chauncey, Ohio, and was said to have attended high school just three days a week; but he was still given a diploma after setting state high school football scoring records. Despite the shaky academic standing, Hayes and the Frontliners got him admitted into Ohio State, where he stayed eligible in 1954, thanks to the efforts of four tutors.

"A modern indoor record," Bobo once joked.

To try to control Bobo, Hayes assigned assistant coach Bill Hess to watch his every move and do whatever was needed to keep him on the field on Saturdays. It was almost a full-time job for Hess. But on the field, Bobo was poised, confident, hypercompetitive, and a team leader even as a sophomore. His teammates responded to his unbridled will to win and natural leadership abilities, and though Cassady was the star, Bobo was just as gifted.

Another member of the backfield was Bobby Watkins, a powerful runner who led the Buckeyes in scoring in 1953. Watkins, along with Jim Parker, were the only black starters and one of the few black players on the team. Parker was one of Woody's first black recruits and was well on his way to becoming one of the best lineman in Buckeye history.

Woody was no racist. Talent, not skin color, was all that really mattered to him, and he tried to be as judicious as possible with his black players. On the 1954 team was a player named Jack Gibbs, who never played high school football and who had worked for two years before enrolling at Ohio State. Hayes saw raw talent in Gibbs and allowed him to try out for the team. He was good enough to make the Buckeyes, and was slated to start at fullback in 1953 until sidelined by a broken ankle. Gibbs returned to the Buckeyes in 1954 and with a Herculean effort, worked a forty-hour week during the night shift in a local factory, went to class during the day, and practiced with the football team in the afternoon. Hayes, who hated it when Cassady skipped spring practice to play baseball, respected Gibbs's work ethic and quietly allowed him to shoehorn football into his schedule.

But Jim Crow was alive and well in Columbus during the early 1950s and it presented some problems. Even though Jesse Owens had starred at Ohio State before his dramatic performance in front of Adolph Hitler in the 1934 Olympics, the school was still mainly closed to black students, most of whom lived in black neighborhoods off the Ohio State campus. Ohio State recruited black players, but the countless quarterback clubs across the state had an unwritten expectation that Ohio State could certainly have blacks on the team as long as the coaches never played more than three black players at a time.

The unspoken racism posed a contradiction for Hayes early in his coaching career at Ohio State. With a mediocre record and mounting pressure on him to satisfy the thousands of boosters who never wanted him hired in the first place, Hayes grudgingly went along with the unspoken rule until he was established enough to force changes. At the same time, Woody had no qualms about inviting the black players over to his neighborhood in Upper Arlington, a place where the only blacks who were seen were at the service entrances of the wealthy. Parker on occasion would stay with Woody and Anne, both of whom would help Parker with his classes. Parker, who played high school football in segregated Macon, was unprepared for college life and needed help to stay eligible. He was a football staff project. Joining the Hayeses was Katy

Hess, wife of assistant Bill Hess, who would tutor Parker throughout his four years at Ohio State.

The development of talented young players like Cassady, Bobo, and Parker gave Hayes hope for the upcoming season, but the assistant coaches were far happier about something else. Larkins, who was supporting Hayes as the pressure to fire him swirled, strongly suggested to Woody that he make a significant coaching change by agreeing to hire Lyal Clark. Larkins convinced Clark, who was defensive line coach at Ohio State under Fesler and had followed Fesler to Minnesota, to come back to Columbus and work with Woody.

Larkins clearly saw the frustrations suffered by the assistant coaches in working under Woody. The problem was Woody's steadfast refusal to delegate. Hayes drove the coaches crazy by trying to control every aspect of the football program. The incessant meddling was not only hard to deal with for the assistant coaches, it was hurting the performance of the team. Woody loved to say that he was never outworked by anyone while he was coaching the Buckeyes, but the demands of his job far exceeded what Hayes could do by himself. It was becoming obvious that the genteel programs at Denison and Miami of Ohio hadn't prepared Hayes to handle all the duties of coaching the Buckeyes. Hayes knew no other way but to run the offense and coach the defense while balancing recruiting efforts and dealing with alumni pressures all at the same time. Advice and suggestion often turned into loud disagreements, especially when they triggered Woody's hair-trigger temper. It was up to Larkins to convince Woody to change his ways.

"I never worked under a big-time coach, so I naturally grew accustomed to doing everything myself," Hayes later admitted.

Hayes had little choice in accepting Larkins's suggestion. His job was in Larkins's hands, and both knew that time was running out. The agreement was to let Clark run the defense to free up Hayes to focus on the offense. For everyone but the Ohio State quarterbacks, it was a welcoming change.

Hayes couldn't have been too pleased to have one of Fesler's former coaches around, but the hiring was more palatable, given that in the 1953 season Minnesota had shut out Michigan 22–0, with Clark's stingy defense holding Michigan star halfback Tony Ranoff to just 27 total yards.

That alone was enough to bring back Clark, and it would prove to be one of the best coaching decisions Hayes would ever make. It was a move that would end up saving his job.

"Woody was still a part of everything, but he began to delegate," Arnsparger said. "It wasn't as if he didn't know what had to be accomplished. He was always in the background and involved, and though he delegated, he knew what was happening."

The difference was immediate. Hayes always more comfortable as an offense coach. Defense, under the one-platoon system, took somewhat of a back seat to what Woody wanted to accomplish on offense. But with Clark now coaching the defense, the Buckeyes improved dramatically. They opened the 1954 season with a 28–0 shutout over Indiana that included four turnovers. Suddenly, it didn't matter that Clark was part of the former Fesler regime. It was the first shutout by the Buckeyes since Hayes's first season in 1951.

The Buckeyes rolled through the early part of the season, piling up points behind Parker's blocking and Cassady's shifty running ability. After trouncing Illinois 40–7, Ohio State beat Iowa and improved their record to 4-0. The Buckeyes, who were ranked fifth in the Big Ten before the start of the season, suddenly found themselves ranked fourth in the nation.

The strong start was beginning to take some of the heat off Hayes, but second-ranked Wisconsin came to Columbus on October 23 with an undefeated record. Though doubts swirled around the Buckeyes' unproven chances, their number-one offense clashing with the Badgers number-one-ranked defense, made the matchup one of the season's top games, with more than four hundred press credentials issued to accommodate all of the big-city sportswriters who came to Columbus for the Homecoming Day game.

Homecoming at Ohio State was full of pageantry and tradition. It began in 1912, then called "Ohio State Day" by a professor named George Rightmire, who later went on to be the school president. Parades, homecoming queens, and parties filled the weekend, creating a week full of distractions for the players and coaches. But Hayes kept the same practice schedule, made the same Friday afternoon plans for dinner at the country club before retiring his team to a local hotel. The only bow to tradition was the captain's breakfast, a time-honored homecoming ritual that began in 1934 and that brings all past captains together for breakfast to recognize the team's current captains. No game, no matter what the stakes, would ever derail the event that took Hayes and his two team leaders away from their preparations.

For most of the game, all of the criticism and doubt that shrouded Hayes seemed justified. Though the Buckeyes were playing at home and the Badgers hadn't beaten Ohio State in Columbus since 1918, Hayes had yet to prove that he could consistently win. Something bad, it seemed, always occurred. A key turnover, maybe a defensive lapse, always seemed to strike the Buckeyes at the wrong time. But Hayes had run the Buckeyes hard during the week of practice and the team was in great condition. The plodding, physical pace of the Wisconsin game was just what he wanted. He ran a steady attack of belly plays into the line, forcing a bruising contest that he felt his team could win. The Badgers, though, were just as tough, with fullback Alan Ameche leading their offense. The game was close late into the third quarter, with Wisconsin leading 7–3 and the Badgers driving deep into Ohio State territory. The Buckeyes seemed destined to lose.

With second and four on the Buckeyes 20-yard line, the Badgers were looking to put the game out of reach. Clark's defense had stymied Ameche all afternoon, so Wisconsin coach Ivy Williamson ordered quarterback Jim Miller to throw downfield. Cassady, who was as talented on defense as he was on offense, intercepted Miller's pass at the 12-yard line and weaved across the field to the sideline. With a Badgers defender angling for a tackle, Cassady cut back sharply against the grain on Ohio State's 30-yard line and sprinted 88 yards for a touchdown. The dazzling play left the fans gasping. Janowicz was a great runner, but Cassady displayed such spectacular athleticism that his heroics on the field stunned fans.

The Badgers, too, seemed stunned by the play. It changed the tone of the game so abruptly that the Buckeyes went on to win 31–14, scoring three touchdowns in the next twelve minutes.

After two years of unrelenting pressure, Hayes was vindicated and rewarded by the press, who ranked the Buckeyes first in the Associated Press poll.

The team was halfway through the season and undefeated. Now, with the soft part of the schedule ahead, the players still didn't believe that they could run the table. It wasn't as if the Buckeyes weren't good enough. They had already shown their deep talent on offense, and more unexpectedly, on defense. Rather, it was whether their luck would hold. Good teams had talent. Great teams had just as much luck as talent. So far, the Buckeyes had avoided any serious injuries to key players, and they also had one other mark of a great team: a knack for creating a key turnover or a touchdown when they most needed it.

But Hayes refused to recognize their accomplishments. As always, he demanded the coaches show up for work early Sunday morning after the Wisconsin game. Woody wouldn't let the coaches or himself linger over the big win. His typical Saturday night after the game meant work. Hayes spent much of Saturday night after the Wisconsin game in his office watching the newly developed game film before heading downtown to WBNS-TV, where he would host *The Woody Hayes Show* after every game during the season. With the team's success, the show was growing in popularity, and each week Woody would trot out two of the game's best players and ask them easy questions that didn't need a lot of answering.

"You'd worked hard all week in practice, and that was the reason you played so well, right?" he'd pose his question to his players, who would just nod and stammer, "Right, coach."

Hayes, always worried about some force he couldn't control, immediately began to fret about the upcoming Northwestern contest. As the players slowly made their way to the training room on Sunday morning, they were greeted with a number-one ranking after their huge Homecoming win, but by then whatever satisfaction Hayes felt by beating the Badgers was long gone. Already, he was barking at his coaches, studying film, and worrying how the Buckeyes could beat overmatched Northwestern.

The Buckeyes practiced hard the week after the Wisconsin game. Typically, the bigger the Buckeyes victory, the harder Hayes would practice the players the following week. It was his way of preventing his players—and his coaches—from getting overconfident in victory. It was after the losses when he would generally back off practice a bit to rebuild his team's confidence. He'd be more patient with mistakes on the practice field, run them a little less, and pull the throttle back on his demands.

As it turned out, Hayes was right to worry about a letdown following the Wisconsin game. The Buckeyes traveled to Evanston and squeaked by for a 14–7 win. But the poor performance was eclipsed by the news that Indiana had upset Michigan, putting the Buckeyes all alone atop of the Big Ten standings. After easy wins over Pittsburgh and Purdue over the next two weeks, the stage was finally set for the game everyone had been anticipating since the Wisconsin win. Michigan would come to Columbus with the Big Ten's number-one-ranked defense to meet the Buckeyes and their powerful offense, with the Rose Bowl on the line.

Michigan week. The most important week of the year for Hayes. Not of the season, but of the entire twelve-month calendar. No matter how successful their season, it would all be for naught if the Buckeyes lost to Michigan. The incredible Wisconsin game, Cassady's season full of dazzling exploits, Parker's dominating line play—none of it would mean a thing if they didn't beat Michigan. The pressure to win was even greater on Hayes. A loss to Michigan at home could cost him his job. Larkins, who had spent the past three years defending Hayes, also knew of the consequences. But the players were immune to how vital the game was to their coach. Woody never impressed it on his players, never allowed the personal pressure to get in the way of coaching the team. The players cared only about beating the rival Wolverines.

"None of us were personally aware of what the game meant to Woody," Brubaker said. "We had lost to Michigan the year before and that was all that mattered."

The game was a constant source of concern that caused endless days and nights of watching reels of film, and of plotting various plays and formations to somehow find the edge. These planning sessions weren't saved just for the week leading up to the Michigan game. Hayes would spend slow days in the summer in his office gearing up for the Michigan game—a game that wouldn't be played for months. It would be a gorgeous summer day, and Hayes would call one of his assistants and demand that he leave his family or his golf game and come in to watch film. Or Hayes would spend nights alone in his office, order dinner, and then eat by the light of the film projector, while scouring the screen for the slightest clues to winning.

The week would be the most intense of the season, with a renewed sense of energy crackling through the locker room as Hayes put his team through its paces. Woody would order team managers to put pictures of the Michigan players in the Ohio State locker room, a trick he felt would help his players personalize the battle that lay ahead. He would be even more intense than usual, compared to a normal week during the season. Every mistake on the practice field was magnified and each play had to be perfect. He would barely see Anne and Steve all week. He'd either work late and leave early, or spend the nights on a cot in his office, obsessing over every detail, plotting, planning, fretting, meddling, and focusing solely on the upcoming game.

Out behind Ohio Stadium the Buckeyes practiced all week under gray and rainy skies, preparing for Michigan, drilling over and over the same running plays they'd run all season. There would be few offensive surprises on Saturday. Hayes would beat Michigan by dominating the line of scrimmage and by pounding Cassady and Bobo into the Michigan defense. Power versus power. By the end of the week the Buckeyes had reached the point where no more drilling could make them better. Hayes was in a particularly surly mood, ordering reporters and other bystanders to wear scarlet jerseys during practice so he could identify any outsiders who he feared could spy on practice.

On Monday Hayes snarled at writers, during a press luncheon, who dared question the coach's strategy.

"You have no more right to tell me how to coach my team in front of fifteen other writers than I would have to tell you how to write your stories in front of fifteen other coaches," he barked at the press.

On Tuesday an irritated Hayes drilled his team with an hour-long, rugged scrimmage that resulted in Cassady dislocating a finger, and risking injury to other key players. Wednesday and Thursday brought other tough practices, but the Buckeyes were razor sharp. As the team wrapped up practice, the sun popped through the rain.

"Boys," he said. "There's the omen we need."

When the team gathered for its traditional Friday night dinner at the university golf course, the players felt as if they were as prepared and confident as they had been for any game under Hayes. Despite the optimism, problems loomed. Dave Leggett was admitted to University Hospital on Friday after badly reacting to a penicillin shot. It had caused a bad rash over both hands. Bobo too was hobbling after reinjuring his foot during Thursday's practice.

November 20 dawned cold and damp. Hayes was even more edgy than usual, as he put his quarterbacks through their final pregame review of the game plan just before the team breakfast at the Seneca Hotel. Two hours before the game Hayes's intensity was raging. He stormed into Larkins's office and demanded his boss stop both the Michigan and Ohio State bands from performing before the game and during half-time, so as to protect the damp field. An incredulous Larkins dodged the confrontation by steering his request to both the Michigan and Ohio State presidents.

"I listened to Woody carry on for a while," Larkins said. "Then I told him I wouldn't think of ordering off the bands. But it seemed to me that he was working himself into a state of mind where he might not be able to direct the team to its best advantage during the game. So I told him that if he wished, we would put it up to the president, Dr. Howard Bevis, who was at a pregame luncheon in the stadium dining room. Woody said he was all for that. We got Doctor Bevis's ear. Both he and Michigan president Doctor Hatcher said it would be unthinkable."

The denial seemed more of an omen than Hayes's reference to the sunshine at Friday's practice. By the time the game began under gray skies in front of eighty-two thousand fans, five hundred members of the press, and a national television audience, the Buckeyes looked as bad as they had all season.

Michigan was loaded with talent, especially on defense. They came into Ohio Stadium with a 6-2 record, but of the six wins, three were shutouts. In two others, they gave up just seven points. The team was led by the all-American left tackle Art Walker and captain Ted Cachey, who played next to Walker at left guard. At left end was Ron Kramer, who was voted to the Big Ten all-conference team and who would follow Walker as an all-American. The star-studded line was one of the best in the country, and though Michigan came to Columbus with two losses, they were confident of shutting down Cassady and the potent Buckeyes. They had the stats to back up their confidence. In the eight games played, they had given up just 66 points while scoring 132 points.

Michigan took the kickoff and drove sixty-eight yards in eleven plays for a touchdown. The Buckeyes had spent hours practicing against the end-around play that Michigan had been successfully using to take advantage of Kramer's prodigious talents at end. But during the game's opening drive, the Wolverines faked the end around to Kramer and suckered the overaggressive Brubaker, who had left his end position to cover Kramer. Brubaker could only watch as the Wolverines engineered a double reverse handoff that led to a touchdown, courtesy of his mental error. It was a horrifying moment for the cocaptain, who as a senior was playing for the last time in Columbus, and he didn't dare go near Hayes on the sideline later. The Buckeyes spent the rest of the first half chasing Michigan all over the field, as the Wolverines completely dominated the game. But an Ohio State interception just before halftime led to a fifteen-yard touchdown pass from Leggett to end Fred Kriss that tied the score at 7–7.

Despite being outgained 190 yards to just 42, the Buckeyes remained confident in the locker room at halftime.

"At no time did we feel they were better than us," Brubaker said. "We still felt they could be had, because other than the screwup by me, we never thought we couldn't win. But personally I was concerned that, if we did lose, I'd have to live for the rest of my life with giving up the touchdown hanging over my head."

The teams returned to the field for a scoreless third quarter, and the homecoming crowd was in full throat, singing the Ohio State fight song, putting the stadium in near bedlam. But the fans grew quiet at the start of the fourth quarter, as Michigan drove to the Buckeyes' four-yard line for a first down. Four yards was all that stood between the Wolverines and the goal line, and they had easily moved the ball all over the field for the entire game. It took Michigan three plunges to get the ball to the six-inch line. Both teams dug in at the line of scrimmage for the fourth-down play. On the snap, Michigan fullback Dave Hill dove into the pile of players as Jim Parker penetrated the line, rose up and put the first hit on Hill. Frank Machinsky and Bobo rushed up to drive Hill back for no gain, giving the ball back to the Buckeyes. After the pandemonium of the dramatic goal-line stand ebbed, Hayes realized that his offense stood over the ball that lay just six inches from their own goal line—ninety-nine-and-a-half yards away from the Michigan end zone.

If there ever was a time for all the physical and mental abuse that Hayes had heaped upon his team during those brutal summer practices to pay off, this was it. When it's first and goal on your own six-inch line, in front of 82,438 screaming fans and a national television audience, with the Rose Bowl, an undefeated season, and a national championship on the line, it's easy for a lineman to jump offsides, or the quarterback to bobble the snap from center. Which is why Hayes had nearly killed the players in spring and summer practice. All the running, hitting, and endless drilling that drove them into the ground was to prepare them for situations as dire as the one they now found themselves in, as they broke the huddle in the shadow of their own goal post. The players, especially the quarterbacks, were used to pressure. Hayes put so much pressure on his quarterbacks during practice that the toughest games compared to what they had endured during the training week. Leggett felt the pressure of the entire state of Ohio on his back near that goal line, but he was steeled to the chaos that surrounded him. He had already dealt with the demands of Woody nearly every day throughout the season. Even though he was just inches from his own goal line, Leggett took refuge on the field. It was still better than having to stand next to Hayes on the sideline.

Hayes would take no chances on handling the ball at his own goal line. Instead, he simply pit the strength of his linemen against Michigan's defense and sent Leggett into the line on three straight quarterback sneaks. The simple and safe strategy paid off, with Leggett advancing to the twelve-yard line for a first down, giving the Buckeyes some precious breathing room. The Buckeyes' offensive line now dominated the Michigan defense, but Hayes was not about to open things up. Instead, he turned once again to Cassady—who on the next play took the ball off a fake to Bobo and busted through the right side of the line for a fifty-two-yard run to the Michigan thirty-seven. It was a stunning play, set up by a great fake by Bobo that pulled the Michigan defense away from Cassady for the split-second he needed to break into the secondary. From there, the Buckeyes marched down to the Michigan eight-yard line, where the drive stalled as the Michigan defense keyed on Cassady and Bobo. On third down, Hayes called for Leggett to fake to Cassady on a roll-out pass, which he calmly drilled to Brubaker, who was crossing over the middle along the goal line for a touchdown. In that instant, the only thought that crossed Brubaker's mind was pure relief. He no longer had to face Hayes for his earlier blunder that had allowed Michigan to score. It was a deep-seated fear that would stay with him for years. Even after playing in the NFL for the St. Louis Cardinals and Buffalo Bills before becoming a lawyer, Brubaker couldn't shake the feeling that he'd disappointed Hayes and his Buckeyes teammates. Decades later, Brubaker would wake up in the middle of the night in a cold sweat, shivering from his recurring nightmare that he had dropped the Leggett touchdown pass and had to face his old coach.

Michigan recovered from the stunning turn of events and regained their momentum, driving deep into Ohio State territory. But once again Cassady stepped in. Deep into the fourth quarter, he intercepted a Michigan pass, giving the Buckeyes the ball on the thirty-eight-yard line. Bobo ripped off a twenty-eight-yard run and Cassady finished off the eleven-play, sixty-two-yard drive by plunging the ball into the end zone from the one-yard line with just seconds remaining on the clock, giving the Buckeyes a 21–7 win. The crowd, joyous about the dramatic win, refused to leave after the game. Some of the Ohio State players had showered and dressed, only to return to the stadium to revel in the win as fans showered the field with roses.

There, in the pandemonium of the crowd, Hayes had finally quieted the thousands of critics who wanted him fired. Cassady and the rest of the Buckeyes finally elevated Hayes to the stature of his predecessors. Never again would Hayes hear the cry from the fans to bring back Paul Brown. In his post-game meeting with the press, Hayes broke from his typically grim routine of downplaying a win. Now even Hayes finally had to publicly praise his team, pointing out Parker's line play as the key to the win, offering rare praise to a lineman's typically anonymous performance.

"It is a real team that can stop Michigan on the one and then come back ninety-nine yards for a touchdown," he told the press. "Jim Parker gave us the defensive strength we needed in the clutch. This is the greatest team with the greatest fighting heart I've ever known."

Hayes was then ceremoniously thrown fully clothed into the showers by his jubilant players, who a few months earlier would have liked to have killed him for the way he was treating them.

The reality of an undefeated season was lost even on Hayes, who knew that luck as much as skill had played a part in the team's success.

"Every coach thinks at the beginning of the season that he can go all the way, even if he doesn't say it," he told the *Columbus Dispatch* after the game. "But you need luck. I can look back and say 'gee' if this had happened or that had happened, we'd have been beaten here or there. But you better expect to win them all or you'd better get out of coaching."

The chartered Ohio State plane touched down in Los Angeles on Saturday, December 18, two weeks before the Rose Bowl that was to be played against a 9-2 USC team. For most of the homegrown Buckeyes players California was an exotic place. But Hayes, fearing distractions, ordered the team bus to drive straight from the airport to the practice field at East Los Angeles Junior College Stadium, which suited his demand for secrecy. The twenty-thousand-seat facility featured a stone fence ringing the stands, compared to the usual Big Ten practice field at Brookside Park, which offered just a flimsy canvas fence for privacy.

Hayes's paranoia caught the West Coast writers by surprise, but they were just beginning to encounter his deep disdain for the press. Just hours after landing in California, Hayes and the West Coast writers were already beginning what would become a most contentious relationship. Hayes was instantly and automatically suspicious of the California writers, feeling that they were a threat to his militaristic strategy planning for the Rose Bowl. The feeling would only build during the two weeks in California, as he continually hid injuries and illnesses from the newspapers.

"The coast scribes are already showing signs of disapproval, and they break into their usual screams of protest when they learn Hayes intends to exclude them—and just about everyone else—for most of the Buckeyes workouts," Paul Hornung of the *Columbus Dispatch* wrote the day the team arrived in California.

On the bus from the airport to the practice field, Hayes took a seat next to Brubaker. As the bus rambled north from the airport, Brubaker was taken aback by the sight of the palm trees, and he remarked to his coach about the beauty of the place.

"Goddamn it, Dick," Hayes said, slapping Brubaker's thigh to make his point, "turn away from that window. We're not here for the sights. In two weeks we are going to beat USC."

The two didn't speak another word for the rest of the bus ride. Brubaker, who didn't dare look out the window, stared straight ahead, while Hayes glared at his feet, oblivious to the Southern California splendor. But other Buckeyes didn't share in the early focus. The team was headquartered at the plush Huntington Hotel, but Hayes planned to keep the Buckeyes free from distraction, with a heavy practice schedule and a host of official events leading up to the game. Still, many of the players found ways to enjoy California on their own, aided by Hayes's demand that the Rose Bowl Committee provide twenty Desotos for the team's disposal, with the first priority in using the cars to go to the players, then the coaches, and then the administration. The arrangement gave the players some unexpected freedom, of which they took full advantage. Kicker Tad Weed snuck off to go swimming, and while he was on the beach he turned away when he saw an official OSU car heading his way. His first thought was that it was Hayes coming to get him and send him back to Columbus. But those fears disappeared when Weed recognized some of his teammates in the car that sped south along the ocean, south toward Tijuana, where nobody had ever heard of Woody Hayes and where the players could drink in peace.

Try as he might, Hayes couldn't control the actions of all his players for the entire trip. The lure of Los Angeles proved too much for the players, who were tired of the season-long discipline. Curfews were regularly broken, and players showed up for practice with hangovers.

The attitude among many of the players was that the Rose Bowl was a reward for their season, so what was wrong with having a little fun? If they won the game, then the trip was all the better.

To be sure, a Rose Bowl win meant a shot at an undefeated season and the national championship for the Buckeyes; but for nearly all of the players, this would be their last football game. There was still so little money in professional football during the mid-1950s that nobody had their eyes out for the NFL. Whoever had the ability to go to the pros had already demonstrated their talents during the Big Ten season. So, in Los Angeles everyone knew everyone was out breaking curfew except Hayes, who either chose not to know or was successfully kept unaware. On one morning, Leggett returned from his night on the town just as practice began. In a panic, the trainers and assistant coaches put him in a huge footlocker and covered him with raincoats to keep him hidden from the old man, who would have fired the entire coaching staff if he knew of Leggett's condition.

Hayes never found out about his players' antics. But he moved his team to a monastery up in the hills on New Year's Eve, in order to isolate his team from the temptations and to try to get them to focus on nothing but the game. For the players, some of whom were married, spending New Year's Eve in seclusion wasn't exactly what they had imagined when they boarded the airplane two weeks earlier for Southern California.

NCAA rules allowed sixteen days of practice in the weeks leading up to the Rose Bowl, and Hayes used every allotted hour, including calling double sessions. Nearly six weeks would pass between the regular season finale against Michigan and the Rose Bowl, and Hayes made sure the Buckeyes didn't get rusty. The practices sometimes were brutal, with live scrimmages during most of the two weeks in Los Angeles. Hayes was bent on making sure his team was well conditioned—and too tired to cause much trouble at night—but his aggressive approach nearly cost him. The week before the game, Hayes, furious at his team's lackluster practice, abruptly ordered the players into a live scrimmage. Cassady proceeded to crack a rib throwing a block, threatening his chances of playing on New Year's Day, while guard Bill Jobko sprained his ankle. Center Bud Bond suffered a cut that needed three stitches, and dozens of other players were banged up. Then, two days before the game, a flu bug raged through the team, causing Hayes to close practices to hide the illness from the press.

Hayes awoke on New Year's morning, his stomach churning with anxiety when he called his quarterbacks down to his room for their pregame meeting where he would grill them over the game plan. After excusing Leggett, Borton, and third-stringer Bill Booth, from the meeting, Hayes stepped outside into a misty rain.

The rain had steadily intensified all morning. Hayes, pacing back and forth, was growing increasingly agitated that the horrible weather would ruin his team's chances. When the Buckeyes arrived at the Rose Bowl, the floor of the massive stadium was turning into a quagmire. Like the Michigan game six weeks earlier, Hayes was obsessed with the notion that outside forces, especially the band, would damage the field, and he demanded that the USC and Ohio State bands be prohibited from playing, even though the Ohio State band traveled by train from Columbus at the request of the Rose Bowl committee. It was an irrational thought. The pounding the field would take by the players from both teams wearing cleats would do far greater damage to the turf than any of the flat-soled shoes worn by the band members. But in his mind, the concerns of the Buckeyes were far bigger than anyone or anything else. No matter where he played, he felt the field belonged to him, so he thundered his concerns to perplexed Rose Bowl officials.

By game time the field was a complete mess, and the downpour made for one of the smallest crowds in Rose Bowl history, with little more than eighty-nine thousand people braving the elements to watch the heavily favored Buckeyes take on the Trojans. USC wasn't even the Pacific Coast Conference's best team. UCLA captured the conference championship, but because the Bruins played in the 1954 Rose Bowl, Pacific Coast Conference rules, just like the Big Ten's, prevented the same team from playing in the Rose Bowl in consecutive seasons.

The rain dampened any distant USC chances for an upset. The Buckeyes splashed to a 20–7 win, with Leggett throwing for one touchdown and running for another. In the poor weather, the Buckeyes played their best game by racking up 370 total yards with twenty-two first downs and no turnovers. The defense, anchored by Parker, held the Trojans to only six first downs and forced seven fumbles. Leggett, the sure-handed quarterback, took eighty snaps during the heavy rain and never fumbled, a performance that earned him the game's Most Valuable Player award.

In the locker room after the game, Hayes climbed up on a locker and addressed his soaked team. "See, boys," he said, "that's what clean living will do for you."

Bobo, Leggett, and the other Buckeyes who spent the past two weeks chasing women and drinking up as much nightlife as possible, could only look at each other and laugh.

As expected, the Associated Press voted the Buckeyes national champions, while Cassady and end Dean Dugger were named to the all-America team. But Hayes, who arguably deserved to be named coach of the year by his peers, came in a distant second in the voting by the American College Football Coaches Association behind UCLA coach Red Sanders. And United Press International, the other major football poll, determined by a group of thirty-five college coaches, elected to give its national championship to UCLA, which won the Pacific Coast Conference championship but was ineligible to play in the Rose Bowl.

There was no doubt that winning the national championship by beating USC was one of Hayes's finest moments as a coach, but he still couldn't prevent himself from creating controversy when, after the game, a West Coast writer asked him to compare Southern Cal to the rest of the Big Ten football teams.

"In addition to us," Woody began, unable to stop himself, "I'd say that Michigan, Wisconsin, Iowa, Purdue, and possibly Minnesota—although we didn't play them—were better than Southern Cal."

The West Coast papers ripped Hayes after his postgame comments, but back East Hayes was the toast of Columbus—bringing Ohio State its second national championship. He had triumphed over his critics and proved that he was the undisputed leader of one of the most powerful football programs in the country. The Rose Bowl win was even sweeter for Woody because he was able to share it with his older brother Ike, who had traveled by train with his wife Lucy and daughters Mary and Martha from their home in Waterloo, Iowa.

Ike reveled in Woody's successes and stayed close to his younger brother, offering advice, one high school football captain to another. There were games in Hayes's coaching career when Ike, visiting from Iowa, would commandeer the Buckeyes chalkboard at halftime, diagramming plays that he felt would help Woody win. And both were similar in temperament. Like Woody, Ike was more than willing to settle things with his fists. In one instance Ike, enraged at the tailgating driver behind him, motioned for the driver to pull over, jumped out of his car and punched the unfortunate tailgater in the face. When the driver tried to press charges against Ike, the Waterloo police only snickered. There was no way they'd go after Ike, not after he routinely treated their dogs, horses, and other animals free of charge.

"Like Woody, my dad could be volatile," said Mary Hoyt, Ike's daughter. "And they both felt the same way about money. My father never charged cops, firemen, bus drivers, or any working men. He just never had any use for money. And, like Woody, he believed in doing things first class. We didn't have much money, but when we traveled to Pasadena, we went in the dome car on the train, even though we couldn't afford it. But when we got to California, Woody insisted that we be treated as guests of Ohio State, so we did everything with the team."

But the 1955 Rose Bowl would be the last time Woody would see Ike alive. Twenty-five days after the Rose Bowl, Ike suffered a massive heart attack in his sleep and died a few hours later, tempering any joy Woody had taken from the past season.

Hayes rushed to Iowa to share the grief with Ike's wife Lucy and her two daughters.

Woody, heartbroken over the death of his brother, promised Lucy that he'd see to her children's college education, and both daughters eventually ended up attending Ohio State. Woody also brought back his brother's Little all-America certificate and hung it on his office wall between pictures of presidents and generals.

9

POWER GRAB

The Rose Bowl win and the national championship gave Hayes all the credibility he needed to establish himself as one of the hottest coaches in the country. He turned forty-two the month after the Rose Bowl, making him one of the youngest coaches to capture a national championship. But the success of the 1954 season gave him something more coveted than respect. It gave him power. Just a year removed from when he was nearly fired for his mediocre record and losing to Michigan, Hayes now had gained control of the football program. Larkins acted as the buffer, diffusing Hayes's explosive behavior and repairing collateral damage. With a national championship under his belt, Hayes ran the program with few checks and balances, and he was typically outspoken about his change in stature. On the banquet circuit following the Rose Bowl, Hayes took his shots at all the "downtown quarterbacks" who demanded that Larkins fire his coach a year earlier.

"How many of you were here last year?" he'd say to the crowd during alumni gatherings, taunting the now adoring audience.

Hayes had built a protective wall around him during his tumultuous first few years in Columbus. Larkins was one of his biggest supporters, and Ohio State president Howard Bevis banked on the dominating football program. Big Ten titles and Rose Bowls brought prestige that no amount of money could buy. Even more valuable than the prestige of Ohio State football was its power to attract donors for other needs. Ohio State was growing fast in the mid-1950s, its twenty-two-thousand student population would swell during the roaring economy of the postwar years. New facilities, like St. John Arena, were popping up all over the university's huge land grant campus. When asked about the growing emphasis of football under Woody, Bevis liked to joke that "we should have a university of which the football team can be proud."

But Bevis would soon regret his tongue-in-cheek reference to the school's obsession with football.

In the fall of 1955, with the Buckeyes on their way to another Big Ten title, Woody allowed a *Sports Illustrated* writer named Robert Shaplen to come to Columbus to write about the vaunted Buckeyes. Hayes and the Buckeyes were always big news in Ohio, but their success was mostly regional; so when a New York–based writer from a national magazine called, Hayes saw a chance to spread his reputation. Hayes, who manipulated the local Columbus press, expected what he was accustomed to—a fawning feature about the great Ohio State football team led by their impressive young coach. Shaplen instead wrote a scathing cover story about Ohio State football, detailing Woody's obsession for winning. It was an unflattering portrait of Ohio State, that focused on the sins of sports and deified athletes and coaches, especially those who just won a national championship. Shaplen clearly was ahead of his time. He railed against the Ohio State football factory, labeling Woody "the Frankenstein of the system," while detailing Woody's habit of providing financial assistance to some of his players "in need." He also publicly exposed the network of Frontliners who delivered the best prospects to Woody's office door.

Hayes, just as he would for any of his transgressions, saw nothing wrong with giving his players money if they needed it. Just as he helped out his players at Denison, Hayes had no qualms about giving players from difficult economic backgrounds some financial help. According to *Sports Illustrated,* Woody would use some of the four thousand dollars he earned from his weekly television show to pay players. Hayes passed off his loan program as a humanitarian gesture, insisting that he never paid for luxuries for the players and would only help out those in need. The story caught the attention of the NCAA and sparked an immediate investigation by Big Ten commissioner Kenneth "Tug" Wilson. Woody, feeling he'd done nothing wrong, had even mentioned on his weekly television show in 1955 that he loaned small amounts of money to some of his players to help get them through school.

Hayes cooperated with the probe from the start, giving Wilson the names of the players to whom he had given money. Woody also made no apologies. He felt that the players were truly in need, and that whatever money he gave the players was his personal business. Wilson's probe backed Hayes to a point, finding that Woody had paid only an estimated four hundred dollars annually to various players, dating back to 1951, a paltry sum compared to the free cars and suitcases of cash that other schools routinely offered to their prized recruits and their parents. But Wilson's investigation also found that some thirty Ohio State players had been given jobs that required no work or didn't exist at all. Parker, for example, was hired to clean the coaches' offices, but he never lifted a finger. Instead, freshmen players would do the actual work, with Parker on the ghost payroll.

Through it all Hayes pleaded ignorance of the NCAA's rules prohibiting paying players, and again Larkins and the rest of the administration backed Woody, as the Buckeyes kept winning, led by senior Cassady.

The season began with a first-ever meeting with the Nebraska Cornhuskers, with the Bucks winning in come-from-behind fashion, thanks to three touchdowns by Cassady and 170 yards rushing. But then the Buckeyes traveled to Stanford and were upset 6–0, breaking an eleven-game winning streak. The Buckeyes rebounded from their offensive slumber and beat Illinois 27–12 the next weekend at home, but then lost to Duke the following week 20–14, in a sloppy game that saw Ohio State commit six turnovers while the offense sputtered again. Four straight wins, over Wisconsin, Northwestern, Indiana, and Iowa, put the Bucks at 6-2, and the season-ending battle with Michigan awaited in Ann Arbor. The game shaped up to be a battle between the number-nine-ranked Buckeyes and the number-six-ranked Wolverines. At stake for Michigan was a trip to the Rose Bowl; but the Buckeyes could only play the spoiler, since conference rules prohibited consecutive trips to Pasadena. But there was other motivation. Ohio State hadn't won in Ann Arbor since 1937, an embarrassing statistic in the epic rivalry.

The game plan was simple: Run the ball. The Buckeyes ran the ball seventy-one times in the bruising battle, compared to Michigan's thirty-one rushing attempts. Still, the game was tight, with Ohio State leading 3–0 in the third quarter, when Cassady scored on a two-yard plunge, to take a 9–0 lead. A safety and a late Ohio State touchdown sparked a brawl in the game's final minutes, with players from both sides taking cheap shots at one another, while Buckeye fans tore down the north goalpost. The mayhem continued, with fans pelting players and officials with snowballs, as the game ended with a 17–0 shutout.

Hayes was jubilant in victory.

"This is the greatest game Ohio State has ever played for me," he said later.

The statistics gave Hayes reason for his bold statement. The offense completely dominated, gaining 337 yards to Michigan's 109 yards, while racking up twenty first downs to just five for the Wolverines—who managed to cross into Buckeyes territory just one time. The Buckeyes passed only three times, but the lack of a balanced offense meant little to Hayes, who relished his team's physical dominance, as it was displayed in the shutout.

Woody also had displayed some savvy coaching. During the week, he moved Cassady over to right halfback from his typical left halfback position, and the switch surprised and confused the Michigan defenders, who had spent all week preparing to face the all-American back in formations that Hayes never used.

The victory also silenced the critics who complained about the Buckeyes' inability to beat Michigan in Ann Arbor and eased the pressure Hayes felt from the extended losing streak.

The team finished the 1955 season with a 7-2 record. Conference rules sent Michigan State to Pasadena, but the Buckeyes still captured some major honors. Parker and Cassady were named as all-Americans. Cassady also won the Heisman Trophy, captured the prestigious Maxwell Award, and was named Associated Press Male Athlete of the Year, beating out heavyweight champion Rocky Marciano and Cleveland Browns quarterback Otto Graham for the award.

The Buckeyes' two consecutive Big Ten championships firmly cemented Hayes's job. Not even a scandal would hurt Hayes, who was now nearly untouchable. A month after spring practice in 1956, however, Wilson informed Larkins and Bevis that he was putting the Buckeyes on probation for one year, stemming from the investigation that he began in late 1955.

The terms of the probation called for all players involved in the bogus job program to repay in service the money they had been given.

In addition, the one-year probation banned all Ohio State teams from playing in the NCAA's sanctioned postseason tournaments, meaning that the Buckeyes would be prohibited from playing in the Rose Bowl should they win the 1956 Big Ten championship.

Hayes was outraged at the penalty, but he refused to appeal. He may have broken the rules (and in his mind he broke them unknowingly), but his compliance with the probation showed his respect for Wilson's authority. Hayes, as much a military man as a football coach, firmly believed in following orders. He demanded that his players did what he said, and if they didn't they'd either be benched or kicked off the team. But he also held himself to that same standard. He despised Wilson's ruling, truly believing that he was helping his players by lending them money. But he still wouldn't go against Wilson because, as Big Ten commissioner, Wilson outranked Woody. At the same time, taking the punishment didn't mean that Hayes had to apologize to anyone. That was a job he left to Larkins, or in this case, to Bevis.

The two-bit payoffs to players and the phony jobs program would quickly be forgotten, especially since Hayes continued to win; but there was another issue still smoldering from the *Sports Illustrated* story, and winning wouldn't make it go away. In fact, the more Hayes won, the more he found himself battling with Jack Fullen, who headed up Ohio State's powerful alumni association. Fullen, one of few people connected with the university who dared criticize the football program, was beginning to wage an ugly public battle over the dominant stature of Ohio State football.

In an era of conformity, during the late 1950s, Fullen was unafraid to take on the university, the city of Columbus, and the state of Ohio, over his view. Universal support of the Buckeyes football team was the expected attitude, but Fullen firmly believed that the university was putting far too much emphasis on athletics, especially football, and it was threatening the quality of education at Ohio State—which in the late 1950s had an enrollment of more than twenty-one thousand students, making it one of the largest schools in the country.

These were inflammatory charges coming from someone who had deep ties to the program. Back in the late 1940s Fullen helped organize the creation of the Frontliners, to build a better football team and stay competitive with the other Big Ten schools. Fullen wasn't intimidated by Hayes and wasn't about to back down from his accusations. He also knew the power of the press, and he made his views known by tipping off *Sports Illustrated* how Hayes and Larkins put football ahead of anything else at the university. Though *Sports Illustrated* was still a fairly new publication, it had a growing national circulation and, just as important, was independent of any influence of Ohio State alumni.

"Larkins has to meet an $800,000-a-year budget in the athletic department," Fullen told *Sports Illustrated*. "If he doesn't fill that stadium every Saturday, he won't be able to make ends meet. Like Woody, Dick is a creature of the system. Little by little, his ideals are disintegrating as he has to use football receipts to pay off the bond issue on the new field house. We'll never be off the hook until we stop worrying about attendance."

Hayes was blindsided by Fullen. The man had backed Hayes when the young coach was under siege during his first few years in Columbus, regularly writing glowing articles in the monthly alumni magazine to help fend off the drive to fire Hayes. Fullen, the longtime head of the alumni association, held a unique position in Columbus. Though technically not a member of the university, he was president of the alumni group since 1928 and had helped the organization grow more powerful. The *Columbus Dispatch* pointed out that the group called itself the Ohio State Association, intentionally leaving out the word "alumni," to be able to include anyone who attended Ohio State but did not graduate. Thus, anyone who had ever attended Ohio State for any length of time could claim a connection to the university, as long as they paid their dues. This allowed for a large membership base. The sheer size of the group, that in 1955 counted thirty-five thousand dues-paying members, allowed Fullen to influence university affairs.

Fullen was also editor of the widely distributed alumni magazine and could easily shape opinion about the school; and he used the power of the press to criticize Woody after the 1955 Rose Bowl game, when Hayes tried to keep the Ohio State and USC bands off the muddy field at halftime.

"I have a right to clobber Woody when he's off base," Fullen wrote in the February 1955 alumni magazine, just weeks after the Rose Bowl win. "A couple of events since returning have convinced me our football team is getting out of hand. One was to find a number of persons agreeing with Woody Hayes that the bands should not have been allowed to perform. The football tail now seems to be wagging the university dog visibly. Since when is the training of musicians less educational than the training of football players?"

Hayes railed against the damning editorial, but he was also taken aback by Fullen's comments. After all, Fullen attended the Rose Bowl in 1955 on the association's dime, and he took the train out to Southern California for the game along with the band. But the comments in the alumni magazine paled in comparison to Fullen's devastating blow, fired at Hayes and Larkins later in the year when he tipped off *Sports Illustrated* about Hayes's habit of paying players and the athletic department's policy of giving phony jobs to football players. Fullen, sensing a backlash against his association with the damaging *Sports Illustrated* article, claimed that Shaplen misrepresented the facts by printing "gossip," but by then it was too late. The investigation was underway—and it would end with the one-year probation.

The feud between Hayes and Fullen would not end when the Buckeyes completed their probationary year. Fullen remained a constant critic of Hayes, and kept close watch on the football program that was unquestionably a powerhouse. From 1954 through 1957, the Buckeyes won three conference championships and two Rose Bowls. The 1957 team went 9–1 and beat Oregon 10–7 in the Rose Bowl, finished second in the AP poll. UPI voted the Buckeyes national champions and Hayes was voted Coach of the Year.

But in a 1957 issue of The *Ohio State University Monthly,* the alumni magazine edited by Fullen printed an entire page of pictures of Hayes from a recent game where he had charged onto the field, waving his fists in anger toward the officials and opposing players. The pictures showed Hayes in full rage and carried the caption: "The gentle art of teaching." It was a most unflattering portrait of Hayes, and for the embarrassed the university's board of trustees that was charged with setting the academic roadmap for the growing university.

But the Buckeyes kept winning, which deflected the criticism.

From October 5, 1957 through November 1 1958, the Buckeyes

went on an incredible run of fourteen consecutive games without a loss.

The streak began with a 35–7 win over Washington on the road, after being upset in the season opener against Texas Christian University 18–14. The TCU loss gave little clue that the Buckeyes were about to go on their impressive run, a streak that began in Seattle.

The run-oriented offense was led by junior Frank Kremblas at quarterback, but it was backfield by committee, with Hayes shuffling playing time between a half-dozen players, including Don Clark and Galen Cisco.

But the line, led by guards Aurealius Thomas and Bill Jobko, was one of the best in the Big Ten, and Hayes knew he would have to rely on its strength to carry the team.

When conference play began against Illinois, Hayes ran Clark thirty-three times in the Buckeyes' 21–7 win, establishing the run game to become the hallmark of the streak.

After an easy 56–0 win over Indiana, the Buckeyes beat a tough Wisconsin team in Madison 16–13, followed by a dominant 47–6 Homecoming Day win against Northwestern, which put the surprising Buckeyes in first place in the Big Ten.

The streak nearly ended against the Purdue Boilermakers, who trailed 20–0 at halftime, but had the ball five times inside the Buckeyes 20-yard line but failed to score, resulting in the 20–7 loss. The next week pit Ohio State, now ranked sixth by the Associated Press, against fifth-ranked Iowa. The Buckeyes were six-point underdogs and were losing 13–10 in the fourth quarter, when they mounted an eight-play, 68-yard drive that was vintage Hayes. He ran fullback Bob White six times for sixty-six yards, with the Buckeyes' line taking control of the game.

"We knew what was happening, but we were powerless to stop it," said Iowa coach Forest Evashevski.

To Woody it was the ultimate compliment.

The win gave the Buckeyes added confidence, and they headed to Ann Arbor to beat Michigan 31–14 by scoring three second-half touchdowns, also earning the trip to the Rose Bowl to play the Oregon Ducks.

The Buckeyes continued their win streak with a 10–7 win over Oregon, and they were voted national champions in the UPI poll and finished second behind Auburn in the AP poll.

The win completed one of the most satisfying of seasons for Hayes and the Buckeyes, who at the start of the year were picked by sports writers to finish fifth in the Big Ten. But Hayes found the right mix of talent, and unlike previous Rose Bowl teams, this version of the Buckeyes had few offensive stars other than the two standout guards in Jobko and Thomas.

The winning streak continued in 1958, with a narrow season-opening 23–20 win over Southern Methodist University, followed by wins against Washington, Illinois, and Indiana. The Buckeyes were now 4-0, but were struggling to live up to their number-two ranking. Except for a 49–8 blowout of Indiana, they were dominating games and the offense was struggling when Wisconsin came to Columbus on October 15. Again, the Buckeyes offense sputtered and they managed a 7–7 tie, keeping their undefeated streak intact. The tie was a sign of things to come, because the next week, in Evanston, the Buckeyes winning streak was snapped by Ara Parseghian's Northwestern Wildcats in a 21–0 in loss. It was a sweet win for Parseghian, a Hayes protege at Miami University.

With the streak over, the Buckeyes returned to Columbus the following week and played Purdue to a 7–7 tie, followed by a 38–28 win over Iowa. The season was salvaged by a 20–14 win over Michigan, giving Hayes five wins over Michigan in his eight seasons at Ohio State and finally endearing him to the Buckeye fans.

The formula for Hayes's success was now firmly rooted in the run. In 1956, the Buckeyes garnered 2,468 rushing yards compared to just 278 passing yards. Quarterback Frank Ellwood threw a grand total of twenty passes and completed just seven. The 1957 and 1959 seasons were also run oriented. It was boring, methodical football that, despite its dullness and predictability, was also powerfully effective. Hayes settled on his split T offense and ran the ball down the throats of the Buckeyes' opponents.

★ ★ ★

Hayes's winning ways were now being seen by more people than ever, as television came of age. Sports, especially big-time college football, provided compelling programming on Saturday afternoons. By the mid-1950s, nearly every Ohio State football game was broadcast on local television, with many also shown on national television.

The broadcasts helped fill the university's coffers, but for Hayes the increase in media attention was becoming an intrusion. He detested anyone snooping around the football team, asking questions, and trying to interview players. The additional television coverage brought hordes of unwanted attention from writers he didn't know and certainly didn't trust. Any added television exposure threatened to upset the control that Woody had established with the local media in Columbus. For the most part, Woody dealt with two local writers who covered the Buckeyes. There was Kessler, who wrote for the *Columbus Citizen,* and then the *Citizen-Journal* when the two papers merged. Then there was Paul Hornung of The *Columbus Dispatch,* who eventually became the paper's sports editor. Hayes tolerated Kessler, a bright and gifted writer who took a more objective approach to covering the team, but he befriended and then influenced Hornung, whose coverage was far more positive. Hornung wrote as if he were part of the team, exaggerating the players' abilities and ignoring the mistakes that early on plagued Hayes's teams. He never directly criticized Hayes and wouldn't write a bad word about the players unless Hayes told him to. Hornung's brand of journalism was stuck in a bygone era, where writers like Grantland Rice would spin myths out of the press box, creating heroes out of the players and coaches they covered. Hornung believed that his *Dispatch* readers wanted to root for the Buckeyes, not against them. Hayes, recognizing Hornung's devotion, deftly used him to his own benefit. He granted Hornung more access than Kessler, or anyone else wanting to get close to the team, and as a result Hornung felt he was part of the great Ohio State football tradition. He grew to worship Hayes, and would hold back on writing what really happened at practice.

"Don't put that in the paper," Hayes would snap at Hornung following a practice that revealed a change in strategy, an injury, or a player problem.

And Hornung never would. Instead he'd write about the team's great chances that week, and he'd defend Hayes at every turn with effusive praise.

As much as Hayes wanted to control the newspapers, he allowed the beat writers access to the team. Kessler and Hornung would attend each practice and then wait to talk to Hayes after he sent his players to the showers. He also allowed his players to talk to the writers that he knew. But Hayes would also grow paranoid about spies infiltrating practice, so he would insist that all nonparticipants at practice, including the writers and the longtime team doctor, wear Ohio State football shirts. Woody knew most of these people from the time he began coaching in 1951, but he still insisted that the shirts be worn.

"Then, when I glance over toward the sidelines, I won't have to fret about who so-and-so is," Hayes said.

Access was granted only because Hayes knew that both Kessler and Hornung couldn't risk printing anything that could cause him to cut them off from access to the team. The result was that the local readers weren't learning much about their beloved Buckeyes. Kessler wrote his share of fluffy features, but there was more perspective in his coverage of the team and of Hayes. He clearly saw the city's infatuation with the football team and was able to convey the obsession, yet avoid insulting his readers.

"Woody was great with us, but he was also impossible," Kessler said. "We'd go to all the practices and, though he did things with an iron hand, he didn't put a lot of clamps on his players, so we could get to them. He had his moods, and if he was pissed off after practice, you'd have to wait until tomorrow. And he was very difficult to deal with after games. I was friendly with Woody, but to a point. Paul and I would sit and wait for Woody around six P.M. after practice, but if he didn't show after fifteen minutes, I'd leave. But Paul would sit there all night until Woody came out. He was Woody's mouthpiece."

Each September the Big Ten conducted an annual media tour that brought writers to each school to drum up publicity for the upcoming season. Dubbed the "Skywriters," the newspapermen would be ferried from school to school, visiting with the coaches and players during the day and drinking at night. It was a friendly exchange between the writers and the coaches, and with the season still a few weeks away, the players and coaches were full of optimism. Hayes hated the intrusion but tolerated the writers. But when the writers showed up in September 1958, Hayes was already in a foul mood. His team was in the midst of a ragged practice and Hayes was furious. With the writers looking on from the sidelines, players were missing blocks, forgetting assignments, and were mostly lethargic during the heat of the day. Hayes snapped. The players were used to Hayes's outbursts, but not the writers.

"Everyone get out of here," Hayes screamed at the writers. "We are going to play some football."

Incredulous, the writers were forced to leave the field. Stunned and furious over Hayes's treatment, the writers left town after finishing their stories describing Hayes's behavior, which created more embarrassment for Larkins. Once again, Larkins was forced to issue an apology.

"While the damage is done," Larkins wrote, "the least I can do is apologize to you and our other guests for this kind of treatment."

There was no mention in the apology of Hayes regretting the incident, but Larkins was furious. University officials privately called Hayes on the carpet and he was rebuked for his actions. But the next year Woody was able to make light of his behavior, greeting the same writers, with umbrellas shading the field where he served up cookies and lemonade.

The incidents between 1955 and 1958 were an indication of the nearly absolute power Hayes had garnered at Ohio State. With every winning season, Hayes was growing more invincible, and other than the occasional outburst of concern from Fullen, the university allowed Hayes to continue his bullish ways. It was an odd romance between the university and its coach. Hayes would embarrass the administration, but he also would be a tremendous asset to the school.

He was constantly getting on his players to graduate and the pressure was appreciated, if not applauded by many faculty members. Just as important to Larkins was that Hayes was an upright citizen when it came to recruiting. He never cheated to get a player. He had, in the past, violated rules when the players enrolled at Ohio State, but afterward he was resolute about following the recruiting rules. Stung and embarrassed with a Big Ten investigation that led to the one-year probation in 1956, Hayes paid even more attention, to make certain that he ran a clean football program.

Hayes was riding the crest of his success during the mid-1950s, sustaining his winning record by forging strong bonds with his players. He lorded over his team, nearly choking them with his obsession for perfection, but at the same time Hayes put his players first. He insisted that the athletic department spare no expense on the football team. The players had the best equipment, stayed in the best hotels, ate in the finest restaurants, and received the best medical care. He would complain and grumble about his players, but he was steadfast in his loyalty, and it bred—almost begrudgingly—loyalty in return. The players often hated Woody on the field, but they learned to respect him for driving them to win. In the process, however, Hayes would continue to lose control of his emotions, despite the repeated promises he made to Larkins.

Off the field, Hayes was making good on a promise made in 1955 after his brother, Ike, died unexpectedly. Ike's daughter Mary came to Columbus in the fall of 1958 to attend Ohio State. Hayes had promised to see that his nieces Mary and Martha would get college educations, and he took his responsibility seriously.

"Woody met me at eleven A.M. at the train station after I had traveled overnight from Waterloo, and the first thing he did was take me for ice cream at the Jai Alai restaurant," Mary recalled. "He was just so generous."

Mary would stay with Anne and Woody for a few weeks until the Ohio State dorms opened, and Woody treated Mary like the daughter he never had. He introduced her around town and to his team, and he even took her dress shopping to make sure she had what he felt were proper clothes.

"He took me downtown to the Lazarus department store and sat there while I tried on dresses, and he helped me pick out an outfit," Mary said.

During her years at Ohio State, Woody would stop by Mary's sorority house to check on his niece, and he would visit with her sorority sisters, and Anne would on occasion invite Mary over for dinner. There was just one golden rule that came from being related to Woody Hayes.

"I couldn't date any football players," Mary said. "So I dated a member of the basketball team."

When Mary got married, Uncle Woody walked her down the aisle. Despite Woody's moodiness and the distance he kept between himself and Steve and Anne, his generosity of spirit was also extended to other family. In the mid-1960s, Anne's parents moved into Hayes's house on Cardiff Road. Hospital beds were set up there to care for Woody's ailing in-laws, an act of charity that continued until their deaths.

The winning would come to a sudden halt in 1959, with the Buckeyes' pathetic 3-5-1 record, giving Hayes his first losing season since he was hired in 1951. The season was marred by a series of incidents that at most any other schools would have cost Hayes his job.

On October 2, the Buckeyes traveled to California to play Southern Cal on a Friday night at the Los Angeles Coliseum, and they were beaten badly, by a score of 17–0. Hayes had disparaged the Trojans after the 1955 Rose Bowl and now it was payback time for the Southern Cal players, who utterly and completely dominated the game. The Buckeyes' offense stalled under Hayes's predictable strategy of repeatedly running the off-tackle fullback play and gained just eighty-four yards rushing, averaging just 1.9 yards per carry. Rarely was a Hayes-coached team physically overmatched, but the Buckeyes were pounded by the Trojans, with several Ohio State players suffering injuries during the game. Hayes began addressing his players in the locker room after the game, when he spotted two members of the press, Dick Shafer, the brother of a reporter for the *Pasadena News-Star,* and Al Bine, who worked for the *Los Angeles Examiner.* Both were milling around in the locker room, waiting to interview some of the players just after the game, when Hayes went off.

"Get out! Get out," Hayes screamed. But the two writers apparently didn't move fast enough for Hayes, who lunged after them and took a swing at Bine. Bine ducked and Hayes apparently hit Shafer in the back, knocking him against the wall. Hayes then picked up Shafer by the shoulders and shoved him against a wall near the exit door.

A physical confrontation with two writers was a far different matter than Hayes bullying the bands, as he had done on his previous trips to Southern California. For Hayes, it was simply an extension of what he routinely did to players on the practice field. After locking out the writers for nearly a half hour after the game, Hayes came out denying that he struck either of the writers. He did, however, admit to pushing Shafer out the door.

The matter was taken up by Hayes's peers, and an ethics committee of the American Football Coaches Association decided to publicly admonish Hayes for his assault on the writers. If nothing else, it would at least send Hayes an embarrassing message from his peers. The Ohio State administration quietly admonished Hayes, but failed to take any action against him for the physical confrontation. Neither did the Big Ten conference.

September 1961. After a mediocre 7-2 1960 season that gave the Buckeyes a third-place Big Ten finish, Hayes opened fall practice with an address to his team that he'd given every year for a decade. The thrust of the speech was always the same—duty, honor, country, and pound the hell out of the opposition.

In front of the players stood the forty-eight-year-old coach in the prime of his career. There was no arguing his success. Two Rose Bowl wins, two Heisman Trophy winners, a slew of Big Ten titles, and one national championship—and, just as important, seven wins against Michigan.

Hayes's program was in full gear, with the Frontliners, the talented assistant coaches, and Hayes himself, as sharp as the players who took the field wearing the scarlet and gray. The administration had reason to be happy. For the past five years no fewer than eighty thousand fans packed Ohio Stadium for each home game, and the same could be expected in 1961. The Buckeyes would see the return of twenty-six lettermen from the previous season, and even Hayes, the constant worrier, saw the potential in the upcoming season. He had an all-American in Bob Ferguson at fullback, the most important position on the field in Hayes's running-dominated offense. At halfback were two remarkably gifted players in Matt Snell and Paul Warfield. The only question was who would replace Tom Matte at quarterback. He was the talented signal caller who was the team's most valuable player in 1960 and the top pick in the 1961 NFL draft by the Baltimore Colts. It was hard to say who was happier that Matte was now in the pros. The stubborn quarterback had battled Hayes at every turn, as the coach struggled to control his star player's independent streak.

"I was chasing women and having a great time, and after my freshmen year, I had a one-point-five grade point average, and he called me into in his office and asked if I was having fun," Matte said. "I said yes and he ripped into me. He said, 'Let me tell you something. If you don't get your grades up, you're fucking gone.' It was a rude awakening."

Of course, Hayes won the war, with his quarterback finally conforming to his coach's demands.

"I had to have lunch and dinner with him almost every day, and he basically tucked me in at night," Matte said. "I was allowed to go for dinner for a few hours after games, but then I had to go back and watch film. He really worked me, and it sounds bitter, but what he did for me made me what I am today."

Hayes wasn't used to having to spend so much time and energy beating down his starting quarterback. Usually, the team's starter was a strict disciple of Hayes, one who had the mental makeup to handle the pressure, no matter how rough the treatment. But Matte was different. He was a talented but reluctant quarterback. He never wanted to play the position at Ohio State, but Hayes saw his potential and converted the defensive back into a run–first quarterback. Passing was secondary and not encouraged.

"During the first game against Duke in my junior year, and it is ninety-eight degrees, and I'm playing both ways; and at halftime and he takes me out behind the stadium and makes me take some snaps," he said. "I told him 'I thought you said I didn't have to play quarterback.' He said, 'I just might have to send you in.' We were losing thirteen to seven, and he calls time out and sends me in. I didn't know the offense, and he just told me to roll out right and if somebody's open, then throw it. If not, run. I rolled right but it was the wrong way, and it was a naked reverse. I ran forty-three yards along the sideline with Woody running alongside screaming, 'Where did you get that play?' "

The quarterback experiment worked, but Matte's cavalier practice habits frustrated Hayes no end, while occasionally amusing Bo Schembechler, Woody's assistant and Matte's protector.

"I fumbled on purpose in practice and it drove him nuts," Matte said. "I started pulling my hands out from center and we had six fumbles. He ran over and screamed 'what the fuck are you doing?' and Bo was giggling and I was laughing. Woody said 'this ain't funny' and then he gave me a forearm shiver and knocked me ass over teacup that, if it were today, I could've owned the school. He was so pissed off that he hit himself. Bo told me to get out of there before Woody woke up so I took off and he came looking for me."

Hayes made sure to take his pound of flesh out of his signal caller. Like every other quarterback who played for Hayes, Matte developed ulcers from standing up to the pressure of playing for his overbearing coach.

"I had a tendency to keep things bottled up," Matte said. "Woody beat me down so bad that I had seven bleeds and got a staff infection. He made me a better person. But we did not get along when I played. I wanted to get the fuck away from him."

Hayes also took his revenge by making sure that the team didn't elect the star quarterback as captain. To Woody, it would send the wrong message. It was bad enough that Matte was cocky and defiant. Under no circumstances would that type of player represent the rest of Hayes's team.

"He told everyone in my senior year that there was one player that cannot be captain, and that was me. He told everyone that he thought I was getting enough publicity," Matte said. "He was brutal to play for. But he bailed me out of jail my junior year, and he protected us. He also made sure I graduated, and when I did he called my parents to tell them."

To be sure, it was a rocky relationship between the coach and star quarterback, but in the fall of 1961 Hayes would have loved to have him back, because he had no real standout at quarterback; but then again, it wouldn't matter much. All the quarterback would have to do is hand the ball off to one of the three stars in the backfield, or maybe roll out and look to run first, then pass—but it had better be to an open receiver. In fact, three players would split time at the position. John Mummey and Bill Mrkowksi were used primarily as Woody's running quarterbacks. Joe Sparma was the passing specialist, and he would be sent in on the rare occasion when Woody wanted to throw.

The season began with a 7–7 tie against Texas Christian University, but the Buckeyes would roll through the season undefeated, including a 50–20 whipping put on Michigan in Ann Arbor, in a game that proved Hayes could be equally as bad a winner as a loser. The Buckeyes scored late in the fourth quarter, to go up 48–20, and to put the finishing touches on the humiliating defeat for Michigan. But Hayes wasn't done. He ordered the Buckeyes to go for two points, which they successfully converted to make the score 50–20. Ohio State and Michigan were already mortal enemies, but the decision was seen by critics as a show of poor sportsmanship, and it served to only add another chapter to the rivalry.

All the team had to do now was to beat UCLA on January 1, to put their final stamp on a season that would match the great, undefeated 1954 team. But the Rose Bowl contract between the Big Ten and the Pacific Coast Conference champion had lapsed in 1960, and Big Ten administrators were split about renewing the pact, with Ohio State also being one of the schools that voted against a new deal. Despite the lack of a formal agreement, The Rose Bowl Committee still had extended an invitation to Minnesota, the 1960 Big Ten champions, to play Washington in the 1961 Rose Bowl. The game was rife with hypocrisy. Minnesota accepted the bid to play in the game despite voting against renewing the deal. It was Minnesota's first opportunity to play in the Rose Bowl, and school officials suddenly had a change of heart when they received the first-ever Rose Bowl invitation.

And all the Big Ten schools, even those, like Ohio State, that had voted against renewing the contract, had accepted their share of the Rose Bowl revenue.

In the afterglow of the Michigan win, Hayes and his Buckeyes were banking on the continuation of the informal agreement from a year earlier, and no one doubted there would be any chance that the school would prevent Ohio State from contending for another national championship with a Rose Bowl win on January first, 1962.

But there was the growing sentiment among the faculty that, instead of the school's academics Hayes and his football team was defining Ohio State. And Fullen, who for years had railed against Hayes over the increasingly dominant role that football was having on the university, reportedly was behind an Ohio State Faculty Council vote just after the Michigan game, a vote that denied the Buckeyes from playing in the Rose Bowl. The council agreed with Fullen's long-held view that academics were suffering at the expense of the football team, and on November 28, three days after the Michigan win, the faculty council voted 28–25 to turn down the Rose Bowl invitation. The majority of the council was convinced, with a push by Fullen, that too many financial resources were being allocated to the athletic department, especially to the football team, and the role of the university as a leading academic institution was being shrouded by Ohio State's powerhouse football program. In addition to denying the Buckeyes another trip to Pasadena, the faculty council made an additional decision. They argued back and forth about accepting the school's share of the Rose Bowl revenue, but ultimately decided that even though the Rose Bowl had, in their eyes, become too commercial, it would be financially foolish to turn down Ohio State's share of that year's bowl proceeds.

Ohio State president Novice Fawcett let the decision stand: the Buckeyes were staying home. All over campus students protested the decision, smashing windows and hanging Fullen in effigy. Outraged citizens flooded the *Columbus Dispatch* with complaints, and the paper fanned the flames of dissent by printing the names, addresses, and salaries of the faculty members who voted against sending the Buckeyes to the Rose Bowl. Scattered alumni groups called for Fullen to be fired as head of the alumni association. The players and Hayes were stunned. Their season was over and they lost a chance not just to play in the Rose Bowl, but also to showcase their talents to the nation and garner more support for a national championship. It wasn't as if the Rose Bowl was just another game. It was the biggest postseason college football game, and arguably bigger than the NFL championship game. There was no Super Bowl in the early 1960s. Instead, the Rose Bowl, with all its pageantry, was the biggest football attraction of the season. The Rose Bowl was also the big payoff for the players who had put up with Hayes and all the work, pain, suffering, and abuse he had heaped upon them for the past year. Missing the game due to a decision by their own faculty was almost impossible to believe.

Fortunately for some of the faculty members and Fawcett, Hayes wasn't anywhere near campus to hear the crushing news. He was up in Cleveland for a speaking engagement, and when he was notified of the faculty council's decision, he bolted immediately out of the banquet room and trudged around the city for an hour, furious at what he saw as the ultimate injustice toward himself and his team. After keeping the audience waiting, Hayes returned and delivered his speech (to Hayes, keeping a commitment was as honorable a gesture as one could make) and hurried back to Columbus. There were many people for Hayes to blame. There were the members of the faculty council, there was Fawcett, and there were even the other members of the Big Ten who voted against renewing the contract in the first place.

Hayes tried to be diplomatic with his fellow faculty members.

"I don't agree with those twenty-eight 'no' votes, but I respect the integrity of the men who cast them, if not their intelligence," he said. "I would not want football to drive a line of cleavage in our university. Football is not worth that. . . . We have had to learn to accept defeat under pressure, and that may help us now; although it is difficult to explain to the boys, when, after fifteen years, the Rose Bowl is jerked out from under them."

Hayes instead zeroed in on Fullen. On December 2, Hayes, still incensed by the vote, appeared on his television show and used the public airwaves to blast Fullen over his reported role in the decision.

"Only one man has resorted to personal resentment and called our players professionals, which they are not," Hayes said on camera. "[Fullen] used the [alumni] magazine to attack [the football team] and he used thousands of words in the [school newspaper] *Lantern*. We've all heard him say, on many occasions, 'I select the men who hire me.' He also uses the priority of football tickets, so that, if you quit kicking into his [development] fund, you don't get tickets."

Hayes then called on the students to stop demonstrating against the faculty council. Though Fullen had a lot of power within the university, he had no official standing. He wasn't an employee of the university, and that meant that he couldn't touch Hayes.

The show incited another round of outrage. The *Columbus Dispatch* ran a damming article about Fullen. The paper printed a partial text of Hayes's incendiary attack on Fullen, and then they also attacked Fullen and his position as director of the alumni association. The lengthy article solidly backed Hayes, though on December 10 the paper printed the full text of the ten-minute speech Fullen gave on WBNS-TV on December 8.

But protests and rhetoric weren't going to reverse the faculty's vote, and Ohio State's season was officially over. The team could never measure itself against the other Rose Bowl teams, and the reality of foregoing a trip to Pasadena in the name of academic integrity gnawed at Hayes all winter. The faculty council would vote again in October 1962 to send the Buckeyes to future Rose Bowls if invited. But the Buckeyes weren't nearly the team they were a year earlier, though many starters returned, and they were ranked in the top ten before the start of the season. They opened the season at home with a dominating 41–7 win over North Carolina, but traveled to Los Angeles a week later and scored just seven points in a 9–7 loss to UCLA. Inconsistent play plagued the team. After the loss to UCLA, they beat Illinois 51–15, but then lost 18–14 at home to Northwestern, disappointing the Homecoming crowd. The loss stung Hayes more than usual, given that the Wildcats were coached by Parseghian, Woody's former assistant at Miami.

The up-and-down season continued with a win over Wisconsin, followed by a loss to Iowa, then two consecutive wins, one over Indiana and the other over Oregon. The season ended with a 28–0 drubbing of Michigan, but even that couldn't hide the disappointment of the 6-3 season, good for a tie for third place in the Big Ten.

Fullen would keep his job until his retirement in 1967. There were no more major incidents between the two men; but try as he might, Hayes couldn't force Fullen's ouster. Instead, Fullen kept his eye on Hayes and policed the football program through his position as editor of the alumni magazine.

10

TRANSITION

1961 marked Hayes's ten-year anniversary as coach of the Buckeyes, an unlikely milestone, considering the previous turnover before he came to Columbus. By now, however, the rhythms of the job were deeply ingrained into Hayes and his family, with the months marked by football. On Woody's calendar, the year didn't begin in January, it ended—hopefully with the Buckeyes playing in the Rose Bowl on New Year's Day, with the rest of the month spent buttoning up the next year's recruiting class. In February, the coaches began preparing for the spring practice, which began in late March and ended in the first week of May with the spring game that drew tens of thousands of fans for the scrimmage held in Ohio Stadium. The rest of May and June were spent evaluating the talent from the spring game and fine-tuning the depth chart for the fall. July was quiet, with the campus deserted and the coaches taking their well-deserved vacations. Come mid-August, Hayes would become more intense, as he prepared for the arrival of the team in early September for the start of practice, with the season beginning in the middle of September.

The years had blended together for Hayes since coming to Columbus in 1951, one football season turning into another, then another, until ten years had rolled by. For Woody and Anne, their life together fell into a rhythm all its own. Hayes was like a shadow at home, barely there, totally obsessed by his job, and driven to succeed. Even during the off-season, Hayes was mostly gone, attending out-of-town coaching clinics, or hitting the speakers circuit. He had no real hobbies that were typical of men of his generation. Golf was out of the question. Woody wasn't wired for the game, not with his impatience and his temper. One could only imagine the destruction Hayes would have posed to himself, with what would be a regular barrage of broken and thrown clubs. Fishing was too slow and too full of the unknown for Hayes to enjoy. Hunting was simply out of the question, considering that it coincided with the football season.

So Hayes read and walked to relax. On many nights Hayes would be out late, walking through his Upper Arlington neighborhood, wandering the streets, sorting out the problems at hand. Now that he had stopped playing handball, Hayes would hike. Trips to the mountains in Colorado were a rare getaway, but he liked the peace and solace that the hikes provided. Even when he managed to break free, he couldn't fully divorce himself from what was happening in Columbus. On one trip to Colorado for a combination coaching clinic and vacation, Hayes realized that a young but promising Columbus native, Jack Nicklaus, was playing in a tournament in the Denver area, when Hayes, seeing that the Ohio papers failed to send any writers to cover the performance of the state's golfing prodigy, picked up the phone and every day of the tournament dictated Nicklaus's round back to the *Columbus Dispatch* sports desk.

Anne had learned long ago to deal with her husband. The two mainly led separate lives, with Anne throwing herself into a myriad of charitable activities and becoming a popular speaker in her own right. Long ago the two had reached that place in a marriage where each partner has accepted unfulfilled expectations and learned to live with each other's shortcomings. It was a sometimes combative marriage. Woody didn't just turn off his demand for perfection when he left his office. When he was around, he could be difficult, distant, and demanding; but there was no doubt about his love for his wife.

"He worshiped her, worshiped the ground she walked on," Schembechler told the *Columbus Dispatch*.

But mostly, the two lived their own lives under the roof on Cardiff Road, bonded to each other by the pressures that came with coaching at Ohio State. Anne was independent enough to have a life of her own. Early on in Columbus, her identity was securely tied to that of her husband; but as the years rolled on, Anne stepped out from under the shadows of her celebrity husband and, through the force of her sparkling personality, firmly established herself in town.

Anne was mostly a single parent raising their son Steve. Woody wasn't necessarily a bad father; he was simply absent for much of Steve's childhood. During the team's preseason practice in late August and early September, Hayes would even move out of his house and into the dormitory with the players to completely immerse himself into the team. Plumbing problems, putting in screens, mowing the lawn, or whatever else needed to be done around the house fell squarely on Anne's shoulders. When Steve needed some fatherly guidance, more often than not he turned to his mother.

"She had the unique ability to be a father and a mother at the same time," Steve told the *Columbus Dispatch*. "But I understood. She would say, 'It doesn't mean he doesn't care about us. It doesn't mean he doesn't love us, because he does. But that's just the way he is.'

"Early on, she was always talking to me about him being gone so much, so I wouldn't be bitter, and I never was. I learned a lot from my dad, just by example. He did what he said, meant what he said, and you watch that long enough and it's contagious. You'd always get a straight answer. Sometimes you wished you didn't."

The prolonged absences didn't make it any easier to live up to Woody's expectations. Once, when Steve brought home a poor report card, Hayes lit into his son, making sure that despite the fact that he was gone for much of the time, he was still paying attention.

"He chewed me more ways than I care to think about. But once again he was right," Steve said.

And there were rare times when Hayes would treat his son like some of his players who failed to meet his demands.

"Sometimes you'd get a straight left," Steve told Hornung in the *Dispatch* piece. "I must have been twelve or thirteen, and at the dinner table I was mouthing off to my mother. He warned me three times, and the fourth time he grabbed me and stood me up against the wall and let me have it with the open hand, the first and only time. I was sent up to my room and later he said, 'Do you know why I did that? Because you were mouthing off to your mother, and she's as good a friend as you've got.' I couldn't disagree. I deserved what I got."

Steve turned sixteen in 1961, a critical age for anyone, especially for a boy trying to live up to not only his father's expectations, but also to everyone else's idea of who the son of Woody Hayes should be. The public expectations were enormous. A decent student, Steve played football at Upper Arlington High School, but not even the rare personal coaching sessions with his father could improve Steve's limited natural ability. It shouldn't have been a surprise to Hayes that his son wasn't that talented. Hayes himself was an oft-injured, slow lineman who relied on toughness, not natural ability, to get by on the football field.

Those rare occasions when Woody would work with Steve could turn into lessons of frustration for both father and son. But Steve, despite his athletic limitations, persevered through undistinguished seasons at Upper Arlington High. But that never stopped Anne from going to every game to watch her son pace the sideline on Friday nights, while Woody was sequestered with his Buckeyes team. And the bigger the game, the less Woody was around during the week.

"He wasn't home," Steve recounted to the *Columbus Dispatch*. "He left at five A.M. and came home at midnight. After the game he went to watch films and had his TV show. I wish I could say how he made me wear scarlet and gray underwear, but it's not true. The man was never there. We found out what was going on by reading the paper."

The distance between father and son would narrow as both got older. Steve graduated from Ohio State, became a lawyer, and eventually a Franklin County Municipal Court judge.

When Woody became a grandfather, there was a transformation of sorts, with Woody actually taking some time on a Friday night to spend with his grandson.

"We'd bring him down and Dad would sit there and hold him for a long time. Sometimes, he'd talk to him, mostly he'd just sit and look at him; and a couple of times I think both of them were almost conked out," Steve Hayes later recounted to the *Dispatch*. "It was more than I ever saw of him on Friday nights."

In 1966 Hayes won his hundredth game at Ohio State, with a 7–0 victory over Indiana, marking a milestone few expected, given his early struggles. But the Buckeyes were mostly flat during the early 1960s, with the opposing Big Ten coaches seizing upon Ohio State's decision to turn down the 1961 Rose Bowl invitation as a means to lure recruits away from Columbus. From 1962 through 1966 there were no Big Ten championships, no trips to the Rose Bowl, no Heisman Trophy players, and none of the dramatic games against rival Michigan that marked Hayes's early years.

"See, the old man and the university are de-emphasizing football," the rival coaches would tell blue-chip recruits from Ohio. And too often the recruits would listen, and suddenly many of Ohio's best high school players were on other Big Ten football rosters. What used to be unthinkable was becoming commonplace, as Ohio high school stars passed on the chance to play at Ohio State. Soon the famously deep, homegrown Buckeye talent pool was thinning. Hayes had to work harder to get the players he wanted. No longer could he sit back and pick and choose from dozens of top prospects. Now he had to hit the road in Ohio more often to get the players he wanted, show up at the kid's kitchen table and sell the parents. Mostly it worked, but with steeper competition the Buckeyes were mired in a period of relative mediocrity that brought too many routine 6-3 or 7-2 seasons.

The mediocrity would not change Hayes. By 1967 he was all but institutionalized at Ohio State. He had enough success and power to keep him in Columbus. Yet for a man so full of ambition and ego, getting rich simply never mattered.

There is a misconception that Woody didn't care about money, but that's a half-truth. He didn't care much for amassing wealth, but he was thrifty. Raises weren't emphasized, and there weren't many lucrative offers made to assistants. Instead, Woody liked to bring in young, talented assistants, which helped avoid battles over pay. At the same time, his success was also tied to his assistant coaches. Lyal Clark's return in 1954 resurrected the defense and helped save Woody's job. Ernie Godfrey and Esco Sarkkinen helped buffer the players against Woody, while a strong nucleus of younger coaches continued to add a freshness to the program. His attitude was that it was *his* team, and when times were bad he took the heat. Conversely, when the team was racking up Big Ten titles, he rarely publicly praised the assistants. Most of the coaches quickly learned to stand their ground and challenge their boss, even if it meant getting fired one minute, then being hired back after Hayes had cooled down.

The secret of Hayes's success was his ability to hire skilled assistant coaches. Other schools paid more, but working for Woody allowed the assistants to gain valuable experience and, more importantly, they got exposure that led to head coaching jobs at other schools. Pont, who started with Woody in 1951, went back to coach at Miami, then moved on to Northwestern, and eventually won a Rose Bowl at Indiana. Doyt Perry, another assistant under Woody during the early 1950s, got the head coaching job at Bowling Green. Lou Holtz spent a volatile year under Woody, while Joe Bugel, Bill Mallory, George Chaump, and Earle Bruce all toiled for Hayes before moving on to head-coaching careers. Then there was a young assistant named Bo Schembechler, who would spend six seasons during the late 1950s and early 1960s under Hayes before leaving to coach at Miami of Ohio. Hayes tried to stop Schembechler from leaving, but he couldn't hold Schembechler back any more. After a few years the two would meet again on the field, when Bo would leave Miami and take the head job at Michigan. Hayes should have known of Schembechler's propensity to do battle. Once, when Hayes, in a fit of anger, threw a chair at Schembechler and missed, Schembechler picked up the chair and returned fire. The young line coach would gladly fight Woody, but he also knew that the lessons learned in Columbus could be used to his advantage at Michigan.

"They both made it seem like they hated each other, but they didn't," said former Big Ten Commissioner Wayne Duke, who more than once was involved in controversies with both coaches. "They'd rant and rave at each other, but you'd also see them at the annual Big Ten lunches sitting next to each other. The truth is that they liked each other, except when they coached against each other."

While some of his contemporaries and early assistant coaches were ambitiously heading toward their own NFL coaching careers, Hayes was never serious about joining the pro game. His standard argument was centered around the notion of the student-athlete and the value of academics. It was certainly true that Hayes was drawn to the academic life. He took great pleasure in mingling in the Faculty Club lounges, where he could put himself in the university's collegial atmosphere and share his views on military history, politics, or philosophy. Hayes was a voracious reader, but only on topics that fit his conservative Republican politics. He read widely to support his beliefs, but wouldn't explore, and as a result he limited his breadth of intellectual reach. Hayes could re-create battles fought by Gen. George Patton (he even kept a copy of Patton's orders in his office), or recite speeches by Lincoln or philosophy by Emerson, if anyone cared to engage him. And compared to so many other coaches who only wanted to know how fast Emerson ran the forty-yard dash, Woody's knowledge of history and politics made him seem a scholar. But from a purely academic standpoint, Hayes really never allowed himself to explore, much less accept, different ideas.

Still, he loved the academic setting. He would dine with other professors and administrators at the Faculty Club, taking his customary seat at the ten-person "bachelor's table."

He often would eat quietly, reading a book. And if the Buckeyes lost, an inconsolable Hayes often would demand a private table in order to dine by himself.

It wasn't that Woody was a stranger—his friends said that he knew everyone in the state of Ohio and everybody in Columbus by name. But he didn't have many close friends, only hundreds of acquaintances.

Woody's old college roommate Jim Otis and his wife would stay at Woody's house whenever they came to Columbus, but that practice came to a quick halt when Otis's son played at Ohio State during the late 1960s. Hayes, conscious of claims of favoritism, suspended the friendship until Otis's son graduated. Hayes also counted John Miller as one of his true friends in Columbus. It was an unlikely friendship. Miller was a Presbyterian minister who came to Ohio State in 1929. He met Hayes playing handball and the two became close, though Miller was politically a liberal who studied ways to bring peace, while the conservative Hayes studied past wars.

For decades, Miller was the unofficial football team chaplain, attending practices, eating at the team's training table, and giving the annual invocation at the football banquets. He also presided over weddings and funerals for some members of the Ohio State football program. In return, Hayes would speak at local Presbyterian churches, helping raise money.

"I think they valued their relationship because they never critiqued each other's work or points of view," said Miller's wife Carolyn. "They had fun together. Woody was very kind. And he always was a good man to his friends."

The Faculty Club sustained Hayes's sense of academia. There, he could mix with the rest of the tenured faculty, where he was accepted with a combination of respect and resentment, as some of the professors still didn't approve of the university's academic mission being subordinated to the football team.

In the NFL nobody honored such academic trappings. The motive was pure profit, something Hayes had no interest in. You played football to win, Hayes believed, not to make money, even though the Buckeyes annually brought in millions of dollars to Ohio State. He felt the same way about college coaches making the jump to the pros for higher salaries.

"If they don't want to coach, then get into industry, go to the pros," Hayes said. "It's like a high-priced prostitute. You wonder whether she enjoys her work or just the money."

The crass analogy was another in a string of contradictions. While Hayes was denouncing the commercialism of the NFL, he was busy building one of the greatest brand names in sports: Buckeye football.

College football, even during the late 1950s and early 1960s, was defined by money, particularly at Ohio State. Hayes's righteous views toward the profit-mongering NFL would have held up if he were still coaching at Denison, but not at Ohio State. There was no doubt that Hayes valued education, and that he nobly pushed his players to graduate. But denouncing the NFL as an exercise in pure profit, while generating millions of dollars annually through Ohio State football, smacked of hypocrisy.

There was another reason for Hayes to disdain the professional game. For one thing, he couldn't possibly have as much control over an NFL team that he had at Ohio State, not unless he owned the franchise. He couldn't threaten professional players like he did at Ohio State, where a player's future lay in his hands. His penchant for hitting players in practice certainly wouldn't be tolerated by NFL players, who would more than likely respond in kind. On a more technical level,

Hayes's offense was simple and based on the power game, but the talent in the NFL was relatively even across the league. Those predictable fullback plunges into the line would have been met by far more resistance in the pros than what Woody experienced when he coached in the Big Ten. Three yards and a cloud of dust worked fine on the college level, even on a level as full of talent as the Big Ten, but an NFL coaching job required more offensive imagination.

Despite Hayes's lack of interest in the NFL, he respected pro coaches. He allowed scouts to watch practice, allowed access to his players, and set aside space in the Buckeyes' training facility for scouts to watch film. In the late 1950s, one of the scouts to make his way to Columbus was an assistant coach for the New York Giants named Vince Lombardi. The two coaches hit it off, spending time at a blackboard diagramming plays and pondering the various intricacies of the belly series. In time Hayes grew to almost idolize Lombardi. In a rare Hayes family vacation, of a type that were usually built around a coaching clinic in some resort location, Woody took his son Steve with him to visit the Green Bay Packers training camp during Lombardi's 1960s glory years. Up in Green Bay Hayes spent a few days with the gracious Lombardi, who allowed Hayes to sit in on meetings and film sessions, and attend practices. Lombardi also introduced Steve Hayes to his own son Vince Jr., giving both sons a chance to compare the obsessions of their fathers.

The week spent in Wisconsin was as close to an NFL coaching job as Hayes would get. Paul Brown went on to a legendary NFL career and so did Sid Gillman. But Woody steered clear of his coaching rivals when they reached the pros. And just as Woody shied away from the NFL, the NFL likewise kept its distance from Woody. Still, he had his chances to coach in the pros. In 1956 Hayes, full of ambition and promise, was mulling over an opening with the Pittsburgh Steelers. But he would not pursue it with the kind of fervor he demonstrated in getting the Ohio State job.

"He talked to me about it," Jim Parker, Hayes's star lineman told the *Columbus Dispatch*. "He said the only way he'd go was if I'd go with him. Then he said, 'But, hell, I don't know enough about the passing game.' Passing game? Hell, we were lucky to pass forty times a season."

By 1967 Hayes was again feeling the pressure from the powerful alumni, who were growing restless at the stagnant state of Ohio State football. The previous season, the Buckeyes finished with a 4-5 record, just the second time since Hayes came to Columbus that the Buckeyes had a losing season. Once again the "Bye-Bye Woody" banners were flown over Ohio Stadium. Hayes wasn't bothered by the criticism, but there was real concern among the coaching staff about their futures. After starting out with a 2-3 record, the rumors were flying all over Columbus that Woody's run was over. Only a win at Michigan State, to even the Buckeyes' record at 3-3, deflected the pressure building to fire Hayes. The Buckeyes won again the following week, at home against Wisconsin, but the lackluster past few seasons were catching up to the football program. Interest in the Buckeyes was waning. Only 65,470 fans showed up for the Wisconsin game that was played in the rain, the smallest crowd since the infamous "Snow Bowl" game in 1950 that led to Fesler's departure. The Buckeyes won again the next week against Iowa, and then headed to Ann Arbor to face Michigan and finish the season. His players didn't know it when they took the field, but Hayes felt he was playing for his job.

Just 64,411 fans showed up in Michigan Stadium for the rival game, a clear sign of the apathy that had set in. It was a rare sight to see the massive stadium nearly half empty, but the Wolverines were 4-6 and the Buckeyes 5-3. Both teams were playing for pride. Ohio State hadn't won a conference championship in five years.

Both teams, despite their mediocre records, had three straight victories coming into the game; but it was the Buckeyes that kept up their momentum, scoring on their first two possessions and then scoring again early in the second quarter. It was no contest from then on, with Michigan playing sloppy, giving up four turnovers.

The win brightened for Hayes what was a poor season. His Buckeyes had entered the middle of the season with a 2-3 record, but then rallied to win the final four games. The Michigan win was enough to convince the university officials to keep Hayes. The administration could handle a few losing seasons, as long as fans packed Ohio Stadium; but the prospect of thousands of empty seats each Saturday was not only unheard of at Ohio State, it was unacceptable. A few more football Saturdays like the game against Wisconsin would surely have sent Hayes packing. And the only way to keep the stadium packed was by fielding a winning team.

It didn't take a military historian like Hayes to figure out that the plan of attack had better include attracting a better class of players. The balance of power within college football was shifting, and there was more parity. With the parity came increased competition for talent. No longer could Hayes count on the Frontliners bringing in the best prospects from within the state. And the top Ohio players weren't, in many instances, as good as players from other parts of the country.

It had become clear to Hayes that he'd have to spend even more time recruiting out-of-state players. His offense, never innovative, had become completely predictable. Even worse was that the Buckeyes lacked power and speed, the two essential ingredients of Hayes's success. A year earlier he had put in the orders: find the best talent, no matter where they lived. The quaint notion of homegrown high school players playing for good old Ohio State was over, and after the disappointing 1967 season there was a glaring need for better players.

There were certain disadvantages recruiting out-of-state players. The Buckeyes tradition, so firmly entrenched in Ohio, held little advantage over the larger East Coast cities, where the competition for the top players was fierce. With the competition came the propensity to cheat, with offers of cash, cars, and jobs, almost a staple among many college recruiters. But Hayes negated much of the disadvantage strictly through his natural recruiting abilities. Hayes, a conservative Republican from the bedrock of small-town America, had no problems relating to inner-city players or their parents. He thought nothing of tramping into bad neighborhoods where he was the only middle-aged white man within miles. While other coaches offered ample amounts of cash to sign recruits, Hayes counted on winning over the parents of the recruits.

"I was all set to go to Syracuse to follow in Jim Brown's footsteps," said Jack Tatum. Tatum, from Passaic, New Jersey, had been one of the best high school running backs on the East Coast, and he would go on to star as an all-American defensive back at Ohio State. "But then Woody came to the house and pretty much recruited my mother. He talked to me for ten minutes and talked to my mom for two hours, and he promised her I would get a good education. When he left, my Mom said she liked him because he had little holes in the bottoms of his shoes. She said that a man so famous who had holes in his shoes fit in with us. That turned the tide, and the next thing I knew I was at Ohio State."

If a potential player committed to another school, Hayes would immediately back off. He'd compete hard against other schools, but once the kid had expressed interest in another school it was over. Yet Hayes and his staff, once they made their decision to look outside of Ohio, more often than not got the players they wanted. The focus on talent moved outside of Ohio to places like Newark, New Jersey, New York City, Washington, D.C., and up and down the eastern seaboard. The players were in many cases different from the typical Ohio State recruit. They were faster, flashier, and more stylish, both on and off the field, and convincing them to leave the fast pace of New York or New Jersey for the relative serenity of Columbus took all the charm Hayes could muster. His efforts paid off; the skill level of Ohio State recruits increased noticeably once he expanded beyond the state of Ohio.

While Hayes was ordering his assistant coaches to expand Buckeyes recruiting territory, there was another mission to be accomplished. The war in Vietnam was pulling Hayes toward Southeast Asia. Hayes was an unabashed supporter of the war, though he wasn't about to vote for Lyndon Johnson. Politics aside, Hayes, the military man, took the same view toward Vietnam that he had toward World War II when he left coaching to enlist in the navy. The growing protests about the United States involvement in Vietnam were about to spill over to college campuses, including Ohio State, but Hayes dismissed any disagreement about the war as anti-American sentiment from "longhairs." Though Hayes was a student of military history, he refused to accept any criticism of the war, and he firmly believed in its escalation. To him, the growing number of casualties was the price to be paid in defending democracy. Each generation had to do its part. For Hayes, that meant being a vocal supporter of the war effort. He befriended Gen. Lewis Walt. Hayes was immediately impressed with Walt, the general striking a chord in Hayes's long-term worship of Gen. George

Patton and other war heroes. Hayes was drawn to people in positions of power. He had met Richard Nixon in 1957 at a dinner at the home of one of his early sponsors, Sen. John Bricker. It was there that Nixon and Hayes struck up a friendship over drinks and diagrams of plays. Nixon by then was already a football freak, and Hayes took note of the then vice president's knowledge of the game. Through General Walt, Hayes was able to help satisfy his desire to rub shoulders with presidents and generals. Hayes saw himself among the great commanders of his generation, only his battlefield was on the gridiron, not in the jungles of Southeast Asia. The idolatry of Walt by Hayes was shown in the general's visit to Ohio State in November 1967, when, after a win against Iowa, Hayes closed the locker room for nearly an hour while Walt addressed the team. Afterward Hayes called Walt "a great American hero," and returned the favor of Walt's visit by agreeing to travel to Vietnam after the season. In May of 1967 Hayes made good on his promise.

With spring practice over and the recruiting season completed, Hayes cleared two weeks from his schedule to travel throughout South Vietnam armed with a film projector and reels of Big Ten highlights from the previous season. Though the mission was arranged through the army's entertainment office, Hayes took the trip seriously, with a schedule that would have physically taxed a man twenty years younger. On Friday, May 26, he left Columbus at eight A.M. and flew to Chicago, where he connected to an American Airlines flight to San Francisco at nine-fifty. After landing in San Francisco at eleven-fifty local time, Woody was met by a military aide and driven to Travis Air Force base, where he left at four P.M. on a military plane bound for Saigon. On Sunday at five A.M., Hayes landed in Saigon, where he spent the day sleeping off the jet lag. For the next ten days he would fly all over South Vietnam, visiting bases and hospitals, showing the football movies to the troops. But Hayes did more than the typical glad-handing offered by various American entertainers who were brought in by the army to bolster morale. He took a genuine interest in the soldiers he encountered, talking to them individually and hearing their stories, and, in many instances, vowing to personally deliver messages back home to their families.

Hayes kept a detailed record of his trips to Vietnam, and he reported his activities in crisp military language to the chief of the Armed Forces Professional Entertainment Office as if he were back on the USS *Rinehart* recording the day's events into the ship's log.

"Left at 09:10 by chopper Huey for Duc Mi, arriving at 10:00. Spent the afternoon in a survival village, spent time on a firing range, and watched North Vietnamese Rangers fire captured weapons," read one of Hayes's entries from his 1967 trip. "Spent the rest of the afternoon with noncoms, attended chapel services, and then showed the HiLite films that evening, and spoke to officers and men of this compound."

Every day in Vietnam was nearly the same, with Hayes, dressed in Army fatigues, doing his best to boost morale in a war that would nearly tear America apart. When he returned to Columbus on June 12, he dutifully reported back to the army brass that he had visited fourteen hospitals. And while the military released the body counts for the week, Hayes calculated the impact of his trip and made good on the promises he had made to the soldiers he left in Vietnam.

"I talked with almost every man in each hospital; we showed the films twenty-three times, with estimates that I talked to eleven thousand men, either personally or collectively," he said in his report. "Since I have been home, I have called over one hundred families of men whom I met in Vietnam, and each family has been extremely grateful for a personal but brief contact with their son. I found those men were very eager to talk with someone from back home who wanted to spend time with them. That was the purpose of my trip."

Spending hours on the phone with the parents and family members of the soldiers was typical of Hayes. The ex-navy commander felt compelled to take the time to call complete strangers, introduce himself, and relay a message from a lonely soldier half a world away.

That generosity of spirit wasn't reserved for servicemen. On a regular basis, Hayes would visit local hospitals in Columbus after practice, occasionally bringing a player with him to visit patients he didn't know. Sometimes Hayes would overhear someone talking about a friend or relative who was laid up in a hospital, and without a word he'd show up unannounced to the surprised patient's bed to offer a word or two of encouragement. The visits were usually unannounced and went unpublicized, with Hayes squashing any chance that the local papers would print his visits, by dictating through Hornung at the *Dispatch* what could and couldn't be written. The contradiction within Hayes was obvious. Here was a man who barely spent any time with his own family, yet he routinely found time to roam the halls of the local hospitals to bolster the spirits of people he barely knew. The regular hospital visits were also in some respects Hayes's way of expressing the part of his personality that he struggled to verbalize to his friends and his family. Hayes wasn't a deeply religious man. Sunday mornings during the season were spent at work, for Woody's god was more likely found in game film than in church. But he was deeply influenced by his heroes—generals, presidents, philosophers, and poets, that helped guide his moral compass. Those countless clandestine trips to the hospital were as sustaining to Hayes as they were for the patients he spent time consoling.

Hayes returned from his trip to Vietnam and quickly immersed himself in the upcoming season. The trip had helped dim the frustrations of the previous season, and the spring practice had showed enough promise to give Hayes hope that he could turn the program around. For the past two seasons the Buckeyes had faltered. The 4-5 1966 season was still an embarrassment. Woody hadn't fielded a team that bad since 1959. The 6-3 1967 team was an improvement; but that season featured some humiliating losses, most notably Purdue's 41–6 blowout of the Buckeyes at home.

11

THE KIDDIE CORPS

The combined 10–8 record in the previous two seasons gave rise to a growing sense that the Buckeyes were growing stale under Hayes. It was 1968 and the game was changing, with more passing and wide open offenses, yet Hayes was still bringing out the tired old T-formation power offense that even his opponents knew by heart. Hayes heard from the critics who were charging that the Buckeyes had grown stagnant, but he also sensed the potential surrounding his upcoming season. The new recruiting strategy was beginning to pump new talent into the program. The sophomore class included players from outside of Ohio, like John Brockington, the diesel-like halfback from Brooklyn, New York; Tatum, the quiet but vicious defensive back from Passaic, New Jersey; Jan White, a swift and strong tight end from Harrisburg, Pennsylvania; and Tim Anderson, another all-state high schooler from West Virginia. Like Tatum, Anderson was a talented fullback in high school who had gained more than two thousand yards in two years. But he was converted to defensive back during his freshman season at Ohio State and became an instant starter in the spring. In all, there were thirteen high school all-Americans in the class of 1967.

Since freshmen were ineligible to play varsity, the freshman class spent all of 1967 with little chance to demonstrate their abilities on Saturdays. There were only two freshman games that year, so practice was the only way to impress the coaches. As a result, the freshmen treated their scrimmages against the varsity during the week as their games. Shunned by the rest of the team due to their ineligibility, the freshmen players adopted a sense of camaraderie from being outsiders, and it was a motivating factor. Each week they lived for the chance to make the varsity players look bad in practice. The upperclassmen starters, beat up from the games on Saturday and tired from the grind of the season, did not want to be challenged, or worse, made to look bad in front of the coaches by the freshmen players. But the collective talents of the 1967 freshmen class became obvious to Hayes after watching them dominate against the varsity during the week. Now that they were sophomores, there was really only one thing that Brockington and the other star sophomores needed to prove to the old man: that they perform on game day in front of eighty-two thousand screaming fans and a national television audience.

Hayes, who rarely trusted young players, was inherently suspicious of any of his sophomores until they proved themselves in pressure-packed Big Ten games, especially on the road.

"You're bound to lose one game for every sophomore you start," Hayes said in quarterback club meetings that summer, sending a warning to the devoted followers who kept hearing great things about the 1968 team. Hayes wasn't using the comments to deflect any criticism that would surely come his way if the Buckeyes didn't produce during the upcoming season. He firmly believed that putting the football game in the hands of young players was the fastest way to the bottom of the Big Ten standings, and he dreaded the thought of so many sophomores playing at the same time.

By the start of practice it was obvious that his dim view of underclassmen began to change. The sophomore class was so obviously talented that there would be no way to keep some of them off the field, especially after the lackluster 1967 season.

When Tatum first stepped foot on the Buckeyes' practice field as a freshman, he was stunned by the collective talent in his own class, much less on the whole team. Along with Brockington was Leo Hayden and Larry Zelina, all of whom would end up starting as sophomores in the backfield. Despite his own prodigious running ability, Tatum was switched to defense, joining another promising sophomore linebacker from Mt. Vernon, Ohio, named Jim Stillwagon. The coaches named Stillwagon the team's starting middle guard the moment he took the field during his first spring practice session after his freshman year. He was a tremendous athlete, winning fourteen letters in high school, and the Buckeyes were so loaded with talent at each position that the offensive and defensive coaches would hold a draft of sorts, with each coach trying to get the best players on their respective sides of the ball. It was not a friendly exercise.

Under Hayes's team structure, the defense was in many ways its own separate entity. It practiced on a field separate from the offense, and the defensive coaches were on their own, with little oversight from Woody. The structure bred competition; and when it came to sorting out the talent, the coaches would look to serve their own interests, with Hayes serving as the final arbiter of who would play where. The defense now boasted just as much speed and skill as the offense, and the coaches spent all their time in the weeks following the spring game figuring out where to play all the unproven but tremendously gifted sophomores.

The quarterback position was particularly unsettled. Billy Long, a senior, was the returning starter, but Hayes had to two sophomores pushing for the job. One was rifle-armed Ron Maciejowski, and the other was Rex Kern from Lancaster, Ohio. Kern, the son of a barber, was one of Ohio's great schoolboy athletes. He was wooed by more than one hundred colleges, where he had his choice of playing football, basketball, and baseball. But he was infatuated with Ohio State basketball and it was Ohio State basketball coach Fred Taylor who beat Hayes to the punch in recruiting the six-foot guard who averaged twenty-three points a game.

It wasn't until Kern's senior year in high school that Hayes finally got interested, mainly because Kern wasn't Hayes's prototypical quarterback. Hayes liked his quarterbacks to resemble fullbacks; big, tough, strong, and smart. Kern was tough and plenty smart, but he was just six feet and 185 pounds with catlike balance and quickness.

Hayes could no longer ignore Kern's athleticism; but by now, so late in the recruiting game, he would have to compete against other schools—and Taylor—in convincing Kern to play football. Both Ohio State coaches coveted Kern, so, rather than lose the star recruit to another school, they reached a compromise. They would allow Kern to play both sports, a rare concession by Hayes.

"I was recruited by many other schools before Woody got into the mix, and from the fourth grade on I knew I wanted to play basketball at Ohio State," Kern said. "Woody and Fred both said they wanted me, and said it was incumbent for me to play both sports, and after they told me that I drove down to Columbus and announced my signing there. But Woody and Fred were completely different. Woody would go no nuts and pound players, and it struck the fear of God in you. Fred just looked at you and you knew what he was thinking."

But Kern wasn't easily intimidated by Hayes's bluster, and Hayes, recognizing Kern's cool nature, backed off, a rarity for the coach. Instead, Hayes turned his wrath on Maciejowski.

"Woody and I had a special relationship. He could be the meanest son of a gun in the world, but I was probably the only quarterback he never hit. Unfortunately, Maciejowski became the punching bag. I don't know why that was. I don't know if he saw something in my character, or that my high school coach had played for him. But there was a great amount of respect that I had for him and he had for me."

Fall 1968. A year of protest, war, assassination, rebellion, riots, and civil unrest, and the upheaval rolled along High Street and through the Ohio State campus. Try as he might, Hayes couldn't stop the changes, and a new generation of players swept into Ohio State. Hayes, as he put it, preferred the 1950s "when the air was clean and sex was dirty." It was all so confusing to Hayes, who, despite his broad grasp of history, was perplexed and appalled by what he saw as a breakdown of society in all the turmoil. He defended his views as he did with every other conflict—head on, caring none at all about the enemies he was making with his vociferous support of his beliefs. He continued to back the war in Vietnam with four trips to Southeast Asia.

Though he didn't like it, Hayes allowed his players to have long hair and mustaches and put few limitations on their behavior. He spent team meetings lecturing his players about the perils of drugs and sex, but he was tolerant of the changing ways of his players—as long as they met his demands on the field. He also supported the civil rights movement, preaching to his players about the injustices of segregation and refusing to tolerate any hint of racism among his players. For all his talk of racial tolerance, other Big Ten schools had blacks playing quarterback in 1968, but it would be another few years before Hayes would break the color barrier at his team's prized position.

Kern, though fully aware and engaged in the social changes swirling about, proved to be everything Hayes wanted in his quarterbacks. Clean-cut, respectful, smart, obedient to authority, and most of all a natural leader who could handle a seemingly endless amount of pressure.

While Long spent the spring playing baseball Kern impressed Hayes, and eventually Hayes developed enough faith in Kern to hand over the offense to the untested but confident quarterback.

"I wasn't surprised coming out of spring," Kern said. "Billy played baseball in the spring and 'Mace' and I got all the reps at quarterback."

But one June morning, two months before the start of fall practice, Kern couldn't get out of bed. He had ruptured a disc in his spine and would have to have surgery. With little time for rehabilitation, Kern reported to practice in August weak and out of shape. Still, Hayes made Kern, like he did all his players, pass a brutal conditioning test before being allowed to practice. Kern would have to prove all over to Hayes that he was healthy and skilled enough to start.

"I had no time to rehab or to condition myself, and my back was killing me, but Woody made me run and I didn't know if I'd ever play. But he had also called my parents and told them that even if I never played a down, he's see that I'd graduate. That's how he was. We called him 'schizoid.' You'd see him coming at you throwing that left hook at you and the next minute, he'd have his arm around you."

In a letter to his players just before the start of 1968 season, Hayes warned them that they had better come to camp in shape.

"There will be times when we won't bother to huddle between plays. This will put terrific pressure on the defense, but also great pressure on us, unless we are in perfect shape. Each player that we have will be in better shape than he was last year. I strongly suggest that you finish up this week and early next week real strong, and then take two or three days to freshen your legs before you report to us."

Hayes then closed the letter by reminding his players to bring their own shoes and any spare footballs, "regardless of their condition," for the kickers to use.

It was classic Hayes. Here was the head of one of the biggest football factories in the country, an organization that could afford to buy an endless supply of footballs, yet the frugal pragmatist ingrained in

Woody from his childhood compelled him to ask his own players to donate old footballs for the kickers. The odd request also spoke volumes on how Hayes felt toward his place kickers, having them resort to using scuffed footballs.

Some eighty-four players checked into Smith Hall on Thursday, August 28, 1968, to prepare for the grind of double sessions under the blaze of the summer sun. That same weekend protestors gathered in Chicago's Grant Park during the Democratic convention, and Mayor Richard Daley dispatched twelve thousand police officers and the Illinois National Guard to do battle with the demonstrators, as national television beamed the bloody riots into America's living rooms. The country, it seemed, had reached its boiling point. While Daley was ordering his police force to bash heads along Michigan Avenue, the Buckeyes were preparing for the start of a practice that would begin with Hayes's own brand of punishment—the six-minute mile. Each player, no matter what position, was required by Hayes to run a six-minute mile before being allowed to practice. It was Hayes's way of determining who had followed his orders to stay in shape during the summer. Like his school superintendent father, who would make no exceptions for a first-grader, whose birthday fell a few days short of the cutoff, to be able to go to school with her playmates, Woody cut no slack to any player failing to pass the test. For the skill players, the backs and receivers, the mile-long run was difficult, but not nearly as taxing as it was for the linemen. Physically, these behemoths weren't built to run a six-minute mile. Besides, you didn't run long distance on a football field, you ran in spurts. It was really an unfair test of fitness that nearly killed the linemen, though it would be a few years before Woody finally figured out that it wasn't a true measure of conditioning and switched the fitness requirement to a series of sprints that better measured the level of "football shape" of his players.

The players were greeted on August 30, 1968, by a revamped coaching staff that included three new coaches. Hayes had decided to shake up this staff that he felt was partly to blame for the staleness that had infected the program in the past few seasons. Hayes brought in Ohio native and recent Kent State graduate Lou Holtz to coach the defensive backs, and he hired Rudy Hubbard, who had played for him in 1967 at halfback, to coach the freshman. To help with the offense, Hayes went outside of Ohio to bring in one of the brightest high school coaches in the Northeast, George Chaump. Hayes generally preferred to hire college coaches for his staff, and he rarely recruited coaches from out of state. But Chaump came from John Harris High School in Harrisburg, Pennsylvania, as a young offensive-minded coach who had won six consecutive conference championships and who had impressed Hayes and the other Ohio State coaches when they came to Pennsylvania on recruiting visits. After taking Chaump to lunch in Harrisburg ostensibly to discuss a prospect, Hayes decided to fly him to Columbus to interview for the quarterbacks coach job and ultimately made the offer. It was professionally a big step up for Chaump, but it was a financially lateral move. Ohio State only matched Chaump's high school salary, figuring that just getting the chance to work for a big-time program was enough reward. When it came to hiring his assistants, Hayes felt it was more about opportunity than pay.

"He hired me for $11,500 per year, the same salary I was making as a high school coach," Chaump said.

The only way in Ohio State for assistant coaches to make more money was to threaten to leave the program.

"I got a job offer with the Oakland Raiders and went out and stayed with John Madden and picked out a house, but Woody cornered me and badgered me into staying," Chaump said. "He hated Al Davis and told me he wanted me to stay. He gave me a five-thousand-dollar raise, and that was the only time he showed any generosity. Other than that, there were no bonuses, no big raises, no nothing."

The local sports press cast Woody as someone who loved the game so much that he would have coached for free. It made for a charming feature story and good university public relations. But while it was true that Hayes didn't really care that he was paid as much as his peers like Bear Bryant at Alabama or Bud Wilkinson, he was after a currency of a different sort. Power and control was what Hayes coveted more than cash, and he had amassed an ample amount since coming to Columbus in 1951. But by 1968 Hayes was on the brink of losing his job.

"He was about .500 in 1967 and had to beat Michigan to keep his job," Chaump said. "But he did it, and still there were chants of 'Bye-Bye

Woody.' That year he sent out a Christmas card that had a plane flying over the stadium with a sign saying 'Bye Woody,' but Ohio State was hurting and there was pressure on him to win."

Chaump would spend probably as much time working directly with Hayes as anybody, and it was a rocky transition for the young coach. He was nearly fired before the Buckeyes' first game in 1968, after a fierce battle over the offense with his new boss.

Hayes didn't have much trust in his young new quarterbacks coach, so he assigned him to review the freshmen practice tapes while the other coaches went off to recruit. It was supposed to be busy work to help ease Chaump into the program, but it proved to be an eye-opening experience for the new coach, who for the first time saw the talents of the freshmen class jump off the screen. It soon became obvious to Chaump that Hayes would have to accept playing the young sophomores.

"The guy that really got my attention was Rex, and there was Brockington, Tatum, and Mike Sensibaugh," Chaump said. "Nobody else came close. I told Woody that these guys were impressive, but he was very conservative. But he had no choice, and he really had no say in it, the players were that good."

During the weeks of film evaluation, Chaump, who favored a more wide-open offensive philosophy, was eager to use the abundant skills of the Ohio State players that he dutifully charted during the weeks he was assigned to break down the freshmen tapes. But Hayes didn't yet share his new assistant's enthusiasm, and he fully intended to use his tried-and-true "robust" offense, a strategy that featured the fullback running through tight line splits.

In a meeting during the second day of spring practice, Chaump, eager to impress his new boss, raised his hand and boldly suggested that a better way to make use of the talent was to split out the linemen to open up the field and run the offense out of an "I" formation backfield, and spread the field in order to pass to more receivers.

"Woody thought it was illegal to use three receivers," Chaump said. "But I was battling to throw the ball."

The more experienced coaches chuckled under their breaths.

The idea of moving away from his "three yards and a cloud of dust" offense was heresy.

"Woody was tight as hell and was dead set against using the I-formation, and he got so mad at me for suggesting it, and he fired me on the spot," Chaump said. "He said it would never work, that it would make the fullback a glorified guard, and he wasn't going to change his reputation and ruin his image by listening to some high school coach who never coached a college game in his life. I couldn't believe it, but I got up to leave, but then he told me to come back and sit down."

Chaump was now an official member of the coaching staff after receiving the browbeating. Hayes routinely fired and rehired his assistants, sometimes in the same breath.

Hayes's criticism of Chaump's I-formation was rooted in a game between USC and Notre Dame where he served as a guest television analyst. The Notre Dame defense that day dominated USC, which was running out of the I-formation. Hayes was adamant that the I-formation was a "lighthouse" formation that allowed the defense, especially the linebackers, to tee off on the tailback.

He was selling his own players short. The Buckeyes line, anchored by tackle Rufus Mayes and cocaptain Dave Foley, was among the best in the Big Ten. And with so much talent in the backfield, with Kern, Brockington, Zelina, Hayden, and Jim Otis, the son of Hayes's old Denison fraternity brother and roommate, the Buckeyes had the ability to run out of the I-formation. Kern, though not as big and strong as Maciejowksi, had an accurate arm and a good feel for the passing game. The Buckeyes also had Jan White, who Chaump had coached in high school at tight end, and Bruce Jankowski at wide receiver. It was the best talent Hayes would ever have at one time at Ohio State. If he couldn't muster the confidence in his players and staff to adapt in the spring of 1968, he never would.

Hayes soon saw the logic in his new assistant's suggestion to add the I-formation. Then, one by one, each of the assistant coaches backed Chaump. Hugh Hindman, who played for Woody and was his trusted assistant, Earle Bruce who also played for Woody before joining the staff, and Tiger Ellison, the freshman coach who knew the sophomores' abilities more than anyone, all chimed in to convince Hayes to make the change. During spring practice, the Buckeyes installed the new offense, but there was a compromise of sorts. Hayes would run out of the I, but revert back to the old robust power formation when the Buckeyes reached the twenty-yard line. There was no way the old man was going to completely abandon the only thing he felt he had mastered in football, especially when his team was near the goal line.

With Kern, the frail but talented leader at quarterback, the Buckeyes soon mastered the new attack during the practice sessions leading up to the season opener. But with about a week away from the first game, Hayes suddenly changed his mind. The thought of changing the offense left him far too uneasy. After weeks of planning and practicing, he ordered his coaches to scrap the I formation and go back to the old, familiar formation. But Hindman, who played for Hayes at Miami of Ohio and was an OSU assistant, fended off Hayes's hasty decision.

"We had run the I formation all spring and in fall practice, but Woody, Christ, he was a worrier and a stewer and he wanted to go away from it," Chaump said. "But Hugh just told Woody that we had gone too far to go back and the rest of us coaches insisted."

Ohio State opened its seventy-ninth football season in 1968 season at home against the Southern Methodist University Mustangs, on Saturday September 28. On the Thursday before the game, Hayes spent more than an hour lecturing the local writers on a wide range of topics, from instilling in them confidence in the nine sophomores that would start for the Buckeyes to "the problems of the younger generation."

It was vintage Hayes, who at times would pontificate on matters outside of football in front of writers he felt comfortable with. With the fall practice season over, Hayes was anxious and excited to get the season started, and he was in fine form for the first meeting of the season with the newspapermen.

"You name it, Woody covered it in an hour and twenty minutes after his club had showered and headed for chow," Kessler wrote in the *Columbus Citizen*.

Ohio State fans cared little about Hayes's views on the Vietnam War, and more about his decision to start three sophomores in the four-member defensive backfield against an SMU team that brought a wide open passing offense that featured some twenty-five different passing formations. The Mustangs scored 37 points in their season-opening win against Auburn, passing the ball fifty-two times in ninety-one plays out of every conceivable formation that included pro splits, flankers, twin formations, trips, quads, and quints with five receivers spread across the field with only the quarterback in the backfield.

For an ultraconservative team like Ohio State, that used maybe two receivers in its passing formations, the SMU offense may as well have been from Mars, and the thought of defending the wide-open attack with such an inexperienced team was giving defensive coaches fits.

"There are a lot of teams in our league that they could score forty points on—and I hope we're not one," said defensive coordinator Lou McCullough. "They've got twelve different formations from each side, meaning twenty-four different looks. It's not a helter-skelter, spread-'em-out offense. It's well conceived."

Holtz, who coached the secondary, was already gearing up for what could be a defensive disaster in the making, after he returned to Columbus after scouting the SMU–Auburn game for Hayes. Not only did SMU have a strong-armed quarterback out of the Don Meredith mold named Chuck Hixson, but the SMU receivers were speedier than anyone on the Buckeyes.

"I'm a pessimist by nature," Holtz warned the *Columbus Citizen*. "A pessimist actually is an optimist with experience, but it looks like it could be a long day for us. Only way to prepare is find a rabbit that can catch a football. They'll pass on their own one, on our one, or anywhere in between."

Hayes privately shared Holtz's concern that SMU's high-powered, gambling offense would overwhelm his young players, especially his unproven secondary. But the master psychologist spent all week showering his new players with praise in the papers, though the glowing comments served to convince himself as much as it bolstered the young player's confidence.

"They are good ones, and those three sophomores in the secondary have been there pretty nearly every day since last spring," he said, noting that the major overhaul of his team would take fans by surprise, given the number of new starters.

"They better buy a scorecard," Hayes said of the changes made to the team. "We will run with more different people that we have in years—a four-running-back attack. We've also got fellas who can catch, and we might even throw two or three times. Seriously, we will throw a lot, but we will run more."

Hayes then meandered into a discussion about how an enemy steals from his opponent, citing how the Japanese gleaned key information from the 1933 U.S. war games that was used in the bombing of Pearl Harbor.

Hayes took the military history lesson to heart and refused to allow SMU scouts to attend the Buckeyes' spring game. He also refused to exchange game tapes with the Mustangs, who were led by a cocky young coach named Hayden Fry.

On Saturday, September 28, Lyndon Johnson's presidency was on its last legs, even as he continued to bomb Vietnam, but the lead stories in both the *Dispatch* and the *Citizen-Journal* trumpeted the start of the Ohio State football season. NEW MODEL BUCKS AWAIT WHISTLE was the featured, page-one story in the *Citizen-Journal,* with another front-page story detailing the drop in football season ticket sales that resulted from the past years of mediocrity, a record that was putting the pressure on school administrators to fire Hayes. Average attendance at the Horseshoe was expected to drop to 74,200, compared to 76,700 during the five home games played in 1967, which was almost 7,000 off from the peak of 83,391 during the 1964 season. Still, OSU ticket director George Staten defended the steady declines.

"We'll still be number one in the nation," he said, putting the university's spin on the growing disinterest in the Buckeyes.

The Ohio State season usually included two nonconference opponents, scheduled the first two weeks of the season to not only pad the gate, but to give Hayes a couple of weeks to iron out wrinkles before Big Ten play began. Typically, Woody treated the first two weeks of the season as mere exhibitions, holding back the throttle on his team to make it more difficult for the rival Big Ten scouts to prepare. But Hayes knew he had to break from the norm against SMU. There were too many questions surrounding his young team, and the nine unproven sophomore starters needed all the game experience they could get. When a visiting writer challenged Hayes's cautious approach to the nonconference games by asking "How much you gonna show?" Hayes, who normally would have berated the out-of-town writer for posing what he considered an insulting question, was unnaturally calm in his answer.

"We'll show all we've got and hope it's enough," he said. "We've got to get back into that win column. This team coming in here is a good one."

Nobody, not even Hayes, knew how his young team would fare in their first real test of major college football in front of a crowd of 73,845 on that pleasant early autumn afternoon. There was legitimate concern about the young defense, but Hayes was even more worried about his new offense. Not only was it untested, but at the controls was Kern, who despite his innate sense of calm, had never taken a snap on a game day inside Ohio Stadium.

Kern, strung out from all the pressure he had to deal with from Hayes during the weeks leading up to the season, couldn't wait for the game. He was a natural leader with an uncommon amount of poise, qualities that wouldn't allow him to get rattled, even before the huge crowd. He was also quicker and more agile than most at quarterback, and he had a quiet confidence in his athletic ability and in dealing with his coach.

"He'd go nuts and pound players, so when it came to game day, he wasn't in the huddle and he couldn't grab you," Kern recalled. "You were free mentally."

Hayes's heavy demands on Kern during the preseason practice would pay off. He realized Kern's firm grasp of the offense, and before the SMU game bolstered the confidence of his young quarterback with some advice that took Kern by surprise.

"Rex, sometimes when you are on the field you'll see things that I don't see and you'll get a sense and feeling that I won't," Hayes told his young quarterback.

The message was for Kern to take total control on the field, and with that came the option for Kern to check off plays at the line of scrimmage that Hayes had sent in from the sideline.

"When he said that, I felt I had the green light to go with my gut instincts," Kern remembered.

It took Kern less than a half to set the tone for the entire season, and to erase any doubts the coaching staff had about his abilities. After a first quarter interception of a Mustangs pass deep in Ohio State territory, the young quarterback led the Buckeyes on an eighty-yard scoring drive, highlighted by a forty-four-yard pass to John Brockington. Kern finished the drive with a two-yard run off the option so perfectly executed that not a single defender got a hand on him as he sprinted into the end zone. After SMU fumbled the kickoff, the Buckeyes scored again, this time via Jim Otis.

SMU countered with a seventy-yard scoring drive of their own. It was a classic, with Hixson completing eleven passes in the twelve-play drive, calmly picking apart the Ohio State defense. It was the potent offense feared by the Ohio State coaches, and it cut the lead to 14–7. But the young Buckeyes showed their resilience and belied their inexperience by quickly scoring again on a three-play, fifty-one-yard drive, led by a forty-one-yard scoring run by Dave Brungard.

Then, just before halftime, with a 20–7 lead, Kern sent Hayes a message. The Buckeyes faced a fourth down and eleven at the Mustangs forty-one-yard line. Hayes, just wanting to survive the first half with a lead, was sending in the punt team to pin SMU deep in their own territory with less than a minute left in the half. But Kern, remembering what Hayes had said about getting a feel of the game that nobody else could get, boldly waved off the punt team and quickly called a play. Hayes, astounded at his young quarterback's defiance, was helpless.

"I felt we were just one play away from breaking the game wide open and our defense was playing great," Kern said later. "Woody had punted earlier in the game on third down and there was no reason to do that, so I called a play before he could change it. I had talked to the lineman and asked if they could take them. Everyone was looking at me in the huddle so I took the liberty to call a play. Then I waved off Woody and got on with it."

"Robust fullback delay," Kern barked out to his stunned teammates in the huddle.

The play was the wrong call. Robust fullback delay was a play from Hayes's old playbook that sent out one receiver. So familiar was the SMU defense with the play that they triple-teamed the receiver and blitzed another defensive back as Kern went into a five-step drop.

But Kern improvised, and with his great balance danced around right end, dodging defenders and spinning out of tackle to somehow get the first down.

"I evaded the blitz and spun around and landed on my feet for a first down," Kern said. "I felt as if I was running for my life. That play ushered in a new era of football at Ohio State."

On the sideline, defensive end Jim Roman turned to Billy Long, the senior backup quarterback who lost his job to Kern.

"Billy, after that you may be playing after all," Roman said.

But there was no way Hayes could have benched Kern, even after he defied his coach in front of seventy-three thousand fans.

On the next play, Kern hit Brungard for an eighteen-yard touchdown pass, giving the Bucks a 26–7 halftime lead, putting the dagger in the heart of the SMU defense.

It was a defining moment for Kern and the Buckeyes, as they went on to beat SMU 35–14. The young quarterback directed the offense that rushed for 227 yards with ten different ball carriers. He also completed eight of fourteen passes for 139 yards in a performance that drew rave reviews.

"There was indeed, a new look about the Buckeyes, and much of it was provided by the inventive Kern, boldly defying some of Woody's theories and substitutions right out there in front the Methodists and 73,855 fans," Kessler wrote in the *Citizen-Journal*. "The six-foot, 185-pound stimulant was a ballet dancer leaping SMU tacklers one time, a traffic cop directing his own blockers. He was a fourth-down gambler. He was also a pinpoint passer with the quickie or the bomb. Finally, he was the most inspirational guy to put on the scarlet and gray in years, as the crowd acknowledged with a standing ovation shortly before halftime."

It wasn't just Kern's heroics that captured the fans and Hayes. SMU threw the ball an amazing seventy-six times to test the Buckeyes' young secondary, but completed only forty passes and scored just two touchdowns. The Buckeyes picked off Hixson five times, three of them by the sophomores on the team. It was a dazzling performance, one that boded well for the rest of the season and even drew the praise of the snubbed Fry.

"Ohio State looked like great football team," he said to the press after the game. "Particularly defensively. We sure ate up a lot of grass, must have been inside their twenty about ten times. But their fine secondary always made the big play."

Kern's performance wowed his teammates, the fans, and the press; but Hayes still didn't see Kern's heroics worthy of being awarded the game ball. Instead, Hayes gave it to a junior linebacker named Mike Radtke, whose wife gave birth to twins the night before the game. Twenty-four hours earlier, when Radtke told the coaches that his wife was in the hospital in labor, Radtke, of course, wasn't with his wife. He was in the Buckeyes' hotel with the rest of his teammates when Hayes called Radtke into his room.

"Your wife better not screw this up," Hayes threatened Radtke.

Kern played the game of his life, but Hayes didn't want all the recognition going his way. So he gave the game ball honor to Radtke as way of congratulating—and apologizing to—the new father.

Ohio State University welcomed 40,270 students in late August, 1968, one of the largest university enrollments in the country. Before the SMU game, few had ever heard of Kern, but after just one game the Lancaster native was on his way toward stardom and an all-American career. But that didn't mean Hayes would hesitate to yank Kern whenever the offense got bogged down or he got hurt, which in Rex's case was often.

Kern was tough, but he was fragile, and with the Buckeyes' offense centered on his ball handling, he got hammered. Fortunately, Hayes had Maciejowksi, dubbed the "SuperSub." The sophomore quarterback gave the Buckeyes good balance at quarterback. "Mace" was built more like a fullback and had a strong arm; but more than anything, he had the knack to be able to come off the bench and make a big play. He was like a relief pitcher in baseball, coming in spell Kern. Hayes also had Billy Long, who had led the Big Ten in passing just two seasons earlier, and when Kern went down, Hayes interspersed both Mace and Long, depending on the situation, giving Hayes probably the deepest talent at quarterback of any team in the country.

THE KIDDIE CORPS   179

He would need all three at various times throughout the season. Kern got hurt the week after the SMU game in the Buckeyes' win over Oregon, but Mace took over at quarterback and led the team to a 21–6 win. The game was almost an afterthought.

Back in the spring, Hayes had spent the team's first practice going over the schedule with his coaches and players, and he began to talk about the past season's game against Purdue. The more Hayes talked, the more incensed he became. Purdue had embarrassed Hayes during the 1967 season with the crushing 41–6 loss in Columbus. During the game, the Boilermakers had built a 35–0 lead before halftime, and their coach Jack Mollenkopf took a seat on the bench, with his hat over his eyes, as he ignored the action on the field for the rest of the game. The Buckeyes game film was shot on the opposite side of Purdue's bench, capturing the sight of Mollenkopf sitting on the bench. Hayes took it as a complete insult, and every time he watched the game film during the off-season, his anger and resentment over his team's failure and Mollenkopf's arrogance rose again. With all of his coaches and players gathered for the first time in the spring, Hayes worked himself into a frenzy, throwing framed pictures against the wall and vowing in front of his team to attack Mollenkopf if the Buckeyes couldn't beat them on the field. The players chuckled to themselves at the outburst, but Hayes proved his point—that no one was more intent on winning than he was, so the team had better match his intensity.

Purdue was coming into Columbus ranked number one in the country, with all-American Mike Phipps at quarterback and Leroy Keyes, the Heisman Trophy candidate, at running back. Hayes spent the week of the Oregon game practicing for the Boilermakers. To Hayes, the Purdue game would be as big or even bigger than the Michigan game. The Buckeyes would be playing the nation's top team in the opening game of the Big Ten season, with his team loaded with sophomores playing in only their third game. No wonder the oddsmakers made Purdue a thirteen-point favorite.

The crowds returned to Ohio Stadium for the Purdue game as 84,834 fans packed into the old Horseshoe on Columbus Day. The players could sense a difference in this crowd, compared to the crowds in the first two home games. More than an hour before they took the field the Buckeyes could hear the buzz of the crowd from inside the locker room. Hayes made it clear that this was no ordinary game, pulling out every trick he could to motivate his team. During the week of practice, Hayes put jerseys emblazoned with Phipps's number 14 and Keyes's number 23 outside the door of the Buckeyes' locker room, so the players could stomp on and spit all over them on their way to and from practice. It was the same trick he used before Michigan games, when he'd put a mat with Michigan colors on the floor, and pictures of the enemy players on the locker room bulletin board. During Hayes's pregame speech before the team took the field to face Purdue, he launched into a lecture about Columbus discovering America, trying to draw parallels about Columbus's struggles and the challenge that awaited the Buckeyes. The history lesson failed to register, and the Buckeyes played poorly in the first half. The Buckeyes missed three field goals in the mistake-filled half, which had Hayes seething at his team, even though they played Purdue to a scoreless first half. Worse was that Brockington and linebacker Dirk Worden suffered knee injuries that limited their play. At halftime Hayes surprised the players by turning the locker room over to his friend Gen. Lewis Walt, commander of the Marine Corps.

It was a masterful bit of psychology. Walt lit into the Buckeyes, talking about how the war in Vietnam related to football, and about the sacrifices and discipline needed to win both on the battlefield and on the football field. Some of the Ohio State players had friends in the war, and Walt's speech stoked the team, whipping them into a frenzy as they charged back onto the field ready to destroy the Boilermakers.

There was no doubting Woody's ability to get his young team ready to play. He knew exactly what was needed to motivate his players, and sending in Walt was a stroke of genius. The emotionally fortified Buckeyes shocked Purdue 13–0, holding the vaunted Boilermakers running attack to just fifty-seven yards in the stunning shutout of the nation's top team. Hayes returned to his pounding running attack as the Buckeyes ground out 333 yards rushing and just seventy-eight yards passing. And the defense played magnificently with the Buckeyes scoring on a thirty-four-yard interception return by defensive back Ted Provost. Hayes's deep quarterback talent also paid off

Lieutenant Commander Hayes on the deck of the USS *Rinehart*.

Woody takes time out of his military
career for some rare family time.
COURTESY MARY HOYT

Woody and his mother, Effie Hupp Hayes.
COURTESY MARY HOYT

Woody with his wife, Anne, and his young son, Steve.

Coach Woody Hayes before the start of his first season at Ohio State in 1951.

A jubilant Woody Hayes with his 1954 team after they beat Michigan to go to the Rose Bowl.

Woody Hayes greets Howard "Hopalong" Cassady as he leaves the field. Cassady was
Hayes's first superstar and helped lead Woody to his first national championship.

Woody and Anne in the early 1960s.

Coach Hayes giving instructions to quarterback Dave Leggett during the rainy 1955
Rose Bowl against USC.

Uncle Woody walks his niece Mary down the aisle. After Woody's brother, Ike, died in 1955, Woody made sure both of Ike's daughters received college educations.

Hayes in 1967 during one of his frequent trips to Vietnam.

Woody with his favorite-son quarterback, Rex Kern, during the 1969 Rose Bowl.

Cornelius Greene, OSU's first African-American quarterback, used his flashy style to add a new dimension to the Buckeyes' offense.

Archie Griffin was the best back to play for Hayes, winning two consecutive Heisman Trophy awards and propelling the Buckeyes to the top of the college football ranks.

Woody Hayes, President Richard M. Nixon (right), and Ohio governor James Rhodes (left). Hayes loved the power that came with political leaders.
COURTESY OSU ARCHIVES

Woody and Bo Schembechler before one of the classic OSU-Michigan games in the 1970s.
COURTESY OSU ARCHIVES

Hayes before the start of the ill-fated 1978 season, his last at Ohio State.

Woody during his commencement address to OSU graduates in March 1986.

when Billy Long, replacing Kern who left the game to wrist injury, scored on a fourteen-yard run. The Buckeyes' winning strategy also included one brutally simple instruction: take out Keyes.

McCullough, Ohio State's defensive coordinator, wasn't about to stop his players from taking shots, as the Buckeyes pounded Keyes every chance they got, including a designed play on a punt where two players would stand Keyes up to allow the fierce-hitting Tatum to take a ten-yard running start before slamming into Keyes. The vicious play worked. Keyes was badly shaken up and left the game. He only gained nineteen yards on seven carries.

Though it was just the second game of the season, the fans mobbed the field and tore down the goalposts. The Buckeyes didn't yet know it, but they were in true championship form.

The Purdue game erased any doubts about the young team's ability to play under pressure, and it left the players swaggering with confidence. They rolled through the rest of the season, beating a tough Michigan State team at home and surviving a scare against Iowa on a miserable rainy day in Iowa City.

The Buckeyes had built a comfortable 19–0 lead at halftime, the defense keeping Iowa star running back Ed Podolak out of the end zone. By the end of the third quarter, Ohio State led 26–6 with Maciejowski again proving to be a worthy sub for Kern at quarterback. During the fourth quarter, the Buckeyes, it seemed, began to think about the upcoming Michigan game. Iowa turned to the pass and scored twenty-one fourth-quarter points, but the Buckeyes hung for a 33–26 win, while holding Podolak to just forty-five yards rushing.

The Buckeyes couldn't wait to get back to Columbus to begin intense preparations for the upcoming Michigan game.

Hayes started nine sophomores when the season began back in mid-September. Three months later the SMU game seemed a lifetime ago, with thirteen sophomores in the starting lineup against number-four-ranked Michigan. Ohio State entered the game ranked number two in the nation, behind USC, and had beaten the Wolverines in Ann Arbor in 1967 in front of a mostly disinterested crowd. But the upcoming rival game was a complete turnabout from the previous season. Michigan, at 8-1, was a vastly improved team, led by Ron Johnson, who just a week earlier had shattered the Big Ten single-game rushing record by running for 347 yards against Wisconsin. The Wolverines defense was better than the Buckeyes', giving up an average of eleven points a game compared to an average of fifteen points allowed by Ohio State.

Though the Buckeyes were undefeated, Hayes spent the second half of the season frustrated by his team. They were winning, but ever since the Purdue game they hadn't been able to put away a team the way Hayes wanted. The offense wasn't crisp, and in the previous week against Iowa Hayes abandoned the I formation in favor of the old T formation offense. But the Buckeyes were also coming around at the right time. Kern, after a season riddled with injury, was back starting, and the defense, led by Stillwagon, Tatum, Sensibaugh, and Anderson—all of whom would become all-Americans—was razor sharp.

The team had also become a particularly close-knit group during the season, with the players also forging strong bonds with their position coaches. On Thursdays when the heavy work of the practice week was over, some of the position coaches would socialize with their players. Holtz had his star-studded secondary over to his house for cokes. Earle Bruce would do the same with his linemen, and defensive assistant Bill Mallory would play basketball against the players during the winter. Chaump did everything he could to shield his quarterbacks from Hayes's unrelenting pressure. Hayes had more contact with the quarterbacks than with any other players, and he demanded more for them than anybody else. Chaump was the buffer, helping diffuse the players' anxieties that were a consequence of having Hayes in their faces all afternoon.

Kern and the other quarterbacks would have to get to practice at 2:30 in the afternoon, an hour earlier than anyone else. They'd head to the field early to take practice snaps and throw into nets. Then, at three, they would attend their position meeting with Woody, before he addressed the whole team.

"He'd talk about life and football, and because it was the late 1960s, he'd go off about how the militants and freeloaders weren't willing to put their reputations on the line," Kern said. "The material would change, but it was always about people who were trying to bring down the establishment, and that no great country could survive if it happened. Sometime he'd go way too far to the right, but his heart was in the right place."

After his civics lectures to the team practice would start, with most of Hayes's attention reserved for the quarterbacks.

"Woody would get very upset over every little thing all the time, things I never even worried about, and I had the task of keeping the quarterbacks focused," Chaump said. "That was my job as an assistant. Rex, Billy, and Mace were great kids, and I tried to protect them from Woody. I chose not to pay attention to him. I just went on with my business."

The business on November 23 was to beat Michigan and return to the Rose Bowl for the first time since the 1957 season.

The week of preparation began on an ominous note. On Tuesday an early snowstorm hit town, but Woody didn't flinch. He led his team through a seventy-five-minute practice in a raging snowstorm, without a jacket, before taking the team inside the French Fieldhouse to hone the passing game. The weather for the rest of the week was arctic, but Hayes would take the field with his team every day without his jacket, to motivate his players during the two-and-a-half-hour practices.

"I'm a great believer in getting the kids acclimated to bad weather," he said. "There's no other way."

Injuries and sickness also plagued the Buckeyes. Tatum, the star defensive back had strep throat and didn't practice until Friday. The defensive star's availability for the season's biggest game was very much in doubt. Brockington was also banged up, his bruised ankle also making him questionable.

Hayes didn't have to worry about motivating his players for the game. They knew what was at stake, and, if anything, the coaches had to prevent the players from peaking too early. It was impossible. At the beginning of the season Hayes had started a new tradition. During the Monday team meetings he would hand out decals of buckeye leaves to the players who performed well during the games. The decals, put on the players' helmets, were symbols of honor and highly coveted.

"Woody was real stingy with those leaves," Kern said.

Come Michigan week, the players were hungrier than ever to earn their recognition. But Hayes also sensed that his players would stand up well under the pressure of such a big game, and he didn't want to alter the practice routine.

"Maybe, because they're sophomores, they don't feel the pressure," he told Kessler. "It pretty much boils down to how I take it. If I don't get mad at them on the practice field, they think something's wrong with me. Sure I rant and rave a little. But it's alright to get mad if you don't stay mad."

By Friday the Buckeyes were ready, after a solid week of practice.

"They were real sharp," Hayes said. "I can't complain."

Hayes stoked his players' emotions at the traditional Senior Tackle ceremony, held annually the Friday before the Michigan game, where the seniors would take one final run at a practice dummy. Then he added to the festivities by agreeing to start the bonfire to kick off a huge student rally.

A record crowd of 85,371 fans packed Ohio Stadium expecting to see a battle between two of college football's titans. The Buckeyes were ranked second in the nation and Michigan was ranked fourth.

Michigan drew first blood with a first-quarter touchdown by Johnson, who a week earlier rushed for 347 yards against Wisconsin. Ohio State came back to score on a five-yard run by fullback Jim Otis ending the first quarter in a 7–7 tie. In the second quarter, Kern scored on a five-yard run of his own, but Michigan came right back to tie the game 14–14. But Otis scored his second touchdown on a two-yard plunge, and the Buckeyes went into their locker room with a 21–14 halftime lead.

The game was living up to its hype. Both teams were driving the ball and exchanging scoring blows, keeping the massive crowd roaring.

Nobody, not even Hayes, expected a second half that saw the Buckeyes score nearly at will, stunning the Wolverines with an onslaught of thirty-six unanswered points to win 50–14. The game turned on the first play of the fourth quarter, when a Michigan linebacker delivered a vicious shot to Kern, slamming him into the Buckeyes bench, while Ohio State was leading 27–14. The hit seemed to spark fire into the Buckeyes, as they reeled off four consecutive scores.

Leading 44–14 with the time winding down on the clock, Hayes ordered his fullback Otis back into the game on a fourth and goal at Michigan's 2-yard line. Otis blasted through the left tackle for his fourth touchdown, and then Hayes allowed the Buckeyes to go for the two-point conversion to put the finishing touch on the rout. The conversion attempt failed, but Hayes and his players weren't about to apologize to critics who accused the Buckeyes of running up the score on the Wolverines.

"We were turned on today, but not too high," Otis told the writers after the game. "The Michigan players were talking to us in the first half, yelling at me that I couldn't run their side, stuff like that; but they quit talking in the second half."

The Buckeyes rushed for 421 yards against one of the best defenses in the country. Otis, the unsung junior, rushed thirty-four times for 143 yards.

"We wanted Otis to carry about thirty times. We are a better team when he's running," Hayes said after the game.

The defense completely shut down Johnson and the rest of the Michigan offense, with Tatum, still not fully recovered, leading the defense with his hard hitting, and with a key interception. He also made a stunning play when he caught the fleet Johnson from behind to prevent a touchdown. The tackle was born of fear as much as talent.

"I had to catch him to keep him from scoring, because we had a 'fire game' on, and I guessed wrong and he whizzed right past me," Tatum told the *Citizen-Journal*.

Hayes deflected the criticism that he ran up the score by pointing to his football team's accomplishments.

"It was the best game ever played by the best football team I've ever had. It deserves to be number one," he said after the game, while outside fans ripped down the goal posts and paraded them down High Street. The celebrating on High Street lasted all night and turned into a near riot, with store windows broken. One goal post found its final resting place on the front lawn of school president Novice Fawcett's house and the other on the steps of the State House. At midnight Hayes and Columbus Mayor James Sensenbenner showed up with members of the marching band and the cheerleaders to help calm the delirious crowd.

Pasadena was next for the Buckeyes, and though it had been a decade since Hayes had been to the Rose Bowl, he took the same approach in preparing for the game. He practiced his team hard leading up to the team's mid-December California departure. Hayes followed nearly the same plan that he had twenty years earlier, when he readied his Miami of Ohio team for their trip to Phoenix to play in the Salad Bowl, by making the Buckeyes practice indoors in the French Fieldhouse with the furnace blasting to simulate the California heat. But Hayes's aggressive approach nearly backfired. On the first day of practice after the Michigan game, Kern dislocated his left shoulder, and though Ernie Biggs, the team's longtime trainer, immediately popped Kern's shoulder back into its socket, Kern didn't practice again until the team got to Los Angeles. "And when I got there I was real rusty," Kern said.

There would be little hint of a vacation when the Buckeyes arrived in Los Angeles. Though the players begged Hayes not to tape their ankles during the flight to California, Hayes ignored their pleas and about an hour out from Los Angeles, he ordered the trainers to begin taping so he could run the players through practice as soon as they landed.

Hayes had led the Buckeyes to Rose Bowl wins in 1955 over USC and in 1958 over Oregon, but now, for the first time, the top-ranked Buckeyes would play the nation's number-two team in USC, a team that was also undefeated, thanks in large part to Heisman Trophy winner O. J. Simpson. But the Bucks' defense wasn't intimidated. They had already shut down two of the country's premier backs in Purdue's Leroy Keyes, Iowa's Ed Podalak, and Michigan's Ron Johnson during the season; only this time Hayes had six weeks to prepare for Simpson. That meant heavy practice sessions both in Columbus and in California, with Hayes taking the same attitude that he displayed the first two trips to Pasadena. Practices would be closed and the team would head to the Pasadena hills the day before the game.

Hayes told the press about sticking to the same routine he used in the last Rose Bowl visit in 1958. "We are a little set in our ways. You know, like taking the team to the mountain retreat, the Passionist Fathers, that's something we started in 1954, and we'll go there again New Year's Eve."

The hard work and isolation paid off. After a Buckeyes slow start that saw Simpson gallop eighty yards for a touchdown to give the

Trojans an early 10–0 lead, Hayes began running the ball, keeping the potent USC offense off the field while wearing out their defense. The Buckeyes ran sixty-seven plays, twenty-five more than USC, and came back to dominate the second half, beating the Trojans 27–16. Kern, who dislocated his shoulder again during the game but returned after the doctors popped it back in, was named the game's most valuable player.

Hayes again had captured the national championship with an undefeated season, but he wouldn't stick around for the glory. Two days later he left on his fourth trip to Vietnam, leaving his players and the rest of Columbus to savor the great season. But before Hayes left for Southeast Asia, he put to rest any debate over where the 1968 team ranked in his already illustrious career.

"It was the best football team I've ever had," he said.

12

OPPORTUNITY LOST

The Buckeyes gathered again in August 1969 to begin what seemed would be an easy run for their second consecutive national championship. Even Woody, the consummate worrier, had reason for optimism when he gathered his team in the North Facility meeting room on the edge of the Ohio State campus to begin practice. It had been a year of triumph for Hayes. The Football Writers Association of America, made up of twelve hundred football writers—many of whom had battled with Hayes over the years—voted him Coach of the Year by a wide margin. When he returned to Columbus from Vietnam in late January, fans were still living off the glory of the previous national championship season, and Hayes was in great demand. The Columbus Area Chamber of Commerce presented Hayes with its prestigious "Columbus Award," in honor of the national championship season. Throughout the year leading up to the 1969 season, various statewide quarterback clubs and other civic groups lined up to honor Hayes, begging him to speak at their luncheons.

Hayes was a master at these public displays of adoration, charming the audiences with a combination of wit, self-righteousness, and self-deprecation, making great theater out of Ohio State football, a show that the mostly male audiences lapped up.

The players got all sides of Woody. Off the field he was the tough-love father who looked out for their best interests, even if that meant showing up at the team's study table to check up on their academic progress. Hayes was one of the first coaches to hire a "brain coach," whose sole responsibility was to monitor the player's academics and, when necessary, arrange tutors and schedule classes to make sure the players stayed eligible.

One of the first "brain coaches" Hayes brought in was Jim Jones, a bright graduate assistant who would eventually become athletic director at Ohio State in the late 1980s. Hayes had his players' best interest at heart when he convinced the athletic department to hire Jones in the late 1960s, but he was also protecting himself. Nearly all of the starters of the national championship team were returning, including the thirteen sophomores that started in the Rose Bowl. Hayes would lose two all-American linemen in Rufus Mayes and Dave Foley, but the overall lack of attrition made the Bucks the overwhelming preseason favorite to repeat as national champions.

On the field Hayes took on an entirely different personality, as he drove his team toward his own view of perfection. Even with a national championship under his belt, Hayes didn't let up on himself or his team. The incredibly heavy demands he put on himself and others seemed only to increase after he won the national championship.

"He was relentless," Chaump said. "But no matter how hard it was for him, he cared about his players and the school. He'd get to work at seven in the morning and he'd go home at midnight. He'd eat alone at work at night."

With a family history of heart trouble, too many fast-food meals eaten by the light of the film projector, and the stress of the job, Woody was heading for health problems. But he wasn't about to back off, even after winning the national championship.

The truth was that Hayes could have eased off a bit, given the immense amount of talent that was returning. The team was mostly set from last year, and it would only improve with another year of experience in running out of the I formation. Kern was entering the season healthy, and was so sharp that it was like he was a coach on the field. He assumed complete command of the offense. Hayes would send plays into the huddle, but Rex was the ultimate arbiter of the offense.

"I had a lot of latitude, but I'd say that eighty or ninety percent of the plays that I checked off at the line of scrimmage were the same plays I would have called," Kern said.

The Buckeyes were in sync the moment they took the field for the season opener against Texas Christian. On the first play from scrimmage, Kern hit Bruce Jankowski on a fifty-eight-yard touchdown pass and the Buckeyes coasted to a 62–0 win. The play was a perfect metaphor for the season. Never before had a team coached by Hayes dominated as the Buckeyes did in the first eight games of the season. With a balanced running and passing attack, they scored seemingly at will: fifty-four points against Michigan State, forty-one against Illinois, sixty-two against Wisconsin, and forty-two against Purdue, as they steamrolled through the season. The Buckeyes defense was equally dominant. With Stillwagon, Tatum, Anderson, and others, the defense posted two shutouts and gave up an average of just over eight points a game. Week after week, Kern and company rolled up yardage, while the defense shut down their opponents almost at will.

The explosive offense barely resembled Hayes's typical, simple strategy of finding the biggest fullback and tackle and letting them blast away at the defense. Now the Buckeyes were throwing regularly on first and second downs, relying on sprint-out plays and the option in a wide open offense that would have been unthinkable in past seasons.

They were, without a doubt, the best team in the nation. Many of their games were nationally televised and, unlike past season, tickets were tough to get for home games. After beating tenth-ranked Purdue 42–14 in the snow in Columbus, Hayes's and the Buckeyes' winning streak reached twenty-two games. The offense was averaging forty-six points and 512 yards per game, gaudy numbers that no one who had spent any time watching a Hayes-coached team could have ever imagined. The Buckeyes were America's team, with late-night congratulatory calls from President Nixon common. Woody and Nixon, by now good friends, would chat over the vagaries of the I formation, foreign policy, and the continuing decline of America's youth.

"By the end of the first quarter the games were already history," Kern said. "We'd score so many points that I'd be out of the game by the second half."

By the last week of the season the Buckeyes had all but wrapped up their second consecutive national championship. All that stood between Hayes and his total dominance of college football were the Michigan Wolverines, who were now coached by former Hayes assistant Bo Schembechler. Unranked and installed as a seventeen-point underdog at the game in Ann Arbor, Michigan, seemingly was a lesser threat than usual to the Buckeyes. Ohio State couldn't play in the Rose

Bowl because of the Big Ten's no-repeat Rose Bowl rule, but a win would still deliver an undisputed national championship.

The Buckeyes had played in a Rose Bowl, but never before had they played before a crowd so large. The record crowd of 103,588 jammed into Michigan Stadium, including 22,000 Buckeyes fans who traveled north to presumably see Hayes capture another national championship; but it remained an intimidating place for the still-young Buckeyes to play.

The junior starters had never played at Michigan, and they had no idea of the vastness of the place when they entered the dressing room from the parking lot. Michigan Stadium is dug into the ground, giving little hint from the outside of its size. When the Buckeyes ran out of the dark tunnel into the bright stadium, they had one universal reaction to the surprisingly hostile surroundings.

"Holy shit!" the players collectively whispered under their breaths as they took the field.

Hayes roamed the sidelines in his trademark short baseball cap and short-sleeve shirt, despite the blustery wintry weather, and immediately it looked the like Buckeyes would continue to do what they had done all season. On the game's first play, Kern scrambled for a twenty-five-yard gain, part of the opening drive that put the ball on the Michigan ten-yard line, where the drive stalled. On fourth down and one, Hayes decided to run Otis up the middle, instead of kicking the short field goal. It was an odd decision for Hayes. Strategy and football logic dictated that on an opening drive in the season's biggest game on the road, you get early points. But Hayes decided to go for the first down and the Wolverines defense held, stuffing Otis for no gain.

The Buckeyes' defense shut down Michigan's first drive and a Larry Zelina thirty-six-yard punt return to the Michigan sixteen-yard line set up a Kern pass to Jan White at the three. Otis then made up for the failed fourth-down try by scoring, and it seemed that the Buckeyes had made up for the earlier lost scoring opportunity.

White missed the extra point attempt and Michigan roared back to score, giving the Wolverines a 7–6 lead. Incredibly, it was the first time the Buckeyes had trailed an opponent all year.

But Kern was his typically cool self in the huddle, and he led the

Buckeyes on a seventy-four-yard drive, hitting White on a twenty-two-yard touchdown pass. This time, White's extra point attempt was good, but a Michigan offsides penalty gave Hayes the chance to go for two points. Hayes committed a cardinal sin. He took points off the scoreboard to go for the two-point conversion. But Kern was sacked, leaving the Buckeyes with a 12–7 lead.

It still appeared that the Buckeyes were on their way to another rout, but inexplicably, their powerful offense stalled. Michigan scored seventeen unanswered points by halftime, as the Buckeyes stumbled and bumbled their way to a 24–12 loss.

It was an embarrassing display for the team. Hayes made some questionable decisions, and his team committed eight turnovers, including six interceptions, and allowed a sixty-yard punt return, to give archenemy Michigan claim to what ABC announcer Bill Fleming called "the upset of the century" during the broadcast. Making the win sweeter for Schembechler and Michigan was that it came after the previous season's 50–14 drubbing.

"You can't talk about the 1969 game without talking about the 1968 game," said Jim Mandich, who played high school football in Solon, Ohio, and was captain of the 1969 Michigan team.

Michigan's win stunned the Buckeyes, who came to Ann Arbor cocky and confident and then left humiliated.

"I was shocked," Kern said. "They were better than us that day. Bo knew Woody so well that he even knew how Woody tied his shoes. Bo got his kids ready to play from the minute he took the job."

A downcast Hayes faced the writers after the game with an honest assessment. In one of the biggest games of his career, his team was ill prepared. No matter how talented the 1969 team was—and it was one of the best college teams ever—the bitter loss not only cost Hayes the national championship, it erased any true measure of the team's greatness.

"We got outplayed and outcoached," he said to the writers after the game.

Five Buckeyes—Kern, Tatum, Otis, Stillwagon, and defensive back Ted Provost—were all-Americans, and a total of eleven Buckeyes were named to the All-Big Ten conference team. None of the honors mattered to Hayes.

The 1969 game was also the first game of the "ten-year war" between Hayes and Schembechler, with nine of the ten games played for the Big Ten Conference championship. Schembechler got the best of Hayes with a 5-4-1 record, but each game was a war unto itself.

"I talked about it all the time. I did something every day to beat Ohio State and to beat Woody. That was the greatest challenge in my coaching, was to beat him. If that added fuel to the fire, so be it," Schembechler said. "You've got to understand, when I came here I was sent to beat one—and only one—team," Schembechler said. "I only wanted Ohio State. That's the team I wanted to beat. Michigan could beat those other guys, but Ohio State was different."

Hayes felt the same way. Upon returning to Columbus following the 1969 loss, Hayes went directly to his office to begin work on the 1970 season.

It would be a far different season both on and off the field. Long-time Ohio State athletic director Dick Larkins retired in 1970 after thirty-four years on the job. Larkins was the driving force behind Hayes's hiring, and he protected him throughout his numerous clashes. More than once Larkins fended off efforts to have Hayes fired, and now Hayes's staunch defender was leaving, an event that could jeopardize Hayes's future. There would be a new athletic director.

Ed Weaver, a longtime member of the Ohio State athletic department, was chosen to be only the third athletic director in school history. Unlike Larkins, who left Hayes alone to build the football program as he saw fit, Weaver was more involved, and he tried to spread the wealth around the athletic department. Under his rocky seven-year tenure, the number of varsity sports jumped to thirty from eighteen. He also was behind the forced resignation of longtime basketball coach Fred Taylor. But Hayes was untouchable. Weaver and Fawcett may not have approved of Hayes's bullying style, and indeed Weaver and Hayes had had their feuds, but come each fall Saturday, the Buckeyes played in front of more than eighty-two thousand paying customers, driving revenues.

"Weaver is scared of Hayes, so also is President Fawcett, whose discrete silence can be heard from coast to coast," Hayes's critic Fullen wrote in the *Ohio State Lantern* after one of Hayes's outbursts against the officials.

Hayes had more to worry about than a new boss. He was stewing over the lost opportunity of the 1969 season. The six interceptions by Kern and Maciejowski haunted him throughout the off-season. He replayed the Michigan tape a million times, going over every play, studying his team's failure, and looking for a way to avoid a repeat of the disaster in Ann Arbor. The upcoming season would be the last for the "super-sophomore" class, and Hayes knew he had to capitalize on a final chance to win with the greatest collection of talent of any recruiting class he'd ever known. His strategy was to retool the offense. Hayes was never comfortable with the I formation, out of which the Buckeyes ran their passing and option formations, the strategy that led to the team's prolific scoring in the past two years. Ohio State may have won one national championship with the souped-up offense, but they also lost one, too. Didn't the six interceptions prove how risky it was? The doubt, the suspicion, and—deep down—the fear of running such a wide-open offense troubled Hayes every time he watched the Michigan debacle on film.

His bitterness over the loss lingered all spring. But there were other, far more serious problems cropping up on the Ohio State campus in April 1970, when Hayes was gearing up his team for the season.

Student demonstrations were sweeping across college campuses, civil unrest was simmering throughout the country, and a new generation rebelled against the Vietnam War, while pushing for sweeping changes in civil rights.

On Wednesday, April 29, a large group of students began to gather for a rally in front of Ohio State's administration building, with other groups heading for campus entrances. All month students had been protesting peacefully, and they were now gathering for a strike rally in front of the administration building. The picketing of several campus buildings began and, according to the police, groups from various student organizations, such as Students for a Democratic Society and the Young Socialist Alliance were leading the protests.

According to university documents, these groups were "observed attempting to work crowds into a frenzy by calling for direct, violent action against the police."

Just after three P.M. university officials asked for help from the state's highway patrol, to open a gate at Eleventh and Neil avenues, where demonstrators had gathered in a sit-down demonstration that blocked the gates. The university's version of what happened next is that the crowd attacked a contingent of plainclothes police officers with rocks and bricks. The undercover cops called in reinforcements consisting of ninety uniformed highway patrol officers, sparking a riot that ended when Columbus police, called in to help by the highway patrol, tear-gassed the crowd. The protestors dispersed, but assembled again on the oval, where speeches were heard. Meanwhile, up and down High Street other violent skirmishes between students and police erupted.

Ohio State University President Fawcett, who earlier during the month had tried to allow the demonstrations and still keep order, gave up, and Ohio Governor James Rhodes wasted no time in calling in the Ohio National Guard.

"Once it became evident that the techniques of negotiation and persuasion were not having the desired effect, the appropriate university officials made the decision to use force to restore order and protect lives and property in the campus area," was the official police version of Fawcett's decision to send in the troops.

Hundreds of Ohio National Guardsmen moved into campus at midnight and began gassing and beating the demonstrators. By the next morning the police reported 175 arrests and the university hospital reported twenty-seven injuries to police officers, eighteen injured students, and eight nonstudents injured in the riot. Eight of the wounded students sustained gunshot wounds.

Ohio State wasn't the only college protesting the war during the tumultuous spring of 1970. On May 4 the National Guard was called in to quell demonstrations at nearby Kent State University, and guardsmen shot and killed four students. The shootings sparked even more violence on the Ohio State campus for the next few days.

Finally, on May 6, following a daylong battle between the students and the National Guard, Fawcett decided to close the campus. According to university documents, a crowd of hundreds of protestors "roared its approval and marched over to Ohio Stadium and rang the victory bell that usually sounded after a Buckeyes win."

That first week in May ended the most violent period in Ohio State history, with hundreds of students hurt and extensive property damage seen along High Street and on campus. Fawcett reopened the university after twelve days, but tensions still ran high. The day after a peaceful "Day of Reflection" was organized on May 20 by the student strike coalition in response to the Kent State shootings, another full-scale riot erupted, with students lowering the American flag that flew atop the campus administration building. The escalating violence spilled onto Columbus streets, and five thousand National Guardsmen were ordered back into the area, as store windows were smashed and looting occurred all along High Street. By the next day the guardsmen had gassed and beaten the students on a large scale once again. Rallies and demonstrations continued, but it seemed that the students and the police both seemed to grow tired of the daily protests. By June curfews were lifted, and the emergency ban on liquor sales was ended. After a month of violence and unrest, calm was restored.

Hayes, guardian of his football empire and defender of the establishment, wasn't about to ignore the strife on campus. Setting aside his intense planning for the upcoming season and yet another trip to Vietnam, he threw himself into the middle of the campus demonstrations and rallies, urging calm restraint, and for the students to back down from their protest demands. He also preached the same beliefs to his players, many of whom were caught between joining in with their fellow student protestors and following the rigid beliefs of their coach.

"Woody was out there on the Oval with the protestors, and he'd grab a bullhorn and tell the students to express their beliefs, but not to be destructive," Kern said. "He believed in Nixon, and he believed in the establishment, but he really wasn't afraid to talk to the students. He wanted to stay close to the action."

The student protests were a paradox to Hayes. His belief in the republic made it difficult to hear the shouts of the antiestablishment students, yet he believed in their right to gather, and he felt that the violence used against the students was completely unjustified.

"There were no pros, no outside agitators," Hayes said. "There were some pretty militant kids, but by God, they were our kids."

With the spring riots over, Hayes again turned his full attention to his Buckeyes. When the team gathered again in August to prepare for the upcoming season, the players quickly discovered a new plan of action.

Despite the juggernaut of an offense, Hayes ordered the coaches to scrap much of the previous season's dynamic offense. It was back to the old three-yards-and-a-cloud-of-dust style that put a drag on Kern, Brockington, and the other former "supersophomores" who were now in their last season.

"We're not going to make the mistakes that we did last year," Hayes thundered to his team.

"After we got beat in nineteen sixty-nine our offense shrunk," Kern said. "So we went from the wide-open offense that was unpredictable to a very predictable offense, to where we were running the ball forty-two times a game."

The Buckeyes started the season just like the previous season, with a 56–13 victory over Texas, but the margin of victory was misleading. Hayes had no intention of taking the shackles off the offense, and though the Buckeyes again came to the Michigan game undefeated, scoring was down by a total of one hundred points, compared to the 1969 season, as Hayes again relied on the fullback to carry the offense.

The games were much closer, with more pressure put on the vaunted Buckeyes defense to win games. By midseason the word was out among other Big Ten coaches that Hayes had fully abandoned his once-explosive offensive attack and was going back to relying almost solely on the fullback.

The Buckeyes were still winning, but the other coaches knew that in Hayes's retreat back to the old days, his team had lost its air of invincibility.

The Buckeyes almost lost to Northwestern at home. Behind 10–7 at halftime, Ohio State struggled to rally and finally did win 24–10. Then the Bucks nearly lost to Purdue, before edging out a 10–7 win.

"[Purdue coach] Alex Agase told me, 'We were so scared of you guys after what you did in nineteen sixty-nine, until we saw Woody come out with the offense. We couldn't believe it. The old man was back to running a Model T,'" Kern said.

Hayes was drilling the Buckeyes into the ground. They'd run the same simple plays over and over—plays they had mastered long ago. Each mistake brought new wrath from Hayes, who knew that the perfection he demanded on the practice field would carry over to the games. The older players sensed that the outbursts were sometimes pre-meditated, but still the practices grew tiresome to both the players and the coaching staff. After a while the team was practicing only for the sake of practice.

"You'd wonder why you couldn't do things more efficiently," Chaump said. "It wasn't that it was all hard work. The truth was that we wasted a lot of time. He'd spend so much time worried about rou-tine stuff like kickoff returns that it got to be ridiculous at times."

Meanwhile, Woody's family life went on without him. Steve, who graduated from Ohio State in 1967, earned his law degree in 1970, and he began a clerkship with Ohio State Supreme Court Justice Robert Leach. Anne took her life as a football widow to the speakers circuit where her vivacious personality and husband's football fame made her a popular draw.

Hayes's preparation during the 1970 season was focused on one game: the November 21 game at home against Michigan. The Buck-eyes were undefeated and ranked fifth in the nation. Michigan was un-defeated and ranked fourth. It would be the first time since 1905 that two undefeated and untied teams would battle for the Big Ten title, but Hayes was more interested in exacting revenge on his former assis-tant Schembechler.

Fans filled the Horseshoe an hour before the game, and when the two teams took the field they did so in front of a national television audience and 87,331 fans, the biggest crowd ever to watch a game in Ohio Stadium.

Hayes was better prepared this time. He put a new wrinkle into the offense, with a two-tight-end formation that put even more blockers at the line of scrimmage to help with the power-run game strategy. The formation caught Schembechler off guard and confused Michigan's defense.

The Buckeyes forced a fumble on the opening kickoff that led to a field goal. Kern later hit Jankowski for a twenty-six-yard touchdown strike to make it a 10–3 game. The Wolverines scored next, but the Buckeyes blocked the extra point attempt, holding to a slim 10–9 lead. The defense did its part by limiting the Wolverines—who averaged 247 rushing yards per game—to just thirty-seven rushing yards. Late in the fourth quarter linebacker Stan White intercepted a Michigan pass and returned it to the Wolverines nine-yard line, the key defensive play in a thrilling 20–9 win.

Hayes called it another one of the greatest games in Ohio State history, and the Buckeyes were again heading back to the Rose Bowl, where they would be favored to beat Stanford. Hayes was back on top and brimming with confidence when he took his team to Pasadena. After the usual two weeks of hard practices on the West Coast, Hayes once again took his team up to the monastery on New Year's Eve. While the assistant coaches stayed up drinking and telling stories with the monks, the players went to bed expecting their second Rose Bowl win in three years.

But the Buckeyes faltered badly. Though they dominated the game with a ground game the chewed up 380 yards, they blew a 17–13 fourth quarter lead to lose to the Jim Plunkett-led Stanford team 27–17. Hayes could only watch hopelessly as Stanford's defense stopped Brockington for no gain on fourth down and inches to go at the Stanford 16. Plunkett then took his team down for the tying touchdown, and then added another to seal the stunning upset.

"It was a game of missed opportunites," a subdued Hayes said after the crushing loss.

Hayes's "kiddie corps" lost just two games in three seasons, for a 27-2 record. Seven players from the class were named all-Americans during their Ohio State careers; Kern, Tatum, Stillwagon, Anderson, White, Brockington, and safety Mike Sensibaugh. But those impressive achievements and personal accomplishments were diminished by the crucial losses that cost Hayes and the Buckeyes a national championship and a Rose Bowl win. Kern, Tatum, Stillwagon, and Brockington moved on and starred in the pros, and the lessons Hayes drummed into them would remain. Kern, especially, stayed close to Hayes. After his professional career with the Baltimore Colts ended, he returned to Columbus, got his doctorate, and remained a central figure in Buckeyes football and a key confidant of Hayes for years.

13

FLAM

Hayes ushered in a new era at Ohio State in 1971 by doing more than replacing Kern and the rest of the departed, star-studded senior class. Ever since Indiana State University became the first college to install Astroturf on their football field in 1967, Hayes was intrigued by the new product. Anything that could eliminate the unknown on a football field captured Hayes's attention, and he demanded that Ohio State install the synthetic turf, invented by Monsanto, because it meant a surer, faster footing for his players, and that meant less uncertainty come game day. Besides, Monsanto was an American company, and to Hayes that made the investment even more attractive. The only problem was getting the university to see it his way. He couldn't convince Ohio State to pay for the new turf, not with the ever-present criticism that football was more important than academics.

The university was struggling to meet its budget, and financial problems would only worsen if the school paid up to $500,000 for the new surface—something that was seen as nothing but a newfangled luxury. But by 1971 an increasing number of other big football schools were installing the turf, and Hayes didn't want to fall behind.

The first college football game on artificial turf was played in 1968 at the newly built Astrodome, between the University of Houston and Washington State University. Since then, the University of Texas installed the plastic turf and so did Tennessee. Hayes wasn't about to sit around and watch a bunch of administrators argue over how to fund it, so he put the word out. Surely, some deep-pocketed Ohio State football supporter would write a check to cover the costs. After all, the quality of the football team was at stake, and after the departure of Kern, Tatum, Stillwagon, and all the others, Hayes needed every advantage available to rebuild his team.

Hayes's call for help was answered by Lou Fischer, a guard from the 1951 team who had gone on to make a fortune in a fast-food restaurant partnership with some former members of the Baltimore Colts that included Gino Marchetti, former Wisconsin star Alan Ameche, and Fischer's former Buckeyes teammate Joe Campanella. Fischer had no problem writing the $380,000 check. By doing so, he could honor his fallen teammate Campanella, who a few years earlier died suddenly of a heart attack. But there was some other satisfaction to be gained by Fischer.

Hayes and Fischer battled each other during those early years of Hayes's career, and Hayes would have much rather preferred the money would have come from a player like Brubaker, Cassady, or any of his favorites; but he had no choice but to accept the donation from Fischer. He couldn't turn down the generous gift, and then turn around and ask the university to spend tax dollars on his pet project.

There would be a greater source of frustration for Hayes in the upcoming season, in addition to the funding of the new turf. The Buckeyes were in a rebuilding year, and Hayes, to put it mildly, wasn't used to losing. But the Buckeyes couldn't come close to the talent level of the past three years, and each week the frustration built. Finally, in front of 104,016 fans in Michigan Stadium, Hayes snapped. Maybe it was the talent drain, or maybe it was having to field his inadequate squad against Schembechler's powerhouse, undefeated team, but Hayes launched into a rage so spectacular that it was the talk of college football for weeks. After the Buckeyes were intercepted late in the fourth quarter to seal a 10–7 Michigan win, Hayes—furious at the officials for missing what he felt was an interference call on the play—stormed out to the middle of the field to confront the officials, halting play. The animated attack on the referee resulted in a fifteen-yard penalty, but Hayes wasn't finished. After screaming at the other officials, Hayes was shown the sideline by some of his own players. Once deposited to the bench. Hayes sprinted down the sideline toward the officials, grabbing a yard marker and busting it over his knee and tossing the mangled equipment onto the field. Then he stormed over to a first down marker and shredded it into pieces. The Buckeyes may have been used to these antics, but to the fans and the national television audience it was shocking. Hayes, still fuming after the game, blew by the press; but the rest of the country had seen what those close to the program saw on a regular basis. Across the country, writers had a field day about Hayes's boorish behavior. Jim Murray, the syndicated columnist for the *Los Angeles Times,* railed into Hayes, pointing out that Hayes for years had gotten his fair share of favorable calls. Murray sarcastically suggested that if Hayes was righteous about the quality of the officiating, then Ohio State should forfeit any games in which the referees had made calls in the Buckeyes' favor.

Weaver and Fawcett never said a word. Still fresh off the string of Rose Bowl wins, few with any connection to the university dared threaten Hayes. Only his old foe Fullen demanded some accountability. In a scathing editorial published in the school newspaper, Fullen indicted the university for excusing Hayes's antics, and condemned college football factories.

"This time the Angry One is not mad at one football official. The *Miami Herald* quotes him as saying, 'I hate them all.' It figures. They're the only persons connected with any phase of his life whom he can't bully and browbeat. In fact, that vindictive nature is why our new athletic director Ed Weaver was quoted as saying 'he understood' the Ann Arbor game disruption. He's scared of Hayes and so also is President Fawcett, whose discreet silence can be heard coast to coast. Our chosen leaders have run for the bushes. So what's new? A winning king can do no wrong. And who spoiled the brat? The university, which could have averted its shame at Ann Arbor by cracking down on Hayes long ago. The line now is 'he went out on the field for his kids.' Weren't ten men out with knee surgery enough for one season, or do we have to *win* at any young man's cost in pain and danger of permanent injury. And the university fosters such wretched contradictions when Reason, Truth, Ethics, and Honor are its symbols. . . . A degraded university is to be condemned more than Hayes, who knows by now what he can get away with. If you don't think our alma mater has lost standing and credibility, here's what somebody at the golf course cracked yesterday: 'Hell, giant emporiums like Ohio State are no longer universities with high standards, they're conglomerate combinations of academic supermarket and amusement park.'"

The harsh criticism had no impact inside the Ohio State program. The players knew that the outside world had seen merely one side, albeit an unattractive one, of Woody's personality. The critics never saw Hayes's commitment to his players. They never saw the guidance or understood the lessons he taught so many of his players. To the players the outbursts were one of the ways Hayes was trying to protect them, and they knew the demands were his way of trying to help them develop not just as players, but as responsible adults.

The general public never knew about the countless private visits between the coach and legions of former players who regularly returned to Columbus. Woody kept track of his former players, many of whom he now counted as friends, and he helped in any way he could. Invariably, his players returned the favors.

Even his Matte, Hayes's old quarterback, who had battled his coach on nearly a daily basis, was a chief ally. Whenever Hayes was recruiting in the Washington-Baltimore area, he stayed with Matte, sleeping in the guest room and regaling Matte's children with stories of their father's past heroics. Then the former adversaries would stay up late, talking not about just football but life.

"We had a love-hate relationship for a long time, but he had a profound impact on me," Matte said.

Kern, Woody's favorite-son quarterback, saw the outbursts as one of the ways his old coach defended the team.

"He fought for his players, and that's why so many of his players loved him," Kern said. "He was totally focused on seeing that we got an education. That meant accountability, and it started with Woody. If it came time for you to go to graduate school or to get a job, Woody led your parade and was behind you."

The Ohio State faithful shrugged it off merely as another indication of Hayes's will to win, and the incident faded, as did the memories of the forgettable 1971 season that saw the 6-4 Buckeyes end their year under a cloud that would hover over program until springtime.

Seventeen freshmen players came to Columbus in August 1972. Just three of the freshman were black; Archie Griffin, the high school all-everything from Columbus, Cornelius Greene, a lithe, cat-quick quarterback from rough-and-tumble Dunbar High School in Northeast Washington, D.C., and Woodrow Roach, a star high school running back, also from the Washington area.

Of the three, Greene looked the least impressive. He was six foot one, barely more than 170 pounds, and lacked the physical strength of the typically fullback-sturdy Ohio State quarterback. Though Greene racked up tremendous statistics at Dunbar High, it was against inferior competition, compared to some of the powerhouse high school programs in Ohio, Pennsylvania, and other Northeastern states. Greene's best sport in high school wasn't even football, it was baseball. He hit .500 his senior year and had racked up a 42-4 pitching record during his high school career, averaging ten strikeouts a game. But football was a way to get a college education, something that precious few eighteen-year-old boys from the Greene's D.C. ghetto were offered.

Greene, who was raised by his aunt and uncle, was one of the Washington area's top prospects, and recruiters flocked to his house, including Rudy Hubbard, who was assigned by Hayes to scour the Washington area for talent. Hubbard showed up to visit Greene and, like the others, was shocked to discover just how small Greene was for someone who was gathering so many headlines. The odds of Hubbard convincing Greene to come to Columbus were long. For one thing, Greene had ties to the state of Michigan. He spent summers staying with family in Flint, and Michigan State University long had been recruiting Greene hard, using Jimmy Ray, the school's first black starting quarterback, to convince Greene to come to East Lansing. And there were the under-the-table offers thrown at Greene and his hard-luck family to help sway his decision. But Greene started to consider Ohio State more seriously after a disastrous recruiting visit to Michigan State, where Greene's host player abandoned him at a party, leaving him to find his own way back to the hotel. A few weeks later, Greene visited Columbus and hit it off with the black players who took him under his wing.

"We hung out, went to some parties, and hung around some white guys, and it gave me a good feeling," Greene said. "I was in an environment with less than five percent blacks, but I felt comfortable, and it was like a fraternity."

At dinner at the top of the Sheraton Hotel during the Friday night of Greene's visit, he met Hayes along with ten other recruits. Hayes wasn't impressed and was brutally honest with Greene.

"Most of the other coaches promised me I'd start right away, but Coach Hayes looked at me and told me my neck was too small and that I might get hurt," Greene said. "He told me that I'd only play if I was good enough, and if I wasn't I wouldn't. It was a little disturbing to hear from him the total opposite of what I'd been hearing from other coaches."

Back home in Washington, other schools were tempting Greene with more than promises of playing time.

"Lots of schools were offering cars and cash, usually between ten and twenty thousand dollars, but my aunt pushed me to go to Ohio State because they were the most honest," Greene said. "Woody also said I could play baseball, so I signed the first day I could."

His decision was met with disdain and doubt. Friends, neighbors, and rival schools shook their heads with regret knowing that Ohio State never had a black starting quarterback. Middle linebackers and quarterbacks: those were the positions at Ohio State reserved for white players only.

"I knew the whole history, that there were no black quarterbacks or middle linebackers, because those were positions supposed to be for the smartest players, but to me it was an old stereotype, and I was cocky," Greene said. "So many people told me I couldn't do it, but I just knew I could."

Greene reported for practice in late August with one hundred other players. His roommate was supposed to be Roach, who was black and from the Washington area. Together, they'd be each other's security blanket against the overwhelmingly white world.

Green walked into a quarterback meeting on the first day of summer practice and he sat down with five other white players. After practice Greene went back to Stradley Hall, opened the door to his room, and found Brian Baschnagel, a suburban white kid, unpacking his bags. Hayes had determined that if there was going to be a black starting quarterback at Ohio State, he'd better learn how to relate to his white teammates, and, without telling Greene, he had switched room assignments.

"I'd never been around white people, but Brian and I ended up as best friends," Greene said. "We did everything as brothers and he taught me a lot. We covered for each other and shared our backgrounds, and the whole experience made me a better person."

The first year at Ohio State was a miserable one for Greene, who found himself at the bottom of the depth chart while he struggled to grasp the offense. It was Griffin, the short but muscular tailback, who blossomed into a dominating player during his freshmen season—while Greene languished at the end of the bench. Both were good friends, but opposite in personality. Griffin was Hayes's favorite, the golden boy who would become the only college player to win consecutive Heisman Trophy awards. Sturdy, dependable, and loyal, Griffin was the unassuming superstar held by Hayes as the epitome of Ohio State football.

Greene was all big city and flash, with a big afro, platform shoes, and stylish clothes that earned him the nickname "Flam" for his flamboyant style and personality. But the outward flamboyance masked Greene's insecurity.

"I was scared to death of Woody," Greene said. "The offense I ran in high school was a split T, and I had no idea what I was doing when I got to practice. I was horrible, and everything was different, and I was a klutz. I was quickly sent to the scout squad and I was the last quarterback. I was lost. But it was like 'you're in the army now,' and I got with the program. I was up at six for breakfast, caught the bus to practice, practiced twice a day, ate dinner, and had meetings at nine at night before going to bed."

Greene quickly found himself in Hayes's doghouse. He had sauntered one evening into the team's meeting room after Hayes took the podium.

"I arrived one minute late for a nine o'clock meeting and he read me the riot act," Greene said. "As I made my way down the aisle, everyone in the room but me knew better, and I was never again late for anything."

One of the ways Hayes liked to gauge the freshmen quarterbacks was to send the player up to the varsity field during practice, to shake up the starter while seeing how the new talent handled himself with the unexpected pressure. Hayes did it with Kern and now he would do it with Greene.

"Greg Hare was having a bad day, so Woody called me up . . . I didn't know the plays, but I had no sense to tell him. Woody called the play in the huddle and I turned the wrong way and ran into the full-back and fumbled, and Woody goes off on me, screaming 'Get him out of here,' so they sent me right back down. I spent about two minutes up with the varsity and I was devastated. For the rest of summer practices I couldn't I sleep, and I was getting ulcers."

Despite the poor first audition Hayes saw the raw talent in Greene, but he knew he wasn't ready. Chaump worked with Greene, making him his personal project. Slowly, Greene responded and he regained his confidence both on the practice field and in the classroom. A decent student at Dunbar, Greene nonetheless had a hard time adjusting to college academics. Mandatory freshman study table helped, and to catch up Greene took to the tutoring during the first semester. At practice, he began to run the scout team with authority, and his incredible scrambling ability made him nearly untouchable, even against the first-string defense.

"George Hill, the defensive coordinator, always wanted me to give the players the look of the opposing team, and one day I went back to pass and scrambled out of the pocket and faked Randy Gradishar so hard that he fell down and hurt his knee," Greene said. "Woody had to call time out and bring out the trainers, and that's when I started getting respect."

Greene's newfound respect didn't mean playing time. The Buckeyes dressed 114 players for the season opener against Iowa. The NCAA had in 1972 reinstated a rule allowing freshmen to play on the varsity, but Greene sat on the bench while Hayes sent Griffin in for one play. If it was any consolation to Greene, it was when Griffin, destined for stardom, committed a cardinal sin, causing Hayes to bench him. Now both were in Hayes's doghouse.

"My only goal was to make the varsity, so Woody sends me in— and I fumbled," Griffin said. "I couldn't believe it. I thought I'd never play for Woody again."

But Griffin's talent was too obvious, even if Hayes despised fumblers. During the next game against lightly regarded North Carolina, the Buckeyes offense stalled. Hayes, furious at the first-team offense, sent fifth-string Griffin into the game to send a message to the starters. Two hundred and thirty nine yards later, Griffin walked off the new artificial turf holding the Buckeyes single-game rushing record, while vaulting to the top of the depth chart. Greene, too, would get noticed when he made his varsity debut that day. Inserted after the Buckeyes had already sealed their 29–14 win, a nervous Greene played poorly, bumping into his running backs with poor ball handling. Hayes didn't need him anyway. With Hare at quarterback and Griffin at tailback, the Buckeyes rattled off seven consecutive wins before losing to Michigan State. The next week the Buckeyes beat Northwestern 27–14 in Evanston, setting up yet another blockbuster game against six-point favorite Michigan in Columbus.

Michigan, ranked third in the country, came into rainy Ohio Stadium favored by six points, an insulting line for the ninth-ranked Buckeyes.

It was a day for defense, given the cold and rainy conditions, but Michigan, behind Ohio native Dennis Franklin at quarterback, the Wolverines rolled up 344 yards to Ohio State's 192 yards and ran eighty-three plays, nearly double the Buckeyes' forty-four plays. But Michigan could only score one touchdown in the 14–11 loss, despite running twelve plays from inside the Buckeyes' five-yard line. Led by linebacker Randy Gradishar, the Buckeyes defense held on two dramatic goal-line stands. Both times the Buckeyes stopped Michigan on fourth and inches, with a stubborn Schembechler refusing to kick what would have been easy field goals to tie the game and send Michigan to the Rose Bowl.

The win gave the Buckeyes the right to go to Pasadena—where trouble awaited. While the Buckeyes were on the field during their pregame warmup, *Los Angeles Times* photographer Art Rogers was training his camera lens on Hayes as he huddled with his coaches. Hayes was incensed at what he saw as an invasion of privacy, even though Rogers was a credentialed member of the press. Hayes shoved the camera into Rogers's face. Hayes insisted he had not used his fist and was grabbing at the camera, but Rogers filed assault charges. The charges were later dropped, but the Big Ten was finally forced to rein in Hayes by putting him on probation. One more incident could lead to his dismissal.

The incident was just the start of what was a decidedly bad day for the Buckeyes. Top-ranked Southern Cal was loaded on offense, with Sam Cunningham and Anthony Davis giving USC the best backfield in the country. Lynn Swann led the team at receiver, and, all told, twenty-three members of the Trojans team would go on to play professional football.

The game, played in front of a record crowd of 106,869 fans, was close at the start, with the first half ending in a 7–7 tie. But then the bigger and faster Trojans took over. Ohio State gained 287 rushing yards, but the senior-laden Trojans ran all over the Buckeyes. Davis gained 157 yards and Cunningham scored four touchdowns, while quarterback Mike Rae completed eighteen of twenty-five passes in the 42–17 drubbing.

The loss and the assault charges against Hayes dampened what had been a remarkable year for the Buckeyes. Gradishar and offensive lineman John Hicks were all-Americans, but Greene contributed little. After his unimpressive performance in the North Carolina game, Greene barely played, seeing only mop-up duty for the rest of the season.

Greene wouldn't make his mark until the spring game, when he ran for two touchdowns and threw for two more. The dominating performance forced Hayes to seriously consider the ramifications of starting Ohio State's first black quarterback. But first Greene would have to beat out Greg Hare during preseason practice.

That summer, Greene heeded Hayes's advice and stayed in Columbus. Hayes had arranged a construction job for Greene and some of the other players, but the main goal was for Greene to improve his quarterbacking skills. Every day after work he met with Chaump, and together they refined the young player's footwork and his understanding of the game.

"George was patient and he worked me out every evening," Greene said. "I really started to come around."

While Chaump was working with Greene, his latest quarterback project, Hayes was spending the summer finishing up a project of his own,

You Win with People, a self-published book on his coaching life that touched only on his great successes. While Hayes was getting ready to publish the book, a writer named Robert Vare showed up unannounced at the team's North Facility in May 1973 with a freelance contract from *Harper's Magazine* to profile the combustible coach. Usually Hayes wouldn't bother with a writer who as an outsider could not be trusted. But Vare wasn't like the other football writers who came looking to sniff the glory of Ohio State Football. Vare had written about Joe Nameth and Muhammad Ali, and Hayes, aware of the more serious and literary approach, wanted to be included in the same company. Besides, *Harper's* had run a piece on Darrell Royal a few years earlier, taking the University of Texas football coach out of the sports pages and exposing him to a more serious, intellectual audience. Hayes wanted the same treatment, and so he made an exception and allowed Vare to hang around the training complex during the summer of 1973.

"He was flattered by the attention of *Harper's* and he was flattered that I wasn't a sports guy, and that was big," Vare recalled. "Sports figures were now being seen much more in social and political terms, as being examples of larger forces. It was the first time Hayes had been paid attention to, and he wanted to be treated as more than just a football coach, he wanted to be treated as a political figure."

Hayes, the ultimate opportunist, also figured that Vare could help him edit his new book.

"He thought I could help him, and he used me as a sounding board. I even did some line editing of his book," Vare said. "We both used each other."

Hayes did his best to impress the Vare, granted him full access around the North Facility and took him to the Faculty Club for lunch or dinner, where the two would talk politics, history, and just about anything but football. They didn't have much in common. Vare was a liberal-minded East Coast writer, and then there was the conservative, Republican Hayes. Vare found himself taken by Hayes's forceful and dynamic personality.

"On a personal level, Hayes was incredibly likable," Vare said. "He was charming, smart, and funny. I just didn't agree with him about anything. But he had an interesting combination of bigheartedness, great values, and he had a great interest in books and philosophy. But he had not grown in a way that he might have, given his brain and generosity of spirit. He took pride in caring for his players, but he could be so brutal. He had this intellectual pursuit, yet he was so inflexible. He long ago had decided how he viewed the world, and he was so set in his ways that there was no changing him. He just didn't see any nuances to the world."

Vare spent all summer with Hayes, and instead of writing a lengthy magazine article, Vare discovered he had enough material to write *Buckeye,* a best-selling book that described the Ohio State football machine during the 1973 season. It was a sometimes unflattering portrait of Hayes that included revelations of his brutality and control over the program. When the book was released, Vare sent Hayes a copy and a letter of explanation and appreciation, but Hayes never spoke to Vare again.

"I never talked to him about it, but he went on his television show and denounced me," Vare said. "He said I had come out and represented myself, but said I turned out to be just like everyone else. He thought I had been set up by the University of Michigan, and his rant helped the book a lot, but then he clammed up."

When the Buckeyes began practice in late August 1973, Greene was already sharp from a summer spent with Chaump, but Hare also reported in great shape to begin his senior season. The incumbent starter had led the Buckeyes to the Rose Bowl, and, as cocaptain, he was again expected to take the Buckeyes to the top of the Big Ten.

A football coach loves nothing more than heated competition to bring out the best in his players, but the battle between Hare and Greene posed some potential problems for Hayes. Married and a father, Hare was popular among his teammates and, most important to Hayes, could be trusted with the ball. A good season could also help his chances of moving on to the NFL, where he could support his young family far better than most recent graduates. Hare fit the part of an Ohio State quarterback with his Jack Armstrong image, his leadership abilities, and his rifle arm; but the reality was that Hare was a one-dimensional quarterback who lacked mobility.

Greene was inexperienced, but his tremendous athletic ability made him far more versatile. Hayes could run him out of the option, or in a more traditional offensive set, and, if he had to, Greene could throw. But it was his scrambling ability that was another dimension that Hare lacked. Greene was far more difficult to defend against, but he was also unproven. There was another far more serious consideration: Hayes had no idea how Greene would stand up to the pressure of starting at quarterback. Race relations had improved in America by 1972, but bigotry and prejudice still existed. Ohio State was one of the last Big Ten schools that didn't have a black starting quarterback, and there was pressure on Hayes to break the color barrier. Hayes wasn't being accused of being a racist. Too many blacks had come through the program to justify any accusation, but there would be a lingering sense of Jim Crow hanging around his football team until a black player lined up at quarterback on fall Saturday afternoons in Ohio Stadium.

Hayes would also have to deal with any impact on team morale that the benching of a senior cocaptain in favor of an unproven sophomore would have on the team. Hayes knew that if he started Greene there would be talk that Greene was only starting because of his color, not his ability, and it put Hayes in a sensitive position. People could rail against Hayes for his boorish behavior toward officials, his violent temper, and his power-hungry ways, but no one could argue that Hayes wasn't fair. He proved time and again that the best players played. Some players might get lost in the shuffle, or some might get hurt, but most got a fair shake. Hayes cared greatly about his reputation, and any whispers that he was playing Greene out of politics rather than merit could damage the team. But the drama of the decision was lessened after Hare hurt his hamstring two weeks before the season opener. It at least gave Hayes more reason to insert the young, flashy Greene at quarterback.

Hayes never made a public issue out of the first black quarterback to start for the Buckeyes. He didn't want to make it a distraction, and, frankly, he didn't make up his mind until just before the first game of the 1973 season, a game against Minnesota. And when he did decide he didn't tell Greene. Instead, Greene read about in the paper.

"I didn't even know he selected me to start," Greene said. "Greg was a great guy, but he was crushed. Here he was the captain, and with a wife and a kid; he couldn't wait for his senior year to start, so he could go to the pros. But you know what. He put it all aside and he helped me out."

Greene immediately made his presence known. He scored a touchdown on the Buckeyes' first possession, and after he scored, he danced in the end zone to celebrate his success.

"I don't know why, but I just broke into a dance after I scored. I didn't even know I was doing it, but it was something you just didn't do. Woody didn't say anything to me. Then we scored again and I kept dancing. Then everyone started being more colorful, but Woody never reprimanded me."

The Buckeyes won easily 56–7. Greene played as if he were a battle-tested senior, leading the Buckeyes to touchdowns on four of the game's first six possessions.

Hayes made sure that Greene's early success did not go to his young quarterback's head.

"I became his whipping boy during practice," Greene said. "He was with the offense every day, and I was so young that I'd drive him crazy. He'd push you around, grab you, and I was still kind of weak and he hurt my feelings. He rode me and I learned to practice like it was a game. It got so bad I couldn't wait for the games when he wasn't in the huddle."

Away from the field, Hayes was sensitive to the sting of racism that Greene endured. A steady stream of hate mail would roll into Greene's mailbox, including threats from the Ku Klux Klan.

"The KKK type of stuff really upset me," Greene said. "I had to go talk to him about it."

"They don't know who you really are," Hayes would tell his quarterback as he ripped up the letters. "Never believe that you are the person they say you are."

Hayes also tried to bridge the color barrier by the choice of movies he'd show his players on Friday nights before the game. Choosing the movie was serious business. Hayes wanted the movies to represent his ideals, and help his players get in the right mood to play the following afternoon. Westerns were big, and of course so were war

movies. Though it was the early 1970s, Hayes forbid any antiestablishment movies like *Easy Rider,* that were so popular. But one Friday
night, Hayes took the team to *Trouble Man,* a blaxploitation film with a
Marvin Gaye soundtrack.

"I couldn't believe it," Greene said. "He took the entire team to a
black movie. It just showed how he didn't discriminate."

Greene was uncomfortable being the one to break the color barrier,
and he said very little publicly about the significance of beating out
Hare. To escape the burden, Greene took refuge by visiting the black
neighborhoods, where he was seen as a hero but treated as an equal.

"I'd get out into the city and I met a lot of folks who were in their
fifties and sixties who, back in the day, could attend Ohio State, but
couldn't live on campus and they'd tell me their stories. They couldn't
believe times had changed and they were proud to know me, and it was
great."

Greene found comfort off the field, but he took a vicious beating
every time he stepped on the field. He played at 170 pounds, and Hayes
used him on rollouts, bootlegs, and the option, exposing Greene to getting hit on nearly every play. Griffin, now the feature back, also took a
pounding under Hayes's run-dominated offense. The difference was
that, during the week Hayes allowed Griffin to rest. Greene, on the other
hand, had to practice no matter how sore he was from the previous
game.

"He beat it into to me that I had to practice," Greene said. "Me
and Archie both got clobbered, and I could be beat to hell, but I had to
practice; but the more I practiced, the better I got."

14

INSURRECTION

By mid-November, the Buckeyes were cruising to an undefeated season, as the team headed into another "game of the century" against undefeated Michigan. Arguments broke out in barber shops and taverns all over the state over which team was better—the undefeated 1968 team with Tatum, Brockington, and Kern, or the 1973 team led by Greene and Griffin and a stout defense. Greene and Griffin were getting the publicity, but it was the crushing Buckeyes defense that had led to nine consecutive wins leading up to the Michigan game. The defense had been so dominating that it had four shutouts and held opponents to a paltry average of 3.7 points per game. Gradishar was the anchor at middle linebacker, with Tim Fox, Neal Colzie, and Steve Luke starring in the almost impenetrable defensive backfield. A win over Michigan would send the Buckeyes back to the Rose Bowl and, like the 1968 team, a shot at yet another national championship.

Nationally, there was another argument raging, this one over the Watergate affair involving Hayes's friend Richard Nixon. A week before the November 24 Michigan game, Nixon uttered to the nation that he was "not a crook," as the Watergate break-in had all but crumbled Nixon's presidency. Just a year earlier Nixon had crushed George McGovern in a landslide election, but now the embattled president was fighting a losing battle for his office. Hayes and Nixon spoke often, mostly after Buckeyes games, when Nixon would reach Hayes by phone to rehash the plays. Needless to say, Hayes saw no evil in Nixon's amateur cover-up and, despite overwhelming evidence to the contrary, Hayes refused to believe that Nixon was wrong. Friendship, loyalty, and respect for the office, made it impossible for Hayes to accept Nixon's crime. Instead, Hayes blamed Watergate on Daniel Ellsworth, a former aide who leaked the Pentagon Papers to the media, calling Ellsworth "a traitor."

Nixon, Hayes said, had every right to cover up the Watergate burglary, because world peace was at stake.

"I think [Nixon] was set up," Hayes said. "If a nation ever tried to commit suicide, the United States tried to do it with the treatment of Richard Nixon. I would have done the same. Do you think he's so stupid to send in a bunch of damn amateurs who didn't even know how to tape a door open? He's not that dumb. He had to cover it up."

While Watergate was toppling a presidency, Greene and the rest of the Buckeyes were preparing to face Michigan. Greene was going into the game hurt, after jamming his right thumb during the previous week's game against Iowa. Hayes had kept the injury from the media, but Greene struggled to grip the ball in practice all week leading up to the Michigan game. Greene refused to sit out, because if he didn't practice he wasn't going to play.

It was a miserable week of practice. Hayes expected perfect execution from his quarterbacks and receivers. The ball, he demanded, should never hit the ground during passing drills, and Hayes would rip his hat to shreds, or smash his watch, if passes were dropped or intercepted. The only problem was that Hayes, who had also installed artificial turf on the Buckeyes practice field, would wet down the turf thinking it softened the turf for his players. But the balls got wet in the process, increasing the odds of a bad throw, especially by a quarterback who could barely hold onto a dry ball, much less a ball made slick by the wet turf. Much of Hayes's dissatisfaction with the quarterbacks was aimed at Chaump, who was responsible for their performance. Making matters worse for the players and Chaump was that Hayes had begun filming every practice, to better monitor the team. Before the coaches ate dinner they'd review the practice tape, and with each dropped or intercepted pass captured on film Hayes would go off again.

"He'd throw the projector and chew me out, but I got to be friends with the team managers who edited the film, and they would edit out the interceptions and bad plays," Chaump said. "They were great kids. Most of the time Woody couldn't remember what had happened on the field."

One Christmas the managers gave Chaump a beautifully wrapped present. Inside was a film compiling the outtakes of Hayes's outbursts.

"I lost that tape; but what I wouldn't give to have it back," Chaump said.

Hayes rested the battered Griffin during the week, but Greene, bad thumb and all, practiced. Greene was healthy enough to start by the time the team was ready on Friday to travel to Ann Arbor. Writers Kessler and Hornung made little mention of Greene's injury in the stories leading up to the game. When the team was ready to depart for Ann Arbor, few knew of the seriousness of Greene's injury.

Hayes's travel plans rarely varied, but Hayes's mood reflected the magnitude of the game. For each road game, the players would be responsible to get to Port Columbus Airport by themselves. Then the team would eat at the airport before boarding the plane. When they arrived, two buses would meet the team. Hayes, the coaches, and the first string would travel in one bus. The second bus was for everyone else. Then, when the team arrived on the visiting campus, Hayes would sometimes take them to a historical place of interest. In Illinois, for example, he'd find some link to Abraham Lincoln and drag the players through an impromptu history lesson. But trips to Michigan did not include any sightseeing. They were tense, quiet trips, with Hayes taking the team right to the stadium upon arrival, instead of to some historical landmark. The starting quarterback got his own seat on the bus, and when Greene boarded the bus to go to the stadium, he was glad to be alone. He was afraid to tell Hayes that he had reinjured his thumb during practice.

At six-thirty the morning of the Michigan game, Hayes called Greene into his room for the ritual quarterback meeting over toast and juice. Hayes wanted to make sure Greene had mastered the game plan, but he also wanted to know about his thumb.

"It was an exam, but it was cool," Greene said. "It helped me prepare, but the problem was my thumb."

The weather was also an issue. It was a rainy day, and Michigan had also installed artificial turf, and the combination of a slick field and Green's injured thumb had Hayes worried. Any ideas of Hayes opening up the offense were deteriorating along with the weather, and by the time the game began in front of an NCAA-record crowd of 105,233 and a national television audience, Hayes was determined to control the ball. Hayes kept the Buckeyes offense under tight wraps during the first half, as both defenses dominated. Hayes decided that with Greene's thumb injured, he'd put the offense in the hands of Griffin. It looked like a promising strategy after Griffin pounded out ninety-nine yards in the first half. Griffin gained forty-one of those yards on five straight carries, putting the ball on the Michigan five-yard line. Freshman fullback Pete Johnson plowed into the end zone for the touchdown, to give the Bucks a 10–0 lead at the half.

Greene and the Buckeyes reached their locker room brimming with confidence. They had shut down Michigan's offense, while managing to score ten points off Michigan's defense—a squad that was just as tough as Ohio State's. A shutout of Michigan at home was a lot to ask of Buckeyes defensive coordinator George Hill, but if Griffin had gained nearly one hundred yards in the first half, the odds were that he could do the same in the second half, and surely that would lead to more points. The coaches also felt that it was time to open things up on offense, and they mentioned it to Hayes as they took the field for the final thirty minutes.

But Hayes ignored the advice. Maybe he was still haunted by the six interceptions thrown in an earlier Michigan loss, or maybe he worried about Greene's thumb, but Hayes ordered nothing but running plays. Even when Michigan put eight men on the line of scrimmage to bottle up the run, Hayes kept running Griffin and Johnson into the line.

"He tightened things up," Griffin said. "He didn't want to pass with Cornelius hurt, so we ran the ball."

Michigan gained confidence on every series, and despite the pleas from the Ohio State assistant coaches, Hayes continued to shrink-wrap the offense, frustrating both the Ohio State players and coaches. On a fourth and two on Michigan's 34-yard line, Greene decided to take matters into his own hands by changing the play at the line of scrimmage with an audible to a quarterback keeper. Michigan held and the Buckeyes turned the ball over on downs. A few plays later the Wolverines kicked a field goal. After stopping Ohio State's next drive, Michigan drove to the Ohio State 10-yard line. On fourth and inches, Michigan quarterback Dennis Franklin faked a run up the middle and scored. After the extra point the game was tied 10–10.

By now the Ohio State coaches were furious with Hayes, who continued to ignore their pleas to balance the offense. Late in the fourth quarter, Griffin was on the sideline, too battered to continue. Franklin again had the Wolverines on the move, but left the game after breaking his collarbone. Hayes then decided to bench Greene, with a minute left in the game, in favor of Hare, a better passer than Greene. But Hare's first pass was intercepted and returned to the Ohio State thirty-three. With twenty-eight seconds left and the ball on the twenty-eight-yard line, Michigan lined up for the winning field goal, but kicker Greg Lantry missed wide right. Hayes then sent in three pass plays, but all fell incomplete and the game ended in a tie.

The Michigan players, confident that they would go to the Rose Bowl, celebrated in their locker room, while across the tunnel confusion, anger, and frustration boiled over in the Buckeyes locker room after the game. The Big Ten athletic directors would meet the following day to determine which team would go to the Rose Bowl, but the Ohio State players and coaches felt defeated, and they fully expected that Michigan would win the vote to go to Pasadena. Even Hayes felt Michigan would go.

"We won the first half and they won the second half, and a tie is never satisfactory," he muttered to the press after the game. "Now it can be told, our passing is no good and has not been all season. We can't pass."

Except for the score, the Buckeyes had been beaten in all phases of the game. Michigan had outgained Ohio State 303 yards compared to 254, had sixteen first downs compared to nine by Ohio State, ran sixty-eight plays compared to the Buckeyes, who ran fifty-three. The assistant coaches were well aware that they had lost the statistical battle and were furious at Hayes's conservative strategy. The old man had refused to listen, stubbornly sticking to play after play of running Griffin into Michigan's defense—a defense that was waiting for him at the line of scrimmage.

Greene left the game after throwing just one pass. Griffin had thirty carries for 163 yards in an heroic effort. Hayes insulted his team further after the game by saying that the 1968 team was better, since they went undefeated.

Even the mostly benevolent Columbus press criticized Hayes for his strategy after the game.

"It might be unkind to say this game was a needless tie because the old coach blew his cool, betrayed his own ball club. But it wouldn't be fair to the effort and preparation of the players not to say it. That may not be entirely fair to the well-organized Bucks, who had too much enthusiasm, too much talent to be hamstrung by an unimaginative attack," Kessler wrote in the *Citizen-Journal*. "The head man may have been too satisfied with that 10–0 first-half cushion, as he went conservative the last half—and paid for it. Conservative! It's a matter of record that they did not make a glaring mistake against the Wolves beyond coaching conservatism."

For the next twenty-four hours rumor and speculation was swirling around the vote. Michigan supporters swore that Hayes would influence the vote and that the athletic directors would use Franklin's injury as an excuse to keep Michigan home, in order to give the Big Ten a better chance to win the Rose Bowl to be played against USC.

They may have been right. The next afternoon, the Big Ten athletic directors gathered in Chicago and in a secret vote elected to send Ohio State to the Rose Bowl. An outraged Schembechler ripped into Big Ten Commissioner Wayne Duke, charging that Duke had swayed the vote to Ohio State because he didn't want Michigan to have to play a second-string quarterback.

"I'm very bitter and very resentful," Schembechler fumed to the press. "Petty jealousies were involved, and they just used the injury to Dennis Franklin as a scapegoat. I'm very disappointed in the administration of the Big Ten. It hasn't been very tough and it hasn't been very good. My team earned the right to go. This is the lowest day of my life as a player and a coach. I'm bitterly resentful at the way this thing was handled."

Then Schembechler said that Duke was "running scared," and he challenged Duke to come to Michigan and tell the players to their faces that they weren't good enough to play in the Rose Bowl.

Duke called Schembechler's charge that the vote was rigged "totally absurd," while Hayes downplayed Franklin's injury and claimed Ohio State was a better team.

"What probably influenced the directors more than Franklin's injury was the fact that the coaches who faced our team and Michigan said Ohio State was the tougher opponent," Hayes said.

While the Big Ten athletic directors were voting, the Ohio State assistant coaches were conducting an informal poll of their own. The coaches were so frustrated that they were threatening to refuse to go to Pasadena if Hayes didn't listen to their concerns and open up the offense against USC.

The players weren't told of the coaches' near-mutiny, but sensed that things were even more tense than usual between Hayes and his assistants.

"We didn't know about it, but we knew the coaches were upset," Greene said. "They were on our side."

The Buckeyes arrived in Pasadena on December 20 and were shocked to learn that Hayes had extended curfew to one A.M. Practices were also easier and, incredibly, there were no double sessions scheduled. Hayes even gave the team two consecutive days off and waived curfew on Christmas Eve. He was more relaxed, even with the hated West Coast press. The only slight occurred during a press conference when a writer asked Gradishar if last year's assault on Rogers had any impact.

"Enough of that," Hayes said, cutting off the question and abruptly ending the press conference. "We came out here to play football, not to rehash things like that."

The California writers nonetheless had a field day with Hayes's return. One columnist from the *Los Angeles Herald-Examiner* ripped into Hayes and USC coach John McKay, who backed Hayes, by writing: "The Rose Bowl game and the parade are covered by 1,000 reporters and cameramen. The way McKay looks at it, 999 were untouched. So what's the big rap at Woody?"

Hayes adjusted his practice schedule to allow the Buckeyes to attend more events, including an extended trip to Disneyland, which met Hayes's wholesome entertainment standards.

"The thing I like about it is it's good, clean entertainment," he said. "It's not like a movie . . . with the porno, the bloodletting. It's extremely difficult to find a good movie. As a father, I always had certain standards and ideas of what my son should see in the way of a movie, and I don't think, as a coach, I should take someone else's son to the wrong movie."

Hayes even allowed himself to be the butt of a joke during the team's Christmas Party when guard Jim Kregel, who had dressed up as Santa Claus to hand out presents to the coaches' kids, put Hayes on his lap as the players roared.

"We may not have a gift for you now, but we will January first," Kregel said. "Are you in a good mood?"

"Yes I am," Hayes said, playing along with the gag.

"Well, that's a switch," Kregel said, with the room in hysterics. "Just for that I have a diet candy cane for you."

Hayes even allowed the team to spend New Year's Eve in the Huntington Hotel, instead of the usual night's lodging at the monastery. The truth was that the players who were making their second consecutive trip to Pasadena had come to almost dread the trip west. For one thing, Hayes brought them to Southern California two weeks before the game, and it was too long to be together. The practices became monotonous. While USC coaches allowed their players three days off for Christmas, the Buckeyes practiced hard all through the holidays. The only break was a Christmas party, when the team put on a show. Griffin and Greene sang a rendition of "White Christmas," and John Hicks, the all-American lineman, dressed up as Santa Claus. It was a night of revelry, but the players would have preferred spending time with their own families.

"We hated it," Greene said. "We went out way too early, and we just got tired of being around each other. And I hated staying in that monastery. Woody did it so we could get rest, but I was a city boy and I was scared to death in those mountains. We slept in single rooms with no curtains and the wolves and coyotes would be howling all night, and it drove me nuts."

Greene was surprised that he didn't have to stay in the monastery before the USC game, but more shocking was the game plan. They didn't know it, but Hayes had acquiesced to his coaches and agreed to open things up against USC.

The first Buckeyes play from scrimmage during the Rose Bowl

was a pass by Greene that was intercepted. Horrified, Greene didn't want to go near Hayes on the sideline, but he tackled the defender out of bounds near Hayes on the Buckeyes' sideline. Hayes immediately called Greene over to where he was standing, but instead of screaming at his quarterback, Hayes was uncharacteristically calm.

"We're still going to pass, so be ready," Hayes said.

Stunned, Greene headed back to the bench for a drink of water.

"I thought he was ready to let me have it, but he was cool and he kept my confidence," Greene said.

With a healthy and confident Greene at quarterback, Ohio State bombed USC 42–21, with a rejuvenated and balanced Buckeyes offense that racked up 449 yards. Griffin gained 149 yards, but Greene was named the game's most valuable player by leading the Buckeyes in the comeback win.

The Buckeyes returned to Columbus with armloads of honors. Griffin and end Van DeCree were selected as all-Americans, and Gradishar and Hicks were repeat all-Americans. Hicks also won the Outland Trophy and the Lombardi Award, and he finished second in the Heisman Trophy voting behind Penn State's John Capeletti. But there was one award the Buckeyes did not win. Hayes's poor coaching during the Michigan game factored heavily into Ohio State vying for a shot at the national championship, which went to undefeated Notre Dame.

On June 5, 1974, the constant work and worry, the rages, the bad diet, and the never-ending pressure to win caught up to the sixty-one-year-old Hayes, and he was admitted to University Hospital after suffering a heart attack. The heart attack was a wake-up call for Hayes. There were too many steak dinners at the Jai Alai, Woody's favorite restaurant, just down the road from his office, where he had a "personal" table. He rarely exercised; and he was also a diabetic who routinely allowed his blood sugars to go out of whack, the imbalance wreaking havoc on his body. The doctors implored Woody to change his diet and to slow down, but all too often he would binge. Someone once sent a tin of smoked sausages to the house. Anne, worried about her husband's weight, hid the tin in a cabinet under the oven, but Hayes sniffed out the goods and ate the entire tin in one sitting.

"I was too damned heavy and too ornery," Hayes said later of his heart attack.

Hayes listened to the diet advice and shed twenty-five pounds by the time late August rolled around, but he wasn't about to change his intensity. When players reported to practice the thinner Hayes was still his old self.

He refused to cut back on his typical fourteen-hour workday, pouring just as much effort and energy into his job as he did before the heart attack; but it was the start of what would become a more steady series of health problems that would plague Hayes for the rest of his life.

Hayes may have been struggling with his health, but his Buckeyes were in fine form. The combination of Greene and Griffin gave them an unprecedented explosiveness on offense, and they roared through the first half of the season, winning eight straight games, scoring an average of forty-five points per game.

Griffin was nearly unstoppable, the workhouse back racking up seventeen consecutive games of rushing for more than a hundred yards, including the 1973 season. Greene's deadly combination of running and passing talents kept opposing defenses off guard, and it seemed that the Buckeyes were invincible. On November 2 Hayes captured his two-hundredth win in this 49–7 rout of Illinois. The team went 8-0, but any hopes for an undefeated season were dashed the following week against Michigan State, when the vaunted Ohio State offense that just a week earlier seemed unstoppable was outscored in the 16–13 controversial loss. Once again, the Buckeyes found themselves at the mercy of Big Ten commissioner Wayne Duke, who spent nearly an hour sorting out the confusion from a crazy last-second play.

With the ball on the goal line and the Buckeyes down 16–13, with seconds remaining, the ball was snapped under Greene's legs before it was picked up by receiver Brian Baschnagal, who ran it into the end zone for what seemed to be a game-winning score. But the officials were confused. While one official ruled that time had expired, another signaled touchdown, causing so much confusion that Duke was called in to sort out the mess. He finally ruled that time had indeed run out, giving Michigan State the win at home.

Inside the visitor locker room Woody exploded upon hearing the decision. He confronted Duke, who was at the game, and berated him in front of his team.

"I wanted that undefeated season more than anything I ever wanted in my life," he later said. "I'd give anything—my house, my bank account, anything but my wife and family—to get it."

Hayes recovered to lead the Buckeyes to wins over Iowa and Michigan, sending the team back to the Rose Bowl to play USC with a 10-1 record. But USC stopped Griffin, who had won the Heisman Trophy, and the Buckeyes lost 18–17.

The 1975 team returned Griffin and Greene and, as expected, Ohio State rolled through the season. They were unstoppable on offense and surprisingly strong on defense, shutting out Michigan State, Iowa, and Wisconsin on their way to an undefeated regular season, a season including another win over Michigan, to go to their fourth consecutive Rose Bowl to face UCLA. They had already beaten the Bruins by 41–20 earlier in the year and were heavily favored, considering that, as the number-one team in the nation, they entered the game giving up a total of seventy-nine points all season. Beating UCLA and capturing another national championship would be the crowning glory for Hayes as he marked, not celebrated, his silver anniversary at Ohio State.

But it was not to be. The lightly regarded Bruins shredded the once-stout Ohio State defense in the second half, gaining 366 yards, and they pounded the Buckeyes 23–10 in one of college football's biggest upsets. Griffin had broken his hand and was limited to seventeen carries, while Greene threw two interceptions to blow a comeback. After the game, a devastated and shaken Hayes took the blame.

"We got outcoached," he said grimly after the game, and then refused to engage the press any further. When pressed for more answers, Hayes angrily left the room, adding to his already legendary reputation of an attitude toward West Coast writers.

The game turned out to be Hayes's last shot at a national championship. Never again under Hayes would there be such a collection of great talent. Griffin again won the Heisman Trophy, establishing himself as one of college football's greatest running backs. Greene was the Big Ten Most Valuable Player in 1975 and three others—Tim Fox, Tom Skladeny, and Ted Smith—joined Griffin as all-Americans. But the successes were dampened by the consecutive Rose Bowl losses and the blown national championships.

It took Hayes just two seasons to rebuild from the great 1970 class led by Kern, but Hayes would have no such luck in replacing the now departed class that featured Griffin and Greene. Rod Gerald, another black quarterback, was waiting to take over for Greene at that position, but there was simply no replacing Griffin at tailback.

In 1976 the Buckeyes still managed a 9-2-1 record, but they lost badly to Michigan 22–0. Instead of a trip to Pasadena, the Bucks went to Miami and played in the Orange Bowl, beating Colorado 27–10. It was the first postseason game for the Buckeyes other than the Rose Bowl. In 1977, the Buckeyes were Big Ten co-champions once again, but lost to Michigan 14–6 for the third consecutive loss. It was an ugly defeat, with a fateful incident. Hayes again lost control of his emotions when the Buckeyes fumbled near Michigan's goal line late in the game. ABC cameraman Mike Freeman then turned his lens on the coach, capturing Hayes slamming his headphones into the ground. Hayes saw Freeman capturing the tantrum from close range and punched Freeman in the stomach. After the game the unrepentant Hayes told the writers he had every reason to punch Freeman.

"How would you like it if they stuck microphones and cameras in your face all the time," he said in his post-game news conference.

Another ugly incident in what was becoming a long list of transgressions.

This time Duke put Hayes on one-year probation. Any more incidents, Hayes was warned, and he would be fired.

It was an ugly end to a frustrating season for Hayes, but the 9-2 record was good enough for an invitation to the Sugar Bowl, to play Alabama. Hayes would coach against Bear Bryant. It was supposed to be a classic matchup of two powerhouse programs, led by two of the greatest coaches in college history. New Orleans wasn't Pasadena, but Hayes took the same martial approach to the game, bringing his team down to New Orleans two weeks early.

It was too long a trip. The players were tired. The coaches and the players, accustomed the grandeur of the Rose Bowl, complained about everything from the food to the field. In contrast, Bryant's refreshed Alabama team arrived in New Orleans just four days before the game and pounded the Buckeyes 35–6 in a game that was never close. It was the worst bowl performance ever by the Buckeyes under Hayes, and for the first time speculation spread that after twenty-six years, maybe the old man was beginning to lose control of the program.

15

THE PUNCH

Art Schlichter came to Columbus in late August 1978, heralded as the next savior of Ohio State football. Arthur, as his friends and family called him, was a rare specimen of a quarterback—tall, smart, athletic, and blessed with a rocket arm, he was one of the most sought-after high school quarterbacks in the country. As an Ohio boy playing in the Buckeyes' backyard, in Blomingburg, a farm town just forty minutes south of Columbus, Schlichter never lost a football game he started at Miami Trace High School, and he was the 1978 national high school player of the year. Every college in America wanted Arthur, and Hayes was pulling out all the stops to get him to commit to Ohio State. Chaump spent so much time recruiting Arthur that he almost became a member of the Schlichter family. But this was no ordinary recruit.

Schlichter was wanted by hundreds of colleges. But so were most other Ohio State recruits, and Hayes could always handle the competition. But this time, things were different. Arthur's father Max was heavily involved in where his son would play, and Max knew how Woody Hayes felt about the pass. To win Schlichter's favor, Hayes promised to change the offense to suit an unproven player's talents, something he'd never done before, not even when Archie Griffin was waffling over signing with Ohio State, or when Kern was considering his options. But the past few years had brought a relative drop in talent to Columbus, and Hayes was so determined to land a player like Schlichter that he had little choice except to acquiesce, to do something he'd never done in twenty-seven years of coaching at Ohio State.

That alone was a sign of the times. Kids were different than they were just a few years earlier. Nowadays they didn't just want a free education, they wanted the fastest route to the NFL. The league was beginning to pay big money to players. As a result, recruiting got more complicated. Kids who hadn't done a thing wanted to play as soon as they stepped on campus, and they wanted to go to schools that could showcase their talents to the NFL. If Schlichter were a running back or a linebacker, then Ohio State would be the place. But nobody from Ohio State had gone on to star in the NFL as a quarterback. The Baltimore Colts turned Tom Matte into a running back. Even Rex Kern couldn't crack the NFL as a quarterback. The Colts drafted him as a defensive back. The Schlichters knew that better than anyone, and their son was definitely professional material so Hayes did what he had to do to get Schlichter to commit. He promised that he'd open up the offense for Arthur and emphasized all the national exposure that would come from playing at Ohio State.

The promise worked. Schlichter signed with Ohio State and he won the starting job in his freshman year, beating out senior Rod Gerald, who Hayes shifted to split end to better his NFL prospects.

"Woody told Arthur that he'd throw eighteen times a game, and that had convinced him," Chaump said. "And when he got here he was fabulous."

On Thursday, August 24 at seven-thirty P.M., Hayes held his first squad meeting for the upcoming season. In his prepared notes Hayes listed eight topics to be covered. None had to do with the actual playing of football. Instead, he preached to his players what he expected. He demanded promptness and that the players stand up straight and be alert. He lectured them to have no self-pity, and he told them that "people will treat you the way you treat people." He also laid out the Buckeyes' winning attitude, which was comprised of "better players, better coaches, better morale, better conditioning, and better people."

The speech was his stock address, full of Hayes's pet sayings. He underlined and spelled out in capital letters in his notes "YOU ARE EITHER GETTING BETTER OR YOU ARE GETTING WORSE. YOU ARE NEVER, NEVER STAYING THE SAME." And, "NO EASY WAY. DON'T OUTSMART 'EM, OUTWORK 'EM," as if he were reminding himself of the importance of the messages. He told his squad: "No haters and no drugs," and that he wouldn't tolerate swearing (though he was exempt from that rule). There would be no

"Levis, T-shirts, wives and girlfriends" at the golf course where the team gathered for dinners. "Get up early," he implored his team, "and put wrinkles on your brain, not your face."

The topic he spent the most time on was behavior, urging his players to treat people well and to be careful choosing friends. Teammates, Hayes wrote in bold print, are "THE BEST PEOPLE YOU WILL EVER KNOW."

Opening day—Penn State, at home, in front of a sold-out crowd. True to his word, Hayes let Schlichter pass, but it was a disaster. The previous summer, Chaump had spent a few weeks with Bill Walsh at Stanford and came back to Columbus praising Walsh's offense, a strategy that featured short passes with multiple receivers. The sophisticated offense protected the quarterback with quick three-step drops, instead of seven-step drops, allowing the quarterback to throw the ball quicker and avoid pressure. It also featured numerous receivers and ball fakes to keep the defense guessing. Schlichter's talents suited the offense perfectly, and at first Hayes embraced the offense, but then he backed off, convinced that sending out multiple receivers left the offense vulnerable to the blitz. Only it was the other way around. When Schlichter or any other quarterback was taking seven step drops with no fakes or audibles, it was an invitation for the defense to tee off on the quarterback, and that's exactly what Penn State did in welcoming Schlichter to major college football.

Unable to cope with a barrage of blitzes, the Buckeyes fell behind early, and Hayes abandoned any suggestions from Chaump to use a scaled-down version of Walsh's offense.

"When we got behind we were dead," Chaump said. "We went to a simple passing attack and we got killed. There were no fakes, no checkoffs, and no short, little passes. We got blitzed and sacked."

Schlichter managed to complete twelve of twenty-seven passes during the Penn State game, but there was too much pressure on the eighteen-year-old quarterback. He threw five interceptions in the 19–0 loss, and suddenly Hayes's promise that he'd open up the offense was all but forgotten.

The rest of the season was a jumble of frustration, confusion, and anger between Hayes, his star freshman quarterback and Max Schlichter, who was holding Hayes to his word. Chaump, who grew close to Arthur, was caught in the middle. Chaump was loyal to Hayes, and after eleven years he was thought to be a frontrunner for the job, whenever Hayes decided to retire. But Chaump was also troubled. In the past, the assistant coaches would confront Hayes if they felt he was straying too far from what they thought was good for the team. Hayes encouraged the questions, and sometimes the conflicts, knowing they served as an effective system of checks and balances.

Hubbard had pushed for Hayes to start Archie Griffin, Chaump had lobbied for Kern, and the coaches nearly quit after the 1973 Michigan game that ended in a tie. But now the coaches seemed to be positioning themselves to win favor with Hayes in order to have a shot at his job, and the Machiavellian drama was taking its toll on the team and the coaching staff. Morale had plummeted, and while it was never easy to play and to coach for Hayes, winning made it fun and worthwhile. Now, with the team struggling, it was approaching pure drudgery.

"Woody was great in getting assistant coaches who were willing to stand up to him, but things had changed," Chaump said. "Instead of standing up to him, some of the coaches were telling him the bullshit he wanted to hear, and that included telling Woody how great he was. It was discouraging."

The turmoil was reflected in the team's record. The Buckeyes finished the season with a 7-3-1 record, but they lost badly to Michigan and finished fourth in the Big Ten. Still, the drawing power of Ohio State football convinced organizers of the Gator Bowl to invite the Buckeyes to play Clemson. The bowl invitation salvaged the season, but behind the scenes the relationship between Hayes and the Schlichters deteriorated week by week, and all the drama was taking its toll on the team.

"Arthur's father was a dominating daddy, and Woody got more conservative as the year went on, and the daddy was upset by it all," Chaump said. "It got ugly. I was close to Arthur and started to be his father, priest, coach, and counselor. Woody was driving Arthur nuts. He was relentless."

One of the Hayes's strongest attributes as a coach was his ability to get close to his players. He took the time to find out about their families, friends, and their circumstances, which helped bridge the gap between coach and player. It gave him a good understanding, and a sense of how to motivate his players, and it kept his finger on the pulse of his team. There weren't many coaches, like Woody, who cared enough to personally tutor players or show up at the player's room at night to make sure he was studying, or show up in the morning to make sure the player went to class.

Woody even liked to shower with his players occasionally after practice, to show everyone that even though he might rip their heads off during practice, they were still a team. He would also stand outside his office door after practice watching the players file out. As the team passed by his office, he'd call in certain players who he was particularly rough on during practice and explain why he did what he did. He'd break the players on the field, then build them up after practice, sending their spirits soaring as they prepared for another game.

Hayes had turned sixty-five earlier in the year and he was aging fast. He tired more easily, his heart and diabetes were constant sources of worry, and he was beaten down by the struggles with Schlichter and the mediocre season. The players too were different, and Woody was becoming more removed from his team.

There had been talk of Hayes retiring after the previous season, but he wasn't about to leave after the disastrous Sugar Bowl loss to Bear Bryant and Alabama. Hayes still felt he could rebuild the Buckeyes into championship form, but instead he had to settle for an invitation to the Gator Bowl. Other schools gladly would have jumped at the chance to play in the game, but it was a second-tier bowl, especially for the Buckeyes. It wasn't even a New Year's Day bowl game. Instead, it was played on a Friday night in Jacksonville, Florida, on December 29, serving as an appetizer to the more prestigious New Year's Day bowl games. The Buckeyes weren't even going to go Jacksonville, but in the end Hayes and the players decided it was better than staying home. The payout to the university was also too good to pass up, and, besides, the game would give Hayes another few weeks of practice for next season. At the least, the game would help his budding freshman quarterback develop more quickly.

The Buckeyes tried to make the most of their trip, at least on the practice field. The bitterness of the Michigan loss had faded some-what, and Hayes and the coaches were anxious to play again, to dis-tance themselves from the disappointing season. Schlichter was also improving. The weeks of preparation leading up to the game helped Arthur get a better grasp on the offense, and he was maturing as a player. Jacksonville was hardly Southern California, but there was still the usual activities for the teams; trips to the local attractions, lunches, din-ners, and banquets where both teams would be feted. During one of the banquets, ABC announcer Keith Jackson presented Hayes with a pair of boxing gloves as a gag. The room howled at the presentation, the laughter recognizing Hayes's earlier battles.

The weather was beautiful during Christmas week in Florida, and the Buckeyes basked in the warmth and sunshine getting ready for the game. But the day before kickoff the weather changed, with wind and rain hitting northern Florida. Clemson was led by thirty-year-old Danny Ford, who would be coaching his first college game ever, after taking over for Charlie Pell, who abruptly quit two weeks before the Gator Bowl to take a job with the University of Florida. Ford can-celled his team's practice the day before the Citrus Bowl, due to the in-clement weather. Hayes, however, insisted his Buckeyes practice, and took his team to a nearby high school field.

"Outlast 'em and outprepare 'em," Hayes had told his squad dur-ing the first meeting back in late August, and four months later Hayes was living up to his philosophy.

The oddsmakers had made Clemson two-point favorites going into the Gator Bowl game, and they were right on the mark. The Buckeyes were trailing 17–15 deep into the fourth quarter. When the Buckeyes recovered the ball on their own 24-yard line with four minutes and twenty-two seconds left in the game, Schlichter calmly marched his team down the field, acting more like a poised senior than an eighteen-year-old freshman playing in his first bowl game. The Buckeyes were already in field-goal territory, when Schlichter went to the line of scrimmage facing third down and five from the Clemson 24-yard line. Schlichter had thrown twenty passes and completed six-teen for 205 yards and two touchdowns, and the coaches upstairs in the booth were arguing about which play to call. Some wanted to ride

Schlichter's hot hand and throw for the first down, allowing the Buckeyes to run more clock off the ball and put themselves into even closer field position. Others wanted to run the ball, shaving some time off the clock and possibly picking up the first down. If not, then they could kick a field goal and go up 19–18, with just a little more than a minute remaining. Hayes sent in the pass play, setting in motion one of the most infamous plays in college football history.

It was a delay pass, where Schlichter would first look downfield and then dump the ball off to running back Ron Springs, who had released out of the backfield, taking a short route, with the ball to be thrown underneath the linebackers.

The play's execution was perfect. Springs released and cleared into the defense, and Schlichter threw a perfect spiral, soft and chesthigh, toward Springs, who was waiting downfield. But Schlichter never saw the Clemson middle guard who had dropped off in coverage instead of rushing the passer. And the ball was intercepted near the Ohio State sideline. Then, out of the Ohio State sideline came a raging Hayes, swinging a beefy right forearm into the face of the defender. For a split second, players on both teams seemed stunned by the punch. It was as if time stopped as the players and coaches struggled to believe what they saw. Then a melee erupted, with players from both teams pushing each other. Ohio State was assessed a fifteen-yard penalty for unsporstmanlike behavior. After the teams settled down, Hayes continued his rage on the sideline, screaming at the officials. The referee threw another flag on Hayes for unsportsmanlike conduct. Clemson then ran out the clock to end the game. "We were in four-down running territory, and we should have never been passing in that situation," Chaump said. "But they called a delay pass and, lo and behold, it gets intercepted and the kid runs right down our sideline and gets tackled in front of Woody. Then he hit the kid."

The "kid" was a twenty-year-old sophomore New Jersey native named Charlie Bauman. Barely six feet tall and around 205 pounds, Bauman was an undersized, but intense defensive lineman who had never before intercepted a pass. After he was run out of bounds in front of the Ohio State bench, Bauman raised his hands in celebration. Hayes's apologists, most of whom weren't anywhere near the sideline when Hayes threw the punch, swear that Bauman was taunting Hayes and subsequently got what he deserved for showing up the legendary coach on national television. But it wasn't the case.

"The kid was just excited and enthusiastic," Chaump said.

Bauman never knew Hayes hit him.

"I never even felt it," Bauman said.

Hayes's supporters missed the reason for the punch entirely. Hayes didn't strike at Bauman out of anger against an unknown defensive lineman. Instead, Hayes was attacking everything that had failed him during the long and frustrating season.

"I didn't hit [Bauman] to hurt him," Hayes said later. "It hurt only me. But you can't always explain everything. Some things are beyond you."

Up in the ABC television booth, announcers Keith Jackson and Ara Parseghian, Hayes's old assistant at Miami of Ohio, never said a word about what had transpired on the field and mostly ignored the incident. ABC was hammered by critics across the country for protecting Hayes and failing to deliver responsible journalism, in what was one of the biggest sports stories in years.

"I didn't see the punch," Parseghian said. "We had a replay monitor out in the booth and we didn't know what had happened."

Even when a producer told both announcers of the incident, they refused to say a word about it.

"We caught hell for it by everyone, but I honestly didn't know what was going on," Parseghian said.

There was a keener awareness of what had just happened in the Ohio State coaches booth, located near the press box.

"I knew it was over for Woody," Chaump said. "And the thing is, here was a guy who never passed when he should have, and when he finally passes the ball look what happened. He got fired by doing what he was thoroughly against."

Ohio State University President Harold Enarson was sitting in the stands across from the Ohio State sideline, unable to see what all the commotion was about. He had no idea that his coach had just slugged an opposing player and thrust Ohio State into a spotlight of shame and embarrassment.

Enarson wouldn't realize what happened until he returned to the Ohio State headquarters in nearby Ponte Verdra Beach. Enarson went outside to get some kindling wood to start a fire to enjoy over a two-A.M. nightcap with some colleagues, when Ohio State Athletic Director Hugh Hindman knocked on his door and informed him of what happened.

"Did you see it in person? Are you absolutely clear on what happened?" Enarson asked Hindman.

"Yes," Hindman said.

"Well, that's just intolerable," Enarson said.

Hindman, who played for Hayes at Miami and coached for him at Ohio State, told Enarson that he had met with Hayes after the game and told Hayes that he needed to resign to protect the reputation and integrity of the university. Hayes flatly refused, and Hindman told him that he was going to talk to Enarson, and in the meantime he would give Hayes until eight A.M. the next morning to resign. If he didn't, he would be fired.

Hindman and Enarson then quickly drafted two statements, one reading that Hayes had resigned, the other reading that he had been terminated. They finally settled on: "Coach Hayes has been relieved of his duties as head football coach at the Ohio State University. This decision has the full support of the president of the university."

At seven-thirty the next morning Hindman went to Hayes's room and again asked for his resignation. Hayes was confrontational in his refusal and Hindman said he had no choice but to fire him.

Shortly after eight A.M. Hindman called Enarson to tell him he had fired Hayes. Hayes, meanwhile, called his friend Hornung at the *Dispatch*. That afternoon, the paper's headline blared: WOODY HAYES RESIGNS. At the same time, the Associated Press, whose Columbus bureau was located adjacent to the *Dispatch* office, was reporting that Hayes had been fired.

Enarson also sent a telegram to Clemson president Robert C. Edwards, apologizing on behalf of Ohio State University. Clemson then issued a press release acknowledging the punch, with Edwards protecting his own university by declaring after he had watched the game film that Bauman was an innocent bystander.

"I can state with certainty there was no provocation on the part of any Clemson player," Edwards said in the release.

Two chartered airplanes ferried the Ohio State traveling party back to Columbus the day after the game. One plane carried the players and coaches. The other carried the coaches' wives and the university brass.

Hayes sat alone in the team plane. So too did Anne Hayes, who was traveling on the other plane. As the team plane made its approach into Columbus, Hayes took the microphone and announced to his players that "I will no longer be the coach of your football team," and then silently returned to his seat.

While Hayes was flying back to Columbus, the university was acting quickly to control the damage. Members of the administration had begun calling the nine members of the school's board of trustees to let them know of Hayes's pending firing. None of the nine members wanted Hayes to stay under any circumstances.

While school administrators hurried to deal with the crisis, Hayes withdrew. He went straight from the airport, under police escort, to his house, shut the door, and refused to speak to anyone. People close to Hayes were getting concerned. No one had heard a word from Hayes since he arrived in Columbus on Saturday afternoon. Dan Heinlan, president of the Ohio State Alumni Association, suggested that to Daryl Sanders, a former all-American who was now a minister, contact Archie Griffin and check up on Hayes. The hope was that Hayes wouldn't turn away his favorite player when Griffin showed up on his doorstep.

The two former players met in a shopping mall parking lot on Lane Avenue near Hayes's house around eleven A.M. Sunday morning.

"We don't know what we're going into; we don't know if the old man's going to be in a rage, or so despondent. There were concerns about his mental condition," Sanders said. "So Archie and I sat in the car and prayed. We asked for guidance and help and just to be a comfort to the old man."

Sanders and Griffin knocked on Hayes's door and got no answer. They knew both Woody and Anne were home, so they kept knocking. Finally, Hayes answered and asked them to come inside.

For eight hours, both men sat in Hayes's living room and listened to Hayes talk about everything but the incident.

"We had no lunch. We didn't drink a glass of water. No dinner. It's dark out, and there's one little light that he ends up turning on, just so we're not totally in the dark. And he was just talking. We said, 'Yes sir' about three times. It was almost like an old highlight discussion. We talked about things in life and politics. I talked to him about the Lord a little bit," Sanders said.

Griffin had no words to say to his coach. He felt that just being with him was enough.

"We just wanted Woody to know we were there for him," Griffin said.

Enarson moved quickly to begin finding a new head coach. The sooner they hired someone, the faster the issue would fade, and the less collateral damaged there would be to the football program. There'd be no search committee. Hindman and trustee chairman Bill Nester would handle the hiring process themselves.

"We must move quickly, or we could lose considerable ground in the recruiting efforts now underway," Enarson wrote in a letter to the board on January 4, a week after Hayes was fired. "We have not ap-pointed a search committee. The responsibility will be vested in Bill Nester and Hugh Hindman. The others will assist in an advisory ca-pacity. They represent the athletic council, which must, under Big Ten Conference rules, be involved in this matter. We all fully understand the great public attention which will be focused on this matter. We also, again, fully understand the need for urgent action."

Eight days later, Hindman announced that Earle Bruce was the choice to replace Hayes. Bruce had deep ties to Ohio State. He played for Hayes in 1951 until a knee injury ended his career during his sophomore season. He stayed with the team, serving as student coach through 1953. He then coached at four Ohio high schools, accruing a record including two consecutive undefeated seasons at Massilion High School, where, years before, Paul Brown had begun his legendary coaching career. Bruce returned to Ohio State in 1966 as an assistant under Hayes. In 1972, he took the head coaching job the University of Tampa, and a year later he was hired by Iowa State University.

It was a smart hire. Bruce was familiar with Ohio State and its administration, yet it also gave the impression that the university was distancing itself from the Hayes regime by not hiring one of Woody's current assistants.

Chaump, who held the longest tenure of any of the assistants, and who wanted the job, was snubbed.

"I got blocked at the president's office," Chaump said. "They wanted a clean sweep."

With the most pressing problem solved, the administration then addressed the delicate issue of what to do with Hayes. There was no debating the firing of Hayes, but how does a university gracefully distance itself from a national icon and a state hero without harming the university's reputation?

Enarson wrestled with the problem for two weeks after firing Hayes. Hayes had yet to contact anyone from the university, though Sanders had enlisted himself to represent Hayes during the termination process. A deal was finally worked out. In a private letter to Hayes dated January 17, 1979, Enarson made the official offer. Hayes, who was earning $43,000 a year in 1978, could retain his faculty position if he wanted to, and the school would provide him an office and a secretary. In addition, Ohio State would contribute $10,000 to a scholarship fund in his name.

"I have valued our relationship over these past six years," Enarson wrote to Hayes. "It has been, I believe, straightforward and candid. For my part I trust it will always continue to be so. We do, after all, love the same university. And we have each spent important years in our lives serving it—as best we knew how.

"As you know, I fully concurred with Hugh Hindman's decision. I'm sure you must realize there was no other choice—whether for the action or its timing. As I said publicly, it was a shame that an illustrious coaching career ended in such tragic fashion.

"Although neither Hugh, nor Bill Nester, nor I have heard from you, I understand through intermediaries that you are considering various options for your future. While I have agreed to meet with Mr. Sanders, who says he represents you, I want you to know that I and others are available to discuss these matters with you.

"It is my understanding that one initial concern you may have is with respect to office space. We will make every effort to accommodate your needs and desires in that regard. This is true whether you choose to stay on as a faculty member or retire—a decision strictly, completely, in your hands.

"It has come to my attention that many of your friends are eager to recognize your contributions over the years. I believe that the most fitting recognition will be the establishment of a scholarship fund in your name. I know of the interest you and Anne have had in your athletes' academic careers and the pride you both have taken in their successes. You both were, in many instances, contributors to those successes. We propose to do this, believing that it is at the core of what you stand for, most wish to be remembered by."

Hayes took the offer and was given a second-floor office in the military sciences building across the street from his old office in St. John Arena, and just north of Woody Hayes Drive, the street named in his honor that ran in front of the stadium. It would be in the new office that Hayes would begin to rebuild his image, but it wouldn't be easy—not with the past two decades of a life tied to the cheering crowds echoing around Ohio Stadium on autumn afternoon.

"Woody's ego came from the glory of winning football games," Chaump said. "But he had to work his way back, and he wanted to be part of it [Ohio State football tradition]."

16

TWILIGHT

Ohio State made the necessary apologies for the punch, Hayes did not. He did call Bauman, but he never said he was sorry. Publicly, he was more defiant. Hayes first ventured out of his house a week after he was fired, driving to Bowling Green to take refuge among his brethren. A few of Hayes's trusted assistants had gathered at Doyt Perry's house to talk with their old boss. Perry, Hayes's former assistant and former head coach at Bowling Green University, had called Bo Schembechler, who knew Hayes as well as any of the assistants, and asked that he come down from Michigan. The agenda was to convince Hayes to apologize to Bauman, but he refused.

"That was the first time Woody left his house after he got fired," Schembechler said. "I had an agenda. I knew we had to get Woody to apologize for what he did to that Clemson kid. Woody said, 'Should I apologize for all the good things I've done?'"

On January 18, Hayes made his first public appearance, honoring a commitment he gave months earlier to speak at a local chamber of commerce meeting in Columbus. He was greeted as a conquering hero by hundreds of people, and while he apologized for his actions during that dismal night in Jacksonville he refused to apologize to Bauman.

"He went back to Columbus to make a speech," Schembechler said. "Cameras were there because it was the first time he was in the public eye. He said, 'Bo thinks I ought to apologize, but Bo doesn't know everything.' That was the extent of his apology."

Hayes, through a connection with Sanders, signed a movie deal for $100,000, to be produced by Gene Kirkwood, who produced *Rocky*. Hayes was flattered, but just to make sure, he checked on Kirkwood through Bob Hope. The movie was never made, but the project occupied Hayes during the months after his firing, and he privately loved the

Hollywood attention. He was always drawn to power and celebrity. On July 7, 1978, a star-studded crowd roasted Hayes in Miami. Stars such as Ann-Margret and Shirley MacLaine joined legends like Don Shula, Bud Wilkinson, and Gerald Ford in a fund-raising roast of Hayes, who basked in the spotlight. Hayes spoke at the end of the night, and he made sure to play to his connection to former president Ford, while alluding to his great influence in Ohio.

"People ask me, if you had to do it over again, would you coach?" Hayes said. "Yes. Excepting for two weeks. Those two weeks would have been late October and early November 1976. We just lagged by seven thousand five hundred votes in Ohio. I should have taken the damn ball and thrown it to my assistant coaches and said 'Fellows, you play the ball game, I'm going into a bigger ball game,' and I could have gotten those seven thousand five hundred votes and [Ford] would have been in the White House where he belongs."

After the event, Hayes had a drink with MacLaine, and he joked that when he returned to Columbus, he woke up Anne to confess to her his night out with MacLaine.

"She yawned, rolled over, and went back to sleep," Hayes said. "I never could impress that woman."

Bruce now was in charge of Ohio State football, but Hayes, ripped by the national press, was still loved in Ohio. Invitations to banquets and speaking engagments flowed through his office.

Legions of former Ohio State players also rallied around their fallen coach, and on March 12, 1979, they feted Hayes with a private gathering that drew more than four hundred former Ohio State players, and they raised enough money to renovate a cabin Hayes had on the land in Noble County where his grandfather had farmed. With no telephone or television, the simple cabin was the one place where he could take refuge. There he would spend a few days or a week alone, reading and walking around his family's homestead, decompressing from the stress of coaching.

Hayes basked in the glory of his generous and loyal players. Representatives from each of the national championship teams under Hayes spoke, honoring their old coach. Dick Brubaker and Dean Dugger from the 1954 squad, Aurealius Thomas from the 1957 team, and Rex

Kern from the 1968 team each gave tributes to Hayes, thanking him for teaching, not how to win games, but for the larger lessons on how to succeed off the football field.

Then Schembechler got up from the dais and delivered an emotion-packed speech. He spoke of playing and coaching with Hayes, and of the battles they fought across the sidelines from one another.

"I am one of the few who can say they played for Woody, coached for Woody, and coached against Woody, and I know him as well as anyone." Schembechler said, his voice rising. "Tonight is as important to Woody as many of his great victories. There are players at Notre Dame who can say they played for the great Rockne. You Ohio State people can say with pride that you played for Woody Hayes. And I want you to know that you played for the greatest football coach this country has every seen." The room erupted into a standing ovation.

Not a word was said about the fateful night in Jacksonville. There wasn't any need to. Only Dugger referred to the "other idiots outside the city" who didn't understand Hayes. Just showing up spoke volumes on how the players felt about their coach. What Hayes did during those ugly moments late in the Gator Bowl didn't define him to his players, as it did to the rest of the world. Only those in the room could know or understand what Hayes had meant to them. The image of the bullying coach screaming at players and officials on the sidelines was for outsiders, for people who didn't hear the speeches of how to be a team player, of how important it was to give back, or "pay it forward," as Hayes called it. The critics had no idea that Hayes had taught his players so much about life outside of football, though it took most of his players years after they left Ohio State to realize the lessons learned. Only those that had been pushed and prodded past exhaustion by Hayes to accomplish more than they ever thought could ever know.

Hayes, his voice cracking, took the microphone after Schembechler, and suddenly it was as if the aging athletes in the room were transformed into the players they once were.

Hayes spoke of the past glories and began to reminisce. He recalled specific situations in games played nearly three decades earlier. He called out certain players and made them stand up to be recognized for the great plays they made long ago, recreating one last time the thrill of competition, as waves of camaraderie washed over the room.

Then, like he did so many times before in the team's meeting room, Hayes veered away from football. He talked of the collective dissatisfaction of students on campus and the lessons learned from Vietnam. He talked about the perseverance of Abraham Lincoln, "who would've been a great pass rusher from splitting all those rails." He spoke about how important it was to play to win, to always compete, and he reminded the players of the satisfaction that came from team effort. He thanked his players and urged them to be productive in their lives and to participate in a "community of interests." Above all, he said, was the importance of respect.

"Lots of people will try to beat you," he said, his voice rising with emotion as he finished his talk. "Make them respect you by what you do."

The players responded with a thunderous ovation, as Hayes, for one final time, delivered what really was a half-time speech. Neither the players nor Hayes said it, but everyone seemed to understand that it would be the last time that so many would be together. From that night on, the light began to fade for Hayes.

He kept regular hours in his office in room 201 in the military sciences building, where he received visitors and read volumes of mail from fans and friends all over the country.

People felt a personal connection to the old coach, with friends and strangers sending gifts and good wishes by the sackload. Woody generally responded personally. A letter dated December 19, 1984, sent to his friend Bob Evans, was a simple thanks for a calendar sent over Christmas.

"Incidentally, your wife sent me some buckwheat flour and cornmeal, and I have been on the road, so that we haven't used the flour yet," Hayes wrote. "We have used the cornmeal in bread, and it is excellent."

Another letter, dated August 31, 1984, was a reply to a request by a man who had met Hayes briefly four years earlier and was now asking for tickets to the Michigan game in November. Remarkably, Hayes responded with a personal note promising to send the tickets.

He also used his pen to lobby for seemingly minor causes. In a letter to the editor of the *Journal News* in Fairfield, Ohio, he urged readers to support a proposed increase in school taxes, a departure from his mostly conservative Republican politics.

He also set an aggressive schedule of speeches that he delivered around the country. The speech was nearly always the same: It would start out with an anecdote about his childhood in Newcomerstown, and then move into how football taught the importance of getting back up after getting knocked down. Then he'd praise the great Ohio State University, and close by urging the audience to give back to their community, to be good Americans. It was, by most standards, hokey, but Hayes believed every word of it, and he mesmerized audiences.

Hayes kept a full calendar the first few years after he retired, giving speeches and raising money for numerous charitable causes. He flirted with the idea of politics, with the state's Republican party even suggesting that Hayes take a run at Sen. John Glenn's seat in Congress. The idea was preposterous. Hayes could never handle the dirty business of politics, though the interest fed his ego. Instead, Hayes made a new life for himself on the speaker's circuit and became a goodwill ambassador for countless causes, both personal and professional. He even spent more time with his family.

"When he was coaching we didn't see him at many family functions, but that changed after he retired," said his niece Mary Hoyt. "He'd come to family parties and holiday dinners, and he loved to play with his grandchildren."

His health held until May of 1981. The *Dispatch* ran the headline "Hayes Has Chest Cold" on May 9, but it turned out to be gallstones, and he underwent an operation in University Hospital. Two weeks later, an X-ray showed that the surgeon had left a sponge inside Hayes, and he was opened up again to remove the foreign object that was causing a life-threatening infection. Hayes hated mistakes on the football field, but he was more forgiving to the horrified surgeons and he graciously excused the potentially deadly error.

In late April 1982, Hayes went to Boston to help commemorate the one hundredth anniversary of the death of his hero Ralph Waldo Emerson. Hayes joined Archibald Cox, the first Watergate special prosecutor who was fired, and former attorney general Elliot Richardson, who resigned from Nixon's cabinet, at the Sanders Theater at Harvard to discuss the meaning of Emerson. Hayes spoke of the early American revolutionary, praising "Compensation" as his favorite piece, espousing the creed "Every excess causes a defect . . . and for everything you have missed you have gained something else, and for everything you gain, you lose something."

"You know," Hayes said of the passage, "Emerson's just as right as hell on that. I've done some research on it."

Even Hayes's obsession with football had begun to fade. He still helped recruit Ohio State players by drawing on his vast network to do background checks on potential players, but now that he was out of the game, he was growing disenchanted with it.

"Sometimes now," Hayes said, "I get a little bored with myself. I might watch a game on TV, but I worry about it a little. I worry about the game getting out of hand. I do. I really do. The money involved, the overcommercialization. Do we even know what is happening? Do we really?"

In November 1983 Hayes was elected into the College Football Hall of Fame. He also received what he felt was an equally great honor when he was asked to dot the "I" during halftime, when the Ohio State marching band performed the famous "Script Ohio" formation. It was an honor reserved for only the most deserving, and Hayes, in coat and tie, ran out on the field and triumphed in his return to the stadium where he had won so many battles. Hayes was living up to the words he delivered time and again in speeches. He had picked himself up after getting fired by punching Bauman during the Gator Bowl, and he had rebuilt himself into a folk hero. The speaking engagements kept piling up, but Hayes's health was declining. He suffered a stroke on May 24, 1985, while in Vancouver, Canada, to make a speech. He was flown back to Ohio and admitted to University Hospital, where he remained for a few weeks to rehabilitate from the stroke damage to his right side. In November Hayes was treated for phlebitis at University Hospital, suffered another heart attack, and had a pacemaker installed. He also needed a wheelchair or a walker to get around.

The National Association of College and High School coaches

gave Hayes the Amos Alonzo Stagg Award in 1986, but the biggest
honor came when Ohio State president Edward Jennings invited Hayes
to address graduates at the school's 295th commencement ceremonies
on Friday, March, 21, 1987.

"In conversations about excellence at The Ohio State University,
your name is invariably mentioned," Jennings wrote. "The achievements and honors that have brought you national recognition and respect over the years also have brought great credit to Ohio State. Your
long record of outstanding accomplishment and your well-known
dedication to the academic enterprise are symbolic to this university.
For these reasons, you have been chosen to receive an honorary degree
to be conferred upon you at the winter commencement exercises. It
is with special pleasure that I also invite you to honor the university
community by delivering the commencement address."

The resurrection of Woody Hayes was now complete.

Hayes entered St. John Arena in a wheelchair and needed help to
take the podium in front of 1,736 winter quarter graduates and 8,000
guests. "It was," Hayes said in a voice filled with emotion, "the greatest day of my life."

For thirty minutes Hayes lectured the graduates in much of the
same way he spoke to his players when they honored him just after
he was fired.

"When you get knocked down, get up in a hurry," he said to the
graduates after receiving an honorary Doctor of Humanities degree.
"You probably need more strength, you get it in the huddle. Together-
ness is what gives you the buildup. In your lifetime, how well you can
work with people will depend on how quickly you get back to them
and work together." Hayes closed his address by imploring the graduates to strive to achieve. "You have the ability to make this a greater
world. Godspeed to you all."

Hayes was then slowly led off the stage to a standing ovation. He
was by now a frail man who couldn't walk without assistance. He tried
to hide his deteriorating health from the public, but word spread quickly
among his former players. For the rest of the year, the number of public appearances slowed, but the number of visits from so many of his
former players increased.

Hayes celebrated his seventy-fourth birthday on February 13, 1987, in quiet fashion with Anne. By now Hayes was very ill. He was confined to a wheelchair, couldn't drive, and his sight had failed to where he couldn't read. But he still tried to get to his office and make limited public appearances. On March 10 Hayes went out for breakfast with Yale University professor Donald Kagen, one of the country's leading classicists, and with Ohio State University history professor Rick Murray.

"We spent an hour and a half talking about things from football to military history to Greek history to Emerson," Murray said. "As we got up, the restaurant manager said, 'This is on the house.' Woody had a very difficult time accepting that, because he had just berated us, saying we weren't going to pay for it. He left a five-dollar tip, which about paid for breakfast."

It was the last breakfast Hayes had outside his house. Sometime during the night of Wednesday, March 11, and the early morning of Thursday, March 12, Hayes died in his sleep of a heart attack. Anne found him dead at six A.M. on March 12 and called Dr. Bob Murphy, Hayes's longtime physician.

"He had a fatalistic look at his problems," Murphy said. "He wanted to live life to the fullest. The quality was more important to him than the length, and that's why he kept going."

Anne and university officials swiftly made arrangements. A family-only service was held following cremation on Saturday, March 14. On Tuesday, March 17, fourteen hundred friends and family packed the First Community Church in Marble Cliff. There, Anne and Steve greeted mourners in a receiving line that lasted for two hours. Former players flocked to the church to mourn. On a table at the altar was a single lit candle, Woody's coaching hat with the trademark block "O," a U.S. Navy flag, and a red rose in a vase.

Former President Richard Nixon delivered the eulogy for his old friend, drawing upon Winston Churchill and Sophocles, while praising Anne.

"For thirty years, I was privileged to know the real Woody Hayes—the man behind the media myth," Nixon said. "Instead of a know-nothing Neanderthal, I found a Renaissance man with a consuming interest in history and a profound understanding of the forces that move the world. Instead of a cold, ruthless tyrant on the football field, I found a warm-hearted softie—very appropriately born on Valentines' Day—who spoke of his affection for 'his boys' and for his family.

"I'm sure Woody wouldn't mind if I shared with you a letter he wrote to me shortly after Mrs. Nixon suffered a stroke ten years ago: 'You and I are about the two luckiest men in the world from the standpoint of our marriages, with your Pat and my Anne. I know you will agree that neither of us could have done better, and neither of us deserves to do so well.'

"In another Ohio State game, on New Year's Day in 1969, the Buckeyes were playing USC. O. J. Simpson electrified the crowd in the first quarter when he sprinted eighty yards for a touchdown. But the Buckeyes came roaring back in the second half and crushed the Trojans twenty-six to sixteen. It was Woody's third national championship. He could have quit with the three national championships and seven Big Ten championships. He had to know that it was a risk to stay on. It is a rule of life that if you take no risks, you will suffer no defeats. But if you take no risks, you will win no victories. Woody did not believe in playing it safe. He played to win.

"In the next nine years, he won some great victories, including a record six straight Big Ten championships from nineteen seventy-two to nineteen seventy-seven. He also suffered some shattering defeats. The incident at the Gator Bowl in nineteen seventy-eight would have destroyed an ordinary man. But Woody was not an ordinary man. Winston Churchill once said, 'Success is never final. Failure is never fatal.' Woody lived by that maxim. He was never satisfied with success; he was never discouraged by failure.

"The last nine years of his life were probably his best. He made scores of inspirational speeches all over the country. He gave all of the honorariums from those speeches to the Woody Hayes Cancer Fund at Ohio State University. He raised tens of thousands of dollars for crippled children. He gave pregame talks to his beloved Ohio State team. He basked in the warm glow of tributes that were showered upon him by those who played for him and others that had come to know him, love him, and respect him. . . . Two thousand years ago, the poet

Sophocles wrote, 'One must wait until the evening to see how splendid the day had been.' We can all be thankful today that, in the evening of his life, Woody Hayes could look back and see that the day has indeed been splendid."

The memorial ended with the singing of "Carmen Ohio," the alma mater of Ohio State University.

The next day, at three P.M., ten thousand people sat in Ohio Stadium during the middle of the week and paid tribute to Hayes in a more public memorial, with Griffin, Kern, Schembechler, and Earle Bruce all speaking. Bruce summed up his former coach and boss by referring to Hayes's favorite power fullback offense, a strategy that defined him as a coach and as a person.

"We will miss," Bruce said, "the idea to run 'robust' and get the job done."

Renditions of "The Navy Hymn" and "Carmen Ohio" followed. Then came the presentation of military honors, and the memorial service then concluded with the playing of taps.

Hayes's ashes are buried in Union Cemetery, just down the road from the team's practice facility. "And in the night of death, hope sees a star, and listening love hears the rustle of a wing," the epitaph reads, quoting from Robert Ingersoll, an Illinois lawyer who became one of the country's great orators in the late 1800s. There is no sign of any coaching accomplishments on his headstone, no marker that would give any indication of Hayes's huge contribution to college football.

He won 76 percent of the games he coached. Forty-two of his players were all-Americans, with Hop Cassady winning one Heisman Trophy and Archie Griffin the first to win two consecutive Heisman awards. But Hayes appreciated his players more than his statistics.

"He had a personal influence on all of us," Griffin said. "He was a great teacher and would talk to you about anything but football; but more than anything else, he simply hated to lose."

EPILOGUE

The direct link between Hayes and Ohio State football would continue until 1988, when Bruce, who played and coached under Woody, was fired just after the season-ending Michigan game in 1988 and replaced by John Cooper. But Woody's presence would never fade. In fact, his legend would grow, particularly as the Buckeyes struggled in subsequent seasons.

Anne Hayes, still vibrant in the years after her husband's death, helped keep the strong connection. She kept the house on Cardiff Road and stayed close to Ohio State and to many former players.

"Pay it forward" was one of Woody's favorite phrases, and she made certain her husband's death would not diminish his maxim of helping others.

She was busy on the speakers circuit, and worked tirelessly to raise money for a number of charitable causes, and to endow the Woody Hayes Chair in National Securities Studies at Ohio State.

In 1990 she donated her husband's papers and other memorabilia to the university, and now dozens of boxes sit in the university's archives, available to anyone.

She also befriended Cooper and his wife Helen, after Cooper replaced Bruce in 1988, knowing the pressures that came with the job of coaching at Ohio State. There was no bitterness or jealousy aimed at the school or football program.

"If I had a problem, all I had to do was pick up the phone," Helen Cooper told the *Columbus Dispatch*. As the years passed, Anne grew to be as beloved by the university as her husband had been.

In February 1994, at her eightieth birthday party, one thousand friends and former players gathered to help her celebrate by raising money to help endow her husband's Ohio State chair. She was given an Ohio State distinguished service award during the 1996 graduation. That same year she received the Ohio Gold Award from the National Football Foundation and Hall of Fame. She died in 1998 at the age of eighty-three of lung disease and congestive heart failure.

"I think she was a lot of strength for Woody Hayes," said former Ohio State all-American Jim Stillwagon in the *Columbus Dispatch* obituary.

While Anne took a very public role in the years following the death of her husband, Steve Hayes, a retired Franklin County judge, has kept a public distance from his father. He refuses interviews, preferring instead to make his own life in a town where his father is now a folk hero.

NOTES

1. NEWCOMERSTOWN

5 "I speak at a lot of banquets," Ohio Elks Newsletter, Aug. 1979, p. 7.

6 "As the youngest . . ." *You Win with People,* by Woody Hayes, p. 199.

6 Wayne's mother would sit him down, *St. Petersburg Times,* by Bruce Lowitt. Courtesy, Denison University archives.

8 (Young) managed the local semipro team, *You Win with People,* by Woody Hayes, p. 201.

9 "That man could make me feel grown up," undated prepared speech by Hayes, OSU archives.

9 There was a contingent of black residents, int. with Barbara Scott.

10 "When Pappy hired me," int. with Gene Riffle.

10 "I believe there's nothing tougher," *You Win with People,* by Woody Hayes.

11 When [Wayne] announced, *St. Petersburg Times,* undated, courtesy of Denison University archives.

12 "He had a personal aura," *You Win with People,* by Woody Hayes, p. 210.

13 They were known as "Eastenders," *Columbus Dispatch,* January 7, 1979.

13 "The Hupps were that kind of people," *Columbus Dispatch,* January 7, 1979.

14 "Out by Cy Young's farm," undated prepared speech by Hayes, OSU archives.

15 The Golden Trojans: *Ohio Football News,* September 10, 1977.

15 "Woody wasn't much of a runner," *Ohio Football News,* September 10, 1977.

16 "He was extremely interested," *Class of '68,* by Harvey Shapiro, p. 178.

16 Even friendly backyard games, *Buckeye,* by Robert Vare, p. 65.

2. DENISON

19 The university was founded, Denison University archives.

20 The discipline imposed int., article by Robert Amos, *Daily Jeffersonian,* undated.

20 Woody "was not a ladies' man," *Daily Jeffersonian,* undated.

20 It cost $125 per semester, *Denison University Handbook,* 1935.

20 There were better football players, *You Win with People,* by Woody Hayes, p. 213.

21 "Rogers was what every college student needs," *You Win with People,* by Woody Hayes, p. 210.

21 "He was musclebound," *Daily Jeffersonian,* undated.

22 "(Woody) was a good student," int. with Robert Amos.

23 "He was an independent soul," *Daily Jeffersonian,* undated.

3. THE APPRENTICESHIP

25 His first teaching assignment, *You Win with People,* by Woody Hayes, pp. 213–214.

25 These youngsters were merely neglected, *You Win with People,* by Woody Hayes, p. 213.

28 He roomed at the Sigma Chi house, *You Win with People,* by Woody Hayes, p. 215.

29 "He lacked patience," *Buckeye,* by Robert Vare, p. 66.

30 "I paid the bill," Ohio Elks Newsletter, August 1979, p. 7.

31 "Football was my game," *Delaware Gazette,* June 12, 1998.

34 "On our first date," *The Booster,* August 26, 1986.

35 "In the last week," the *Daily Times,* December 3, 1940.

37 Athletes and young coaches joined the war effort, yet there was hesitation, "Different Fields," by David Hinkley, *New York Daily News,* February 24, 2003.

37 Detroit Tigers slugger Hank Greenburg enlisted in 1941, "Once Upon a Time, Athletes Really Did Go to War," by Mickey Herskowitz, *Houston Chronicle,* March 23, 2003.

38 The two had dated on and off for six years, *Woody Hayes, the Man and His Dynasty,* edited by Mike Bynum.

39 "How can you stay angry," *Cleveland Plain Dealer,* April 1, 1976.

39 "It gives us a chance," *Dayton Daily News,* February 24, 1951.

4. DENISON AGAIN

40 "I was expecting a guy," int. with Aubrey Engle.

42 "But timing was a problem," *You Win with People,* by Woody Hayes, p. 19.

44 "We had all these veterans returning," int. with Dick Huff.

45 "It took awhile to get everyone on," int. with Rix Yard.

49 Another defining moment, *You Win with People,* by Woody Hayes, p. 22.

51 He brought his team out, *You Win with People,* by Woody Hayes, p. 25.

53 He didn't know football, Denison University 1979, 1981, 1984, p. 132.

53 "On the field, Hayes owned the players," int. with Bill Wehr.

54 "One day I came back from class," int. with Bill Fleitz.

60 (At Denison) one of those administrators was David Reese, *You Win with People,* by Woody Hayes, p. 28.

5. PROVING GROUND

62 Reese liked what he saw, *You Win with People,* by Woody Hayes, p. 28.

62 His contract was for two years, Miami of Ohio University archives.

65 "Sid's approach was that he'd tell you," int. with Mel Olix.

68 "When Woody got to Oxford," int. with John Pont.

73 "Woody was the most emotional guy," int. with Ara Parseghian.

74 He had team dinners, *Dayton Daily News,* February 25, 1951.

77 " 'You know,' Hayes told friends," int. with Mel Olix.

6. A NEW BEGINNING

79 With almost eighty thousand tickets presold, *The Official Ohio State Football Encyclopedia,* by Jack Park, pp. 269–272.

80 "I could see the goal posts," Gannett New Service.

81 "It was like a nightmare," Ohio State University Monthly.

83 By January the screening committee, Ohio State University archives.

84 "If you are interested," *You Win with People,* by Woody Hayes, p. 39.

84 "When the job was open," *Sports Illustrated,* October 24, 1955.

85 Brown was the perfect choice, *Buckeye,* by Robert Vare, p. 75.

85 Larkins and a few other members of the faculty club never forgave Brown, *Buckeye,* by Robert Vare, pp. 74–75.

86 "A decade earlier, Ohio State nearly lured Faurot," *The Official Ohio State University Football Encyclopedia,* by Jack Park, p. 275.

87 Under his command, *Buckeye,* by Robert Vare, p. 76.

88 So tenuous was the board meeting, *Columbus Dispatch,* February 19, 1951.

88 "Hayes has a one-year agreement," OSU archives.

89 "No doubt you recall," Miami of Ohio University archives.

90 By the time Woody took over, *Columbus Citizen,* February 19, 1951.

7. WELCOME TO THE MACHINE

91 "Isn't that the same," *You Win with People,* by Woody Hayes.

93 "I promise you we'll never," *Sports Illustrated,* October 24, 1955, p. 33.

95 With no water on the field, *Sports Illustrated,* October 24, 1955, p. 33.

96 "I believe in overlearning," *Sports Illustrated,* October 24, 1955, p. 33.

96 The Buckeyes players locked Hayes out, *The Official Ohio State University Football Encyclopedia,* by Jack Park, p. 280.

97 Woody showed his appreciation, int. with Dick Brubaker.

98 Members of network called "Frontliners," *Buckeye,* by Robert Vare, p. 82.

100 Hayes would call on John Galbreath, *Buckeye,* by Robert Vare, pp. 80–89.

100 It was an impressive place, *Buckeye,* by Robert Vare, pp. 80–89.

8. THE DRIVE

105 "I walked into his office," int. with Dick Brubaker.

107 A modern indoor record, *Sports Illustrated,* October 24, 1955.

108 Ohio State recruited black players, *Woody's Boys,* by Alan Natali, p. 57.

108 Hayes grudgingly went along, *Woody's Boys,* by Alan Natali, p. 57.

108–109 Joining the Hayeses was Katy Hess, *Columbus Dispatch,* December 12, 1992.

110 With more than four hundred press credentials issued, *The Official Ohio State University Football Encyclopedia,* by Jack Park, p. 292.

113 "It was after the losses," int. with George Chaump.

114 You have no more right, *Columbus Dispatch,* November 16, 1954.

115 "Boys," he said, int. with Dick Brubaker.

115 An incredulous Larkins, *The Lantern,* March 13, 1987.

115 I listened to Woody, *Saturday Evening Post,* November 12, 1955.

119 Hayes was then ceremoniously, *The Ohio State University Lantern,* March 13, 1987.

121 Leggett returned from his night, int. with Tad Weed.

123 In addition to us, *Saturday Evening Post,* November 12, 1955.

124 "Like Woody, my dad could be volatile," int. with Mary Hoyt.

9. POWER GRAB

125 How many of you, *Sports Illustrated,* October 24, 1955.

127 Parker, for example, was hired to clean, *Woody's Boys,* by Alan Natali, p. 68.

128 Parker and Cassady were named, Ohio News Service.

131 The football tail now seems to be wagging, *Saturday Evening Post,* November 12, 1955.

131 Fullen, sensing a backlash against his association, *Columbus Dispatch,* December 3, 1961.

131 It was a most unflattering portrait of Hayes, *Ohio State University Lantern,* December 8, 1971.

133 In 1956, the Buckeyes garnered 2,468 rushing yards, *The Official Ohio State University Football Encyclopedia,* by Jack Park, page 311.

135 Then, when I glance over, *Saturday Evening Post,* November 12, 1955.

136 The next year Woody was able to, *Columbus Dispatch,* January 7, 1979.

140 "I drove him nuts," int. with Tom Matte.

141 Matte's cavalier practice habits, *Woody's Boys,* by Alan Natali, p. 91.

142 Joe Sparma was the passing specialist, *The Official Ohio State University Football Encyclopedia,* by Jack Park, p. 340.

143 The faculty council voted, *The Official Ohio State University Football Encyclopedia,* by Jack Park, p. 359.

144 I don't agree with those, *Beyond the Gridiron, The Life and Times of Woody Hayes.*

10. TRANSITION

154 I think they valued, *On Campus,* March 19, 1987, p. 6.

154 If they don't want to coach, *Cleveland Plain Dealer,* January 21, 1979.

155 Woody took his son Steve, *You Win with People,* by Woody Hayes.

157 "I was all set to go to Syracuse," int. with Jack Tatum.

159 Afterward, Hayes called Walt, *The Official Ohio State University Football Encyclopedia,* by Jack Park, p. 370.

160 "Left at 09:10 by chopper," Woody Hayes personal papers, OSU archives.

11. THE KIDDIE CORPS

164 "You're bound to lose one game for every sophomore," *The Official Ohio State University Football Encyclopedia,* by Jack Park, p. 371.

165 "I was recruited by many other schools," int. with Rex Kern.

167 "There will be times," *Ohio State, 1968 All the Way to the Top,* by Steve Greenburg and Larry Zelina, p. xii.

173 "There are a lot of teams," *Columbus Citizen-Journal,* September 25, 1968.

174 "They better buy a scorecard," *Columbus Citizen-Journal,* September 28, 1968.

174 "He also refused to exchange," *Columbus Citizen-Journal,* September 27, 1968.

175 "We'll show all we've got," *Columbus Citizen-Journal,* September 27, 1968.

178 So he gave the game ball, *Ohio State, 1968 All the Way to the Top,* by Steve Greenburg and Larry Zelina, p. 24.

179 Hayes worked himself into a frenzy, *Ohio State, 1968 All the Way to the Top,* by Steve Greenburg and Larry Zelina, p. 116.

181 McCullough, Ohio State's defensive coordinator, *Ohio State, 1968 All the Way to the Top,* by Steve Greenburg and Larry Zelina, p. 48.

12. OPPORTUNITY LOST

191 The offense was averaging 46 points, *The Official Ohio State University Football Encyclopedia,* by Jack Park, p. 388.

193 "You can't talk about the 1969 game," *USA Today,* November 21, 2003.

194 "I talked about it all the time," *USA Today,* November 21, 2003.

194 Upon returning to Columbus, *The Official Ohio State University Football Encyclopedia,* by Jack Park, p. 390.

197 "There were no pros," *Cleveland Plain Dealer,* January 21, 1979.

199 Fans filled the Horseshoe, *The Official Ohio State University Football Encyclopedia,* by Jack Park, p. 395.

200 It was a game of missed opportunities, *The Official Ohio State University Football Encyclopedia,* by Jack Park, p. 397.

13. FLAM

202 By doing so, he could honor, *The Official Ohio State University Football Encyclopedia,* by Jack Park, p. 399.

202 Hayes and Fischer battled, int. with Jim Steckl.

203 "This time the Angry One," *Ohio State University Lantern,* December 8, 1971.

205 He hit .500 his senior year, *Woody's Boys,* by Alan Natali.

207 "I was scared to death of Woody," int. with Cornelius Greene.

208 "During the next game," int. with Archie Griffin.

208 A decent student at Dunbar, *Woody's Boys,* by Alan Natali, p. 309.

211 "He was flattered by the attention," int. with Robert Vare.

214 Greene played as if he were a battle-tested senior, leading the Buckeyes, *The Official Ohio State Football Encyclopedia,* by Jack Park, p. 416.

14. INSURRECTION

218 "I think Nixon was set up," *Cleveland Plain Dealer,* January 21, 1979.

222 "It's a matter of record," *Columbus Citizen-Journal,* November 26, 1972.

223 "What probably influenced," Schembechler interview, Michigan Board of Regents, 2002.

223 "Enough of that," *Columbus Citizen-Journal,* December 21, 1973.

224 Hayes even allowed himself, *Columbus Citizen-Journal,* December 27, 1973.

225 Greene was named the game's most valuable player, *The Official Ohio State Football Encyclopedia,* by Jack Park, p. 423.

228 "How would you like it," *Columbus Dispatch,* January 7, 1979.

15. THE PUNCH

231 To win Schlichter's favor, Hayes promised, interview with George Chaump.

237 It was a delay pass, interview with George Chaump.

238 "I never even felt it," *The State,* December 28, 2003.

238 "I didn't hit Bauman to hurt him," *Washington Post,* October 1984.

238 "I didn't see the punch," int. with Ara Parseghian.

239 Enarson went outside to get some kindling, *Truth and Consequences: How Colleges and Universities Meet Public Crisis,* by Jerrold Footlick, American Council on Education, Oryx Press, 1997, p. 137.

240 "We don't know what we're going into," *Truth and Consequences: How Colleges and Universities Meet Public Crisis,* by Jerrold Footlick, American Council on Education, Oryx Press, 1997, p. 142.

241 "We had no lunch," *Truth and Consequences: How Colleges and Universities Meet Public Crisis,* by Jerold Footlick, American Council on Education, Oryx Press, 1997, p. 142.

241 "We must move quickly," Enarson papers, OSU archives.

242 "I have valued our relationship," Enarson papers, OSU archives.

16. TWILIGHT

245 "That was the first time," Associated Press, November 21, 2003.

250 "Emerson's just as right as hell," *Boston Globe,* undated.

250 "Sometimes now, I get a little bored," *Washington Post,* October 1985.

251 "In conversations about excellence," *Capital Magazine,* January 25, 1987.

252 "We spent an hour," *On Campus,* March 19, 1987.

252 "He had a fatalistic look," *Columbus Dispatch,* March 13, 1987.

BIBLIOGRAPHY

For much of the football facts and figures, I relied heavily on *The Official Ohio State Football Encyclopedia,* compiled by Jack Park. The book was indispensable in providing the statistical framework for every Ohio State football game. *Woody's Boys,* by Alan Natali, was also a key resource that provided some player perspectives.

    Beyond the Gridiron: The Life and Times of Woody Hayes, a video produced by the Duncan Group, was also helpful in the Research.

The Official Ohio State Football Encyclopedia, edited by Jack Park, Sports Publishing L.L.C., 2003.

Buckeye, by Robert Vare, Popular Library, New York, 1974.

You Win with People, by Woody Hayes, 1973.

Woody Hayes and the 100-Yard War, by Jerry Brondfield, Random House, New York, 1974.

Ohio State '68 All the Way to the Top, by Steve Greenberg and Larry Zelina, Sports Publishing L.L.C., 2001.

Class of '68, A Season to Remember, by Harvey Shapiro, Witness Productions, Marshall, IN, 1998.

Woody's Boys, by Alan Natali, Orange Frazier Press, Wilmington, Ohio, 1995.

Three Yards and a Cloud of Dust, by Bill Levy, Third World Publishing Co., Cleveland, Ohio, 1966.

Truth and Consequences: How Colleges and Universities Meet Public Crisis, by Jerrold K. Footlick, Oryx Press, 1997.

When Pride Still Mattered, A Life of Vince Lombardi, by David Mariness, Simon & Schuster, New York, 1999.

Bo, by Bo Schembechler and Mitch Albom, Warner Books, 1989.

INDEX